PILGRIMS OF PARADOX

Calvinism and Experience

among the Primitive Baptists

of the Blue Ridge

James L. Peacock

and Ruel W. Tyson, Jr.

Smithsonian Institution Press Washington and London

To the Primitive Baptists of the Blue Ridge

Jeanne M. Sexton, *Senior Editor*
Janice Wheeler, *Designer*

Library of Congress Cataloging-in-Publication Data

Peacock, James L.
  Pilgrims of Paradox.
  (Smithsonian series in ethnographic inquiry)
  Includes index.
    1. Primitive Baptists—Blue Ridge Mountains.
  2. Mountain District Primitive Baptist Association.
  3. Calvinism—Blue Ridge Mountains. 4. Experience
  (Religion) 5. Baptists—Blue Ridge Mountains. 6. Blue
  Ridge Mountains—Church history. I. Tyson, Ruel W.,
  1930–   . II. Title. III. Series.
  BX6384.B57P43 1989   305.6′61′0755   89–5853
  ISBN 0–87474–924–7 (alk. paper)
  ISBN 0–87474–923–9 (pbk. :alk. paper)

The paper in this book meets the requirements of the American
National Standard for Permanence of Paper for Printed Materials
Z39.48–1984

PILGRIMS OF PARADOX

Smithsonian Series in Ethnographic Inquiry

Ivan Karp and William L. Merrill, Series Editors

Ethnography as fieldwork, analysis, and literary form is the distinguishing feature of modern anthropology. Guided by the assumption that anthropological theory and ethnography are inextricably linked, this series is devoted to exploring the ethnographic enterprise.

Contents

Acknowledgments

We are grateful to the following agencies for grant support: National Endowment for the Humanities, General Research Division, for grant #RO-20026, 1981–1984, the major source of support for our field research; Wenner-Gren Foundation for Anthropological Research and the University Research Council of the University of North Carolina at Chapel Hill, which also contributed support for our field research; the University of North Carolina at Chapel Hill, for a Pogue Leave for Ruel Tyson during spring semester 1988; the Kenan Professorship research fund, for James Peacock; and Institute for Research in Social Science, for assistance in several areas.

We gratefully acknowledge the continuing cooperation of co-fieldworkers Daniel and Beverly Patterson. We acknowledge the practical and intellectual contributions of our research assistants. Deborah Warner undertook the immense labor of transcribing numerous tapes of sermons and interviews. Tim Pettyjohn helped finalize the manuscript and wrote Appendix I. Barry Saunders accomplished the most remarkable editorial work that either of us has witnessed, including preparation of the index. We thank the editors at the Smithsonian, Daniel Goodwin and Jeanne M. Sexton, and series editors Ivan Karp and William Merrill, for their continuing help. We acknowledge the indispensable help and suggestions of Marilyn Grunkemeyer, Robert P. Smith, Jr., Wesley Serling-Boyd, Joel Brett Sutton, Jean Harris, Beth Rambo,

Steve Davis, Suphronia Cheek, William Peck, Mary Jo Leddy, and Helen Wilson. We are grateful for the kind hospitality of Julius Miller and Jay Branscomb in sharing with us information concerning their kinsman, Max Weber.

We thank the following institutions and publishers for their cooperation: Allen and Unwin and Macmillan for permission to quote passages from Max Weber, *The Protestant Ethic and the Spirit of Capitalism*; The British Library, London; Macmillan for permission to quote passages from Henry James, *The Art of the Novel: The Critical Prefaces*; and Westminster Press for permission to quote passages from John Calvin, *The Institutes of the Christian Religion*.

Our deepest gratitude is to the Primitive Baptists of the Blue Ridge Mountains, especially Elder Walter Evans and Raymond Nichols and Nonnie Lee Nichols. We thank also the late Elder Elmer Sparks, the late Elder Dewey Roten, Elder and Mrs. Eddie Lyle, Elder Jeff Weaver, Mr. and Mrs. Green Ward, Mr. and Mrs. Roy Truitt, Mr. Billy Yates, Mr. and Mrs. Bobby Absher, Mr. and Mrs. Leslie Nichols, Elder Jess Higgins, and many others. The Primitive Baptists of the Blue Ridge have received us and our queries with a hospitality and kindness that we can never repay or forget. We dedicate this book to them, knowing that our portrayal of their lives and doctrines will not in every instance match their self-understanding, but in the hope that it will contribute to understanding and appreciation by outsiders of their remarkable tradition.

We use real names of Primitive Baptist persons, places, and churches, with these exceptions: Low Valley Church, Low Valley Association, Reed, and the Cahooneys, which are pseudonyms.

Our account of the Mountain District Association essentially ends in December 1983, which was when our fieldwork ended; while we are aware of events occurring since then, a few of which we note, we do not attempt to bring our account up to the date of publication.

Preface

The editors for the Smithsonian Series in Ethnographic Inquiry succinctly state the rationale for the works published under their sponsorship. "Ethnography as fieldwork, analysis, and literary form is the distinguishing feature of modern anthropology." The editors continue by stating that the series is guided by "the assumption that anthropological theory and ethnography are inextricably linked."

We want to stress an obvious motif in the statement of this Series, and that is the term inquiry itself. Ethnographic inquiry is complex and cunning in its practice. The key clue is provided by the editors with their phrase, "inextricably linked." They refer, of course, not only to the connection between theory and ethnography, but also to the three other practices they mention, namely, fieldwork, analysis, and literary form.

A preface is a good place to sketch some of these linkages in the course of introducing the case study in ethnographic inquiry that follows. A preface, of course, is really a retrospective set of reflections in the guise of an introduction. A preface is what happens at the threshold where hosts meet guests. What allows hosts to greet strangers is their history in the house. If our readers are our guests, then the way we introduce them to the house we have constructed reveals something about how we have lived there. Such disclosures are no doubt subject to the usual apologies and reservations, but in our case we hope there is also a continuation of the inquiry which prompted the visit and which the ethnography, in part, represents.

Another set of host-stranger relations is the reverse of the author-reader relation. In ethnography as fieldwork, rather than ethnography as analysis and literary form, the authors are the guests. How we represent our relations with the members of the Primitive Baptist churches in the Blue Ridge returns us to the link between literary form and fieldwork, and to that among analysis, theory, and the composition of the ethnography we present. So we begin our introductions not with the fieldwork, or with theory and analysis, but with the literary representation of our case and of its chief protagonists.

In chapter one our first move is to introduce a story related to us by Clerk Nichols, one of the chief protagonists in the story of the case we will soon unfold. This story, about much talking late into the night and "a gritchel," was told to us five years before the writing of this preface. The action the story narrates occurred at least two decades prior to our first fieldwork among the Primitive Baptists. We place it first in our account, much like a Primitive Baptist elder begins his sermon with a text upon which he will expound during the course of his discourse. Like a scriptural text, this story is dense with reference, arresting in its imagery, and provocative in its wit. We find this story typical and we know it to be entirely exemplary of the characters who appear in it. All the main characters in the larger narrative of the case are present in it. While in the context of its telling it was by no means introductory— all the characters had long known each other—we make it introductory to our case, not only because it names the elders, and the clerk who related it, but also because it reveals gestures and manners that tell as much about the Primitive Baptists as any action they take.

So we employ, like the fiction writer and historian, various types of narratives, from small anecdotes to the large story line of the case we relate. Narratives in ethnographic writing may not entirely create social facts, but they certainly frame and display them. The ethnographic writer, like the fiction writer, is worked upon by a variety of genres and tropes. These figures of speech and literary forms are never innocent in their representations. So the links of rhetoric and genre to theory and analysis are not always under the control of the authors. It is the privilege of readers, as guests with fresh perception, to discover how the cunning of words has helped or hindered the representation of the folks met in the course of fieldwork and understood in the course of analysis.

The Primitive Baptists, too, inherit and work within a variety of genres and tropes. They too are victors and victims of the genres and figures they use. Like us, the Baptists employ favored forms, oral and written—for example, sermons and spiritual autobiographies—and, like us, their use of oral and written forms is informed by the history of their reading in authors, such as John Gill, John Bunyan, the Elders Hassell, and song writers like Stennett and Watts. Like us they have critical standards—applied to the use of the sermon form, for example. They distinguish a good performance from a poor one, a good sermon from one that is "not blessed." Like us, the Primitive Baptists are inheritors, makers, and innovators in the forms they use. They are reciprocal practitioners and critics of each others' performances, though their terms of criticism are not strictly aesthetic but also doctrinal and spiritual.

In our writing about the Primitive Baptists we represent the forms they use and the statements they express through them. The way we describe and quote these forms and the content they express inevitably changes as we cast them into the composition of this ethnography. All our representations, then, are re-presentations, and this makes the movement from fieldwork to writing a process of translation. Like linguistic translation, ethnographic translations from fieldwork to writing constitute a performance as much akin to art as to reporting or recording. Within this art reside a number of ambiguities that are epistemological as well as ethical, rhetorical

as well as aesthetic. Again, we assert a certain kinship between our performance as translators from fieldwork to writing and the Primitive Baptists. They too have commitments
to theory, only they call it doctrine. They too are faced with
the task of translating that theory into practice within their
world. In fact, our case is, among other things, a study of how
they perform this translation. We do not intend to go further
into these parallel movements, our own and those of the
Primitive Baptists we studied. Our purpose is to acknowledge
multiple linkages among fieldwork, analysis, literary form,
and theory.

Before we became guests of our hosts, the Primitive Baptists of the Blue Ridge, we were already heirs to intellectual
traditions that gave us an orientation to social life and the
practice of religion. Our own life histories mediated these traditions of social thought to us, primarily through the universi-
ties where we studied. Our biographies in this context are a
part of the social history of ideas, a history we found ourselves
extending in the way we practiced our fieldwork.

Yet our biographies and the social history of our ideas cannot account satisfactorily for the way we engage in fieldwork
practices. There is a simple and not fully understood reason
for this, namely, fieldwork as an ensemble of practices is a
craft, or a practical art, and not a theoretical activity. Theory,
of course, does enter in, but not as theory. It enters into practice as application, as questions, and as directions for focusing
our attention. But the bias of our orientation goes more toward a knack we call "playing by ear," in styles of collabora-
tion with each other as co-investigators, and in the manner
of our relating to our hosts. This practice has as much to do
with skill in construing the gestures of comparative strangers
as with methods and theories in the interpretation of social
facts.[1]

We underscore again some similarities between us and the
Primitive Baptists. They have a problem to solve between the
theological doctrines they explicitly assert and the way they
conduct their lives as individuals and as a group. Each of

these men and women has a strong conviction about how the cosmos works. In the case of the Primitive Baptists their "theory" is the doctrine of predestination. In fact, this self-designation as "Primitive" refers, as we elaborate later, to their own effort at representing the purity of the original church, uncorrupted by the vicissitudes of history. Those who hold this doctrine do so within a life history, their own, as well as within collective histories of churches and regions. Just as in our case we confront the relationship between theories (i.e., of Durkheim and Weber) and our own work in the field, they too have theologians and elders who articulate the meanings of their doctrine and confront them with how to live it. Like us they claim the sponsorship of doctrine in the routines and in the difficulties of their lives: in their conversations among themselves and with their guests; in recollections provoked by song and story; in private meditation and public statement; and in visits with each other. These are some of the ways Primitive Baptists do their "fieldwork," that is, working out their "theories," in custom and conflict. Like us they act under the persuasions of the traditions and figures that nourish them. They too act against some of these traditions when an occasion demands it, modifying and changing the traditions they cherish. Like ethnographers in the field, their experience is not exclusively under the dominance of doctrine or theory.

By pointing out some parallels between our work and the Primitive Baptists, we do not suggest more than a generic similarity. Their theological beliefs and our social theories are of course quite different. We both live out relations between belief or theory and practice, but we do so differently. These differences result in different kinds of consciousness, already inscribed in the metaphors of host and stranger. This is what makes translation necessary, and it is also what makes it difficult and incomplete.

In a series of prefaces to the New York edition of his novels, Henry James wrote:

> There is the story of one's hero, and then, thanks to the intimate connection of things, the story of one's story itself.[2]

While we do not intend to go into a detailed account of the story of our case study, we do wish to tell some of the unsuspected connections we found during our fieldwork. Such an offering appears authorized by the rationale of this Series in Ethnographic Inquiry. Fiction writers can with good conscience and excellent craft exclude some characters and stories in order to include those they judge best for the overall story they intend to tell. Ethnographic writers make such exclusions with a bad conscience and, at best, with only an equivocal sense of mastery of craft. What we discovered in our research becomes part of our inquiry and merits some recognition here.

In the course of our work we discovered taking shape what we called a case study. Already naming what in fact did not yet exist as a case study no doubt formed our ways of thinking about our data. While such thinking is routine with many ethnographers, it does show, when acknowledged, that the genre in which the ethnographer intends to represent his or her fieldwork shapes by anticipation the way that fieldwork in construed. Upon closer examination, we found that the genre of the "case study" is unstable.

What are the boundaries that give an identity to a case? Where does a case begin and end? When does an ethnography, which begins as a case study, end by making the case study an instance, or illustration, of larger patterns of conflict in the group? When does a case study become a kind of allegory of some informing theory brought to the field by the ethnographers so that theory dominates the case narrative as the confirmation of its predictions? An ethnography that began as a synthetic project, an overall presentation of a culture or a dominant segment within it, may break in on itself, thanks to a telling example, that is in effect a case study, which compels attention at the expense of the synthetic project. The history of ethnography provides examples of both tendencies, each supporting our view that the genre of case study is subject to a variety of pulls and tugs. After we have presented our case study, we will have further reflections about its status, but here we wish to warn our readers to notice how we present the case.

The case itself prompts us to do more than present a case study. For example, our case suggests linkages to theory—Durkheim and Weber. We had studied and taught Max Weber's writing for more than twenty years before we made our first trip to visit a Primitive Baptist meeting. As our attendances increased in frequency and duration over the months beginning in the autumn of 1981, we began to note surprising conjunctions between what a German professor wrote in Heidelberg in the years 1886 to 1919 and what we observed in Ashe and Alleghany counties, North Carolina, and Carroll and Grayson counties, Virginia.

We were then unaware of the connections we would establish between chapter four of *The Protestant Ethic and the Spirit of Capitalism*, entitled "The Religious Foundations of Worldly Asceticism," first published in 1904–1905 in the *Archiv für Sozialwissenschaft und Sozialpolitik*, and the Primitive Baptists of the North Carolina and Virginia Blue Ridge.

We had not imagined while teaching this work in seminars that this section would be verified by us as we read the minutes of, and listened to sermons and debates in, the conferences and association meetings of the Primitive Baptists.

Weber had asserted that the most characteristic dogma of Calvinism was predestination. He had noted further that the history of the canonization of this dogma in the great synods of the seventeenth century, most notably those of Dordrecht and Westminster, had affected the culture and politics of the most highly developed countries of Europe. Little did we suppose that the conflicts we were to observe in the 1980s at the annual meetings of the Baptist associations would vibrantly echo Dordrecht and Westminster. Debates about implications of the doctrine of predestination continue to preoccupy these

Old Baptists and permeate their lives and conflicts. These debates continue in modest meeting houses, on front porches, and in rented school auditoria to this day. While these Calvinists are in the minority in modern culture, their theological critique of "the missionaries," as they call the evangelicals, is potent, if largely unnoticed in the majority culture.

We began to grow accustomed to these conjunctions between Weber's historiography and our observations. Yet we admit our renewed surprise when we found in the Articles of Faith of the Mountain District Association, founded in 1798, direct quotations and paraphrases of the Westminster Confession of 1647, which Weber had singled out as the most authoritative for Calvinism.

The doctrine of predestination, Weber wrote,

> . . . served as a rallying point to countless heroes of the Church militant, and in both the eighteenth and nineteenth centuries it caused schisms in the church and formed the battleground of great new awakenings. We cannot pass it by, and since today it can no longer be assumed as known to all educated men, we can best learn its content from the authoritative words of the Westminster Confession of 1647, which in this regard is simply repeated by both Independent and Baptist creeds.[3]

One of us had first read these words in 1956 and the other had studied at Harvard with Talcott Parsons, the translator of Weber's classic. But neither of us then knew that in 1832 there was a schism between "old" and "new" Baptists, and that out of that division at the Black Rock Church in Maryland came the ancestors of the Primitive Baptists we would meet in 1981 in the churches at Baywood, Virginia, and Sparta, North Carolina. The repetition of the doctrine of predestination, since its formulation by the Westminster Confession, has led to complexities in the doctrinal explication and in the politics of the Primitive Baptist polity. But we did not know about that when we set out to follow Elder Evans and to learn about the life of Clerk Nichols.

We had been taught Weber's theories and the debates about

his thesis on Protestantism and Capitalism, but we had not noted, nor had we in turn taught our students, Weber's own travels in America, just after his marriage, and his visit to relatives in the foothills of the Blue Ridge. Lacking ethnographic and historical knowledge of the Primitive Baptists in their creeds and histories, we had dismissed as only anecdotal Weber's account of a baptism in a work subsequent to the *Protestant Ethic*, namely, "The Protestant Sects and the Spirit of Capitalism."[4] Later we appreciated the story because we had heard similar stories; for example, from Elder Evans about his own baptism on a cold winter day in the Little River, which runs through the same "Blue Ridge Mountains, visible in the distance." Weber himself described attending a baptism "in the company of some relatives who were farmers in the backwoods some miles out of M. [a county seat] in North Carolina."[5]

The date of Weber's trip to visit with his relatives was 1904;[6] the time of our first visit was the autumn of 1981. The place he visited was near Mt. Airy, North Carolina.

We had come via the cities of Cambridge (Peacock) and Manchester and Chicago (Tyson), where our graduate work had taken us, to Chapel Hill, where we teach joint courses to graduate students in folklore, anthropology, and religious studies. From Chapel Hill we traveled to the Blue Ridge of North Carolina and Virginia to study Primitive Baptists, and in following our own routes and connections we crossed Weber's, whose visit to those parts had taken place more than seventy-five years before. The site of Weber's brief excursion into fieldwork became the culture and landscape of our own. This new encounter led to a re-reading of some of Weber's work with this question for our focus: what if Weber had done more fieldwork? What if Appalachian practice rather than New England texts had become the model for his construction of Protestantism? Suppose he had left the archives more frequently? We do not go here into these considerations except to note that he was well aware of ethnographic work. For example, see the last paragraphs of the introduction he wrote later to the *Protestant Ethic*.[7] We also note that ethnographic investigation would have advanced his interest in the ways the logic of theological belief not only shapes the psychology of the believer but also becomes expressed in practical conduct in the world, even in facial expressions.[8]

Weber was no longer for us only the author of theories we called, and admired as, Weberian. Our discovery of Weber in the Blue Ridge gave a place to our received genealogy of the man, grounding for us both his theory and his biography. This crossing of paths saved us from viewing his work and theory in "the artificiality of ideal types."[9] Again, we had confirmed, in several particulars, the "intimate connection of things" of which Henry James wrote. While Weber is not the hero of the case we narrate, he is very much a part of the story of our story itself.

What of the story itself? We call it a case study, a classification and genre in ethnographic writing we have already noted as elusive. But what sort of case, and whose case is it?

A conflict emerged involving many members of the several associations of Primitive Baptists we had come to know. What we had come to know about them, in their conventions and routines, began to be recast due to the emergence of the conflict. Doctrinal positions we had heard in discussion began to come into relief in differences between the contending factions. The case framed itself by appearing in our field of inquiry. On the other hand, we organize the story we tell. We weave its segments, follow lines of connection, and, when we cannot follow, make inferences. The case in its parts was given to us; these forms of presentation are the ways we give the case to our readers.

As we engaged in knitting various episodes together, we made a discovery that is by no means new to us or other ethnographers. From the case that emerged as retold by us, it was difficult for the uninitiated reader to appreciate, without background, its significance for Old Baptists. Narrative alone was insufficient to provide readers with an appropriate field of appreciation against which to judge the case. While the structure of the case is, by definition, the consequential events that compose it, the sequence is incomplete without its backdrop of antecedent forms of life and belief. Without such memories of the past, of previous conflicts and latent tensions, without the sedimentations of Primitive Baptist practice in their Blue Ridge habitations, the reader would quite properly ask, "So what?"

Narrative needs supplements. Just as cases in law make sense because they are a part of the history of law, so the conflict among the Primitive Baptists derives its meaning within and from ritual, doctrines, and life histories of the Primitive Baptists. We have embedded our narrative of the case in historical description, for deep linkages with the past of the groups concerned, a past that reaches well beyond the Blue Ridge into the Middle Atlantic States, to Old England, and to Europe of the sixteenth and seventeenth centuries. As we have already said, the past of this project connects Max Weber's studies of Calvinism and its consequences for consciousness and conduct.

But case narrative and historical description, while complementing each other, are still inadequate representations of Primitive Baptists in their ritual dramas. Particular individuals are disclosed in those dramas. We need to understand character as well as plot; actions require actors. The agents of the case were not born by the case but preceded it by many seasons and multiple routes. Characters enact their convictions out of life histories, which are parts of the background of the case and ingredients in the actions that give identity to the case. So again the geometry of the case presentation must be disturbed by another fracture, this time a cluster of narrative lines that enter the circle of conflict well before and far beyond its focus. The prose of lives must suffuse the drama, to secure stronger sinews of intimate connection between character and event, plot and action.

Henry James, in another critical preface, makes the appropriate justification, in conjunction with reference to case studies, for what ethnographers call life histories:

> Intimacy with a man's specific behavior, with his given case,
> is desperately certain to make us see it as a whole . . . . What
> a man thinks and what he feels are the history and character
> of what he does; on all of which things the logic of intensity
> rests.[10]

The various types of discourse we employ in what follows
are related to our chosen routes between the case and its contexts. The narrative of the case, historical and geographical
descriptions, summaries of doctrines and outline of church
polity, stories of lives, and brief allusions to some of the stories behind our story are related in varying measures to what
we have learned in the field and to our choices of literary
forms. We hope our fieldwork lends authority to our literary
composition. We know the relations between them are more
reciprocal than naive theories of representation allow. We
have worked to provide readers with a field of appreciation
against which they can understand the case we present. The
form our own appreciation takes is in the composition of this
ethnography.

We conclude these introductory reflections with a final reference to Weber and a final quotation from the critical prefaces of Henry James. Weber's scholarly asceticism found
many modes of expression and, undoubtedly, several forms
of repression as well. He sternly enjoins himself and his colleagues not to intrude upon the text with personal commentaries, particularly of an evaluative kind. He presents one example of such an imperative to his reader in an introduction
added to the *Protestant Ethic*.[11] Perhaps Weber allowed himself these normative admonitions because he was writing an
introduction. He said, in effect, the author should keep himself outside the text. This was a part of the specialist's ethic
in contrast to the indulgences in fashion and zeal of the literati, whom he accused of offering sermons. Yet anyone who
reads with heart and spirit—in contrast to Weber's quotation
from Faust, "Specialists without spirit, sensualists without
heart . . ."—the closing pages of the *Protestant Ethic* cannot
help feeling the author's presence registered there in power-

fully evaluative tones, made all the more poignant by the strong self-denying ordinances laid down earlier in that volume.[12]

We do not fancy ourselves among the literati. Yet, after Weber's instructive example, we do not imagine we can keep some form of commentary out of our text; nor would we wish to do so. Our commentary takes many forms—a résumé of our fieldwork, analysis, and the literary forms we have selected for the composition of this ethnography, all of which are "inextricably linked." With an economy we have not been able to match, Henry James makes an admirable statement about the best kind of commentary, the strongest mode of evaluation.

> My report of people's experience—my report as a "storyteller"—is essentially my appreciation of it. . . .[13]

CHAPTER ONE

The Primitive Baptists

Nichols, clerk of the Mountain District Primitive Baptist Association, tells this story about Evans, moderator of the association.

Once Evans and other elders were preaching the Sunday communion sermon at Cross Roads Church in Baywood, Virginia. They were spending Saturday night at the house of Nichols. Among the elders was old Cahooney, now dead, a respected preacher from the Low Valley Association, whose sons will play a part in our later narrative. As is always reported by laymen about elders, Evans and Cahooney were having a heated discussion about doctrine and scripture. Nichols told them at ten o'clock that it was time to go to bed since he had to get up early to milk his cows. Evans and Cahooney asked for a few minutes more. Nichols told them again at eleven, but the same thing happened. Then he told them at twelve, again at one, each time encountering the same resistance. Finally, at two, he laid down the law and commanded them to go to bed. They went upstairs, and Cahooney asked Nichols: "Where's my gritchel [grip, satchel]?" Nichols got it, then Cahooney asked, "Where's old Evans sleeping?" Told where, Cahooney slipped into the bedroom and they got the discussion going again. At four a.m. Nichols had to get up to milk his cows, so he stole softly downstairs, carrying his shoes. Outside, he found Elder Cahooney awake, chewing tobacco while sitting in Nichols's old car in front of the house. Cahooney told Nichols, "Two winks came in that room last night, and Evans got both of them."

Later, after church and communion, they proceeded to the baptism, down at the New River, in Nichols's old car. He was driving with the two elders in the back and his wife, Nonnie Lee, in the front. The two elders were singing so loudly and stirringly that Nichols's hair stood on end, and he got carried away. The louder they sang, the faster he drove, until, as they rounded a curve, his car was on only two wheels. Nonnie Lee told them to be quiet and slow down lest they be thought drunk.

Stories like this distill and foreshadow the personalities and social forces that come into our analysis. Nichols and Evans will be the protagonists in our case, while the Cahooney family will be the catalyst. As in this story, Nichols will appear as the down-to-earth pragmatist, Evans as the above-the-world intellectual. Nichols will be the layman host of the contending elders, the provider of food and lodging and the stabilizing mediator between them. And he is the wry but respectful observer and commentator on Evans, and the Cahooneys, and the other elders who are the stars of the Primitive Baptist universe.

The story hints, too, at the ritual, communal, and doctrinal framework within which the lives and relationships of the Primitive Baptists are carried out: communion Sunday, traveling elders staying at the house of a farmer who, regardless of their emancipated religious late-night doctrinal discussion, must carry on his schedule of milking his cows. One imagines it is dawn, on a bright summer mountain morning (we know it is summer, for communion Sunday at Mountain District churches is only in summer, a custom begun when winter weather made mountain travel difficult). Nichols has returned from his chores, and the elders join the Nicholses in a breakfast of sausage, biscuits, and gravy—Cahooney bleary-eyed, having spent the night in the car, Evans bright and lively in his usual fashion, smoking cigarettes and drinking coffee, Nichols the host and Nonnie Lee the hostess spreading food in the kitchen built partly by Nichols's own hand. By 9:30 they set out for church, the men dressed up in their starched white shirts and dark Sunday suits, Nonnie Lee in Sunday dress. Maybe they drive, as later they have to drive to the river for a baptism. Or maybe they walk the half-mile or so (in past times Evans would have walked fifteen miles to church) to the nearby church of Cross Roads, which is part of the little village of Baywood. Nichols, the clerk, church handyman, and lay leader, opens the church and starts the singing—unaccompanied, slow, and stately, in dissonant harmonies, said to be as close to the American singing at the time of the Plymouth pilgrims as it is still possible to hear. The songs are from as long ago as the English Puritan writers of the sixteen hundreds, and they express a Calvinist doctrine: "Mixture of Joy and Sorrow," "Guide Me O Thy Great Jehovah," and "Amazing Grace."

If Nichols leads the singing, in his strong baritone, the guest Elder Evans excites it, soaring above the melody in a powerful tenor. After the singing, one of the elders delivers the pastoral prayer, then both preach: as "ocupella" as the unaccompanied singing, without the crutch of notes, constructing an argument "at the stand," drawing on the memorized King James Bible. After an intermission, they meet again at the sound of singing, for communion, with wine made by the deacon and unleavened bread baked by the deacon's wife. A foot washing follows: all the men and all the women, separated, divide into pairs; each person, whether low or high in social standing, washes the feet of the other in a tin bowl, wiping them with a white towel girded about the waist. While singing a final hymn they celebrate the hand of fellowship: each shaking hands with every other one; gnarled, calloused powerful hands grasping younger, more tender ones, some embracing while silent tears are shed. They then go outside for dinner on the grounds: ham, chicken, beans, squash, tomatoes, cakes, pies, and iced tea. A little while later, now early afternoon, Evans, Cahooney, Nichols, and Nonnie Lee get in Nichols's car and set off, singing loudly, for the baptism at the

New River, down curvy and dusty roads where Nichols in his excitement rises to two wheels. As crowds gather on the banks, the elders wade into the water with the candidates, immerse them, pray and speak, and the candidates come out wet but beaming to be received, as new members, by their friends and kin on the bank. Cahooney and Evans then go back to Nichols's, fetch their "gritchels," get in their own cars or trucks, and drive home across the Blue Ridge Mountains— Cahooney to his farm to the southwest in Virginia, Evans to his place to the southeast in North Carolina. Before the sun sets, they have to get on with their own farm chores, which will not wait until Monday morning.

Issues

The bucolic setting of the Blue Ridge masks besetting issues that are grounded in existential conditions of human life as formulated by the Calvinism of the Primitive Baptists. The essential problem is that Calvinism denies the ultimate morality and authenticity of any human community. Primitive Baptists treasure community with ambivalence—loving it, yet knowing that love must remain limited and suspect. Within the frame of this paradox they struggle to sustain a meaningful and decent life on this earth, knowing nothing, and forbidden to know anything, of their destiny in the next life. They cherish history, yet history is a flawed source of understanding; they cherish the group, yet the group is not privileged in terms of the ultimate; they admire their leaders, yet leaders too have only limited powers in terms of doctrine. As part of the paradoxes and dilemmas that confront the Primitive Baptists they encounter their own tendency toward schism and division, but doctrine limits the significance of this too: for romanticized rebellion and revolution are as suspect as sycophantic obedience, sentimental sense of belonging, or any other seduction into fascination with the social order.

These qualities and paradoxes will become apparent in our narrative. The case that follows does not develop into a theatrical climax with all tensions resolved, but it does show the serious deliberations of the members who played a part, and the narrative provides a thread to follow as we strive to capture the strains between doctrine and experience of Primitive Baptists of the Blue Ridge.

Sacred Geography

The Blue Ridge is the eastern margin of the Appalachian mountain ranges. Less sharply cut and elevated than the Rockies or the Sierras, more so than the carpeted green hills of Wales or Devonshire, this area forms a complex topography of coves, basins, and narrow river valleys. The upland streams do not have wide valley courses and extensive alluvial plains such as those of the Piedmont, and the topography does not support dense and extensive agricultural settlements.

Climatically, the area varies dramatically. Rain in a valley turns into snow on the peaks, and one can experience strong winds and cold rains on a mountain while the weather is mild a few hundred feet below. Oak, chestnut, and pine grow on intermediate slopes, northern hardwoods and spruce/fir at higher elevations. Squirrel, rabbit, raccoon, opossum, beaver, and deer, as well as turkey and other birds, are found and hunted with dog, bow, and rifle or shotgun. While large-scale farming is not possible in this terrain, the people of these mountains raise cattle, sheep, and goats, and they plant tobacco fields, vegetable gardens, and apple orchards.

Land and space are fundamental in the life experience of the Primitive Baptists of the Mountain District. Most of them work outdoors and hunt, fish, or garden when they are not working, and their environment imposes itself through rugged terrain and the sometimes harsh climate—which can bring heavy snow, treacherous ice, and zero temperatures in winter, as well as strong winds on the peaks. The difficulty of traveling by foot or horse or wagon is still part of the memory of those past middle age, and for all, travel over rough roads, curves, and hills for long distances to town and church is part of life; large-wheeled trucks pulling into yards of small churches set the social scene on Saturdays and Sundays. Preaching to oneself while cutting briars, or singing hymns behind the plow, are part of the worship experience on other days. Landmark religious experiences are situated in briar patches and on mountain peaks as well as publicized in churches. Elder Evans allowed us to trace with him a number of locales identified in his spiritual autobiography. He showed us the cabin where he was born, the one-room school (now a barn filled with hay) he had attended, fields where he had worked, the house, in a field, where he had first prayed publicly, the country house where he had had supper afterwards, the road along which he had walked fifteen miles to preach publicly for the first time the doctrine of predestination, the icy river where he was baptized on the cold November day when he joined the Primitive Baptists, and the church graveyards where his parents and other kinfolk and parishioners were buried. A site he would not take us to, ostensibly because of its distance away, was a ridge where he experienced his great "translation" into a spiritual state analogous to that of Elijah being taken up by God.

"This country" is a phrase that these mountain Primitive Baptists use for the land that comprises their domain, more or less coterminous with the boundaries of their association. For most of them this is the area in which they have lived their lives, for even when, like Elder Evans, they have traveled and worked far away, they have returned for work and preaching to "this country." As religious allusions suggest, "this country" is more than just territory. Yet the Old Baptists are not a Nature cult, and their people are hardly *Naturvölker*. They do not mythologize the land as sacred or as the dwelling place of spirits. As Calvinists, who have, in Max Weber's terms, stripped the land of enchantment, and as Americans of Calvinistic heritage, they do not hesitate to exploit the land for survival. They are bulldozer operators, lumberjacks, and stone quarriers. And while they appreciate natural beauty, situating their churches and houses on picturesque ridges overlooking beautiful valleys, they shield themselves from nature, with storm doors and picture windows and wood stoves, in their homes and churches.

Even if the land is fallen, it is still identified with, or at least designated in terms of, biblical names. There is a Mount Pisgah locally as well as in their hymns, an Antioch church, and a wealth of expressions taken from the Song of Solomon. In sermons, elders vividly evoke meanings of local natural objects, such as mountains, valleys, birds, animals, streams, storms, floods, and winds, that are also part of the biblical world. Elder Roten proclaims, in a memorable sermon, "I preach the God of these hills!" The Primitive Baptists do plot, then, a sacred geography, though they lace it with the usual Calvinistic interdictions about identifying the transcendent with the sensed.

Coming from the east to the Blue Ridge Mountains, country of the Mountain District Association, one leaves heavily traveled expressways (Interstates 85, 40, and 77), rimmed with factories, motels, and restaurants, that link the middle-sized cities of the Piedmont. In summer (when we made most of our trips) these expressways are hot and humid, crowded and noisy—concrete passages of smog. They create a certain urban intensity in a region still half-rural.

As one leaves the expressways and starts on the winding incline (Route 21) to Sparta, the noise, heat, and crowdedness all diminish. By the time one has crossed the Blue Ridge Parkway (at an elevation of some three thousand feet, within sight of Sparta), the temperature is markedly cooler, and the national-chain motels, restaurants, and factories have been replaced with local garages, small stores, and houses or mobile homes. The town of Sparta itself is at an intersection of mountain roads. The largest building is the courthouse, for, though small (pop. 1,687), Sparta is the county seat. On the courthouse lawn is a small cage that was once the jail. A cafe, clothing stores, a tractor repair shop, a building supply store, a real estate office, and a store selling electronic devices, guitars, and country music records and tapes are among the establishments that cater to the substantial flow of traffic, often pickup trucks, issuing from the country surrounding the town. Slightly off town center is a large brick but stone-faced Missionary Baptist church. This stone facing was constructed by Elder Evans, master stone mason. But no Primitive Baptist church is to be found on the main street of this town or any other in the Mountain District.

On the outskirts, some miles east, lives Elder Evans, moderator of the Mountain District Association, in a house on a high ridge overlooking fields that spread toward the Blue Ridge Parkway in the far distance.

If one continues through Sparta, going north, one comes shortly to the line dividing North Carolina from Virginia. This line is marked by the New River, which is spanned by a metal bridge. Crossing the bridge, one comes to the town of Independence, Virginia. Like Sparta, Independence is a county seat, and it boasts two imposing courthouses, an old one on the town square and a new one overlooking the square from a hill. Like Sparta, Independence is a small town (pop. 1,112) at the intersection of four highways that connect it to the rural residences of its shoppers. Similar to Sparta, here are a small cafe, clothing stores, repair shops, also a funeral home and a school. The most prominent church here is Methodist, attached to a graveyard with tombstones dating back to the eighteenth century. As in Sparta, no Primitive Baptist church is within the town proper.

On the outskirts, on a high ridge reachable via dirt roads, lives Elder Reed, at the outset of our fieldwork (1981–83) the assistant moderator of the association.

Independence and Sparta are two of the three towns within the Mountain District Association. The third and largest town in this association territory is Galax, Virginia, some twenty miles down the New River to the east. Boasting a population of some six thousand, Galax is more than a convergence of mountain highways. Opening onto its long main street are department stores, a religious bookstore, a Blue Ridge craft center staffed by local Virginia ladies, a large motel, restaurants,

and a drug store. A block off the main street are large furniture factories; residential areas include large homes. Galax
has a Primitive Baptist church within the town limits, though
not at its center.

Mountain District Primitive Baptist Association, then, surrounds three urbanized points: Sparta, Independence, and
Galax, each approximately a half-hour drive from the others.
While the three towns do constitute points of reference, they
do not constitute critical locales for the Primitive Baptists.
The network of churches is located not in the towns but in
the country, along the tortuous roads criss-crossing and surrounding this triangle. The minutes of the association (prepared by the clerk of the association, Raymond Nichols, now
a retired supervisor with the Virginia Highway Department)
locate churches with reference both to towns and to rural
roads, as in these examples:

> Elk Creek Church, Sparta, North Carolina. Located five miles
> west of Sparta. From Route 21 at Twin Oaks, North Carolina,
> take 221 south, turn right on Route 93, just two miles to church
> on right of road.
> Antioch Church, Stratford, North Carolina. Located six miles
> southwest of Sparta, North Carolina. Turn off Route 221 onto
> Route 1167 (Antioch Church Road), go two miles, turn left on
> Route 1163. Just .4 mile to brick church on left of road.
> Peach Bottom Church, Independence, Virginia. Located one
> mile north of Independence at intersection of Route 21 and 654.
> Cross Roads Church, Baywood, Virginia. Located seven miles
> west of Galax, Virginia. Turn off Route 58 (five miles west of
> Galax) onto Route 636 for .3 mile. Turn right on Route 626, and
> church is just beyond Baywood Elementary School.

Equally precise directions are supplied for the remainder
of the nine churches of the Mountain Association (see Appendix A).

While these town-referenced directions serve to direct new-
comers such as ourselves to the churches, members who live
scattered throughout the rural areas (homes, like churches,
are rarely in town) plot their own mental maps that connect

the churches along unmarked roads and in terms of natural features. Creeks, for example, serve as landmarks—reflecting former days, no doubt, when members came overland rather than on roads. Four of the nine Mountain Association churches are named for creeks (Elk Creek, Rock Creek, Saddle Creek, and Peach Bottom) and one for a river (Little River), whereas only one is named for roads (Cross Roads). Mr. Green Ward, a farmer, once indicated from his porch, at the top of a hill near Independence, the systems of creeks that led across the county—a classification system so pervasive that in a nearby area a Primitive Baptist church that happens not to be on a creek is named simply "No Creek."

Networks and Exchanges: How the Dispersed Stay Versed

The nine churches of the Mountain District Association meet according to the following schedule:

Church	Sunday of Meeting
Virginia Churches	
Cross Roads	first and third
Rock Creek	first
Galax	second
Peach Bottom	second
Saddle Creek	fourth
North Carolina Churches	
Union	first
Elk Creek	second
Little River	third
Antioch	fourth

Primitive Baptists understand that when a church meets on a Sunday, it also meets on the Saturday of that weekend—a custom that is said to have originated when travel was so difficult that anyone who had traveled to church for service on

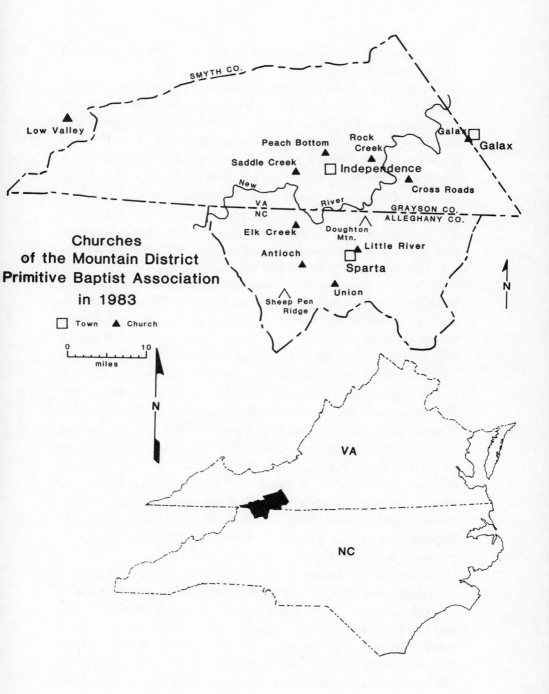

Churches
of the Mountain District
Primitive Baptist Association
in 1983

one day would spend the night in order to attend a second day as well.

In this table, the churches are divided by location and ordered by Sunday of meeting. The map shows that there is a cluster of churches some five to ten miles apart on the North Carolina side of the line and another such cluster on the Virginia side, with Galax Church slightly outside this cluster. A member living on the Virginia side can go through the entire monthly cycle, from first to fourth Sundays, within the Virginia cluster (with a choice between two churches on the first and second Sundays), and a resident on the North Carolina side can go through the cycle within the North Carolina cluster. This pattern becomes relevant later.

"Primitive Baptists will drive the furtherest to hear the least" is an aphorism quoted by them but attributed to outsiders. "When we're not having church at Senter, we just decide where we'll go that Sunday . . . sometimes we drive three or four hours . . . wherever we decide to go, we know some one will take us in," remarks Bobby Absher of the Senter Church in the Senter Association in neighboring Ashe County, confirming at least the first part of the aphorism. Such movement is encouraged by the fact that members' home churches do not meet weekly, so that during off-weeks they can choose to go to another church within the association or travel to a church elsewhere. If a respected elder is preaching at a church several hours away, a layman may well go to that church, and, when a church holds its association meeting, the opportunity to hear a number of visiting elders will draw people from a radius of more than a hundred miles.

"Wherever we decide to go, we know some one will take us in" alludes not only to hospitable reception at church but also to food and lodging. Primitive Baptists are affronted if any visitor, even non-Primitive Baptists like ourselves, stay in a motel. They are accustomed to overnight guests, for whom they spread good tables of country food: biscuits, gravy, and eggs for breakfast; beef, ham, salads, fresh garden vegetables, and cakes and pies. Everyone has a garden; likely the meats are home-butchered and cured. The wife, who does the cooking, may very well have woven the bedspread, an Appalachian craft, and the husband may have constructed the bed or even the house, for many are excellent craftsmen. The self-grown and self-made are combined with modern conveniences, however, such as refrigerators, freezers, and electric stoves. Host and hostess take pleasure in putting their own as well as purchased provisions at the service of guests, toward whom they are gracious without reservation but also without pretense and display—a directness and simplicity that contrast with the more elaborate style associated with gentry of the Southern lowlands. Also in contrast with lowland gentry, Primitive Baptists have no servants. Primitive Baptists speak with pleasure of harnessing their energies toward providing shelter and hospitality for guests among "our people." Nonnie Lee Nichols describes the formidable amount of food and cooking she produced for a set of elders who stayed with them, and Elder Reed, co-pastor of Cross Roads Church, describes how pleased he is that he has been able to expand his house to accommodate guests. These comments are expressed in tones of pleasure rather than complaint, for hospitality is seen as part of a religious way of life that is not onerous duty but a chance to contribute materially to the church community.

The Traveling Elders
While the laity may drive a long way to attend a service and may entertain guests who have come for that purpose, circles of travel for elders are even larger. Within the association, each elder pastors at least one church; one of them pastors three, and another pastors several within the neighboring Senter Association as well as one within the Mountain District Association. Customarily, at a given service more than one elder preaches, so that the pastor almost always is joined by a visiting elder, either someone within the association whose own church is not meeting that weekend or a visitor from out-

side. Thus, elders are moving about among local churches more frequently and for greater distances than the laity, in a sort of "circuit rider" pattern.

Elders who become better known expand their travel circle beyond the association. Elders of Mountain District Association such as Evans or Yates travel as far as Texas to the southwest, Pennsylvania to the north, and Georgia to the southeast, while visitors from that same radius regularly come to the Mountain District Association. One visiting elder, Charles Alexander, even came from Liverpool, England (in England, as will be noted, there is a tradition congruent with that of the Primitive Baptists in America). Traveling away and drawing in visitors from away are reciprocal arrangements, based on mutual invitation and exchange.

After the principle of "A Prophet is without honor in his own Land," distance serves to enhance reputations of elders. An elder from far away is listened to with special attention. Laity recount marvelous sermons they have heard, and which they now tape and listen to repeatedly, from visiting elders. Elders recall wonderful meetings far away in which they were blessed and given liberty to transcend themselves in preaching; such experiences tend to occur during visits, rather than in the elders' home churches.

For an elder caught up in the crush of work around the clock during the week, weekend travel can be wearying. Young Elder Yates, despite powerful physique and forceful character, once collapsed under the strain (though his collapse was, in fact, a kind of shell shock, repeating traumatic experiences from wartime service in Vietnam). But as we observed elders visiting in local churches, we saw mainly conviviality. For most elders, traveling is remembered with exhilaration. They recall the scriptural text, the rousing hymns sung, the congregational crowds, their inspired sermons. Hosts and hostesses are apt to recall them as, in the words of Mary Absher, "having a good time." As in the anecdote of Raymond Nichols, the visits are when elders can talk and argue issues of scripture and doctrine. Losing sleep, released from their chores, they eat well, and enjoy a kind of intellectual effervescence, which then carries over to their excitement in preaching—and maybe even to lusty singing in the car on the way to the river on a Sunday afternoon.

The Ritual Cycle

The Primitive Baptist ritual cycles that occur within a church building, or under the auspices of the church, can be categorized according to the length of the cycles: weekly (the Saturday/Sunday services) and yearly (communion and the association meeting). Other rituals are gauged according to the life cycle of an individual (weddings and funerals) or the intersection of the individual's life cycle and the developmental cycles of a church as it expands and shrinks, losing and gaining members, and replaces officers (baptism, ordination). A third type of ritual is occasional: special services (rather like revivals in more evangelical churches) when visiting elders preach for several days running, or special meetings if and when troubles in a church call for them.

The Weekly Service

If you ask "What time is the service?" an hour will be stated, but you will be later than anyone else if you wait until that hour to arrive. More than half an hour before the official time, whether on a Sunday or Saturday, trucks and cars begin to pull into the yards of churches. People often sit in their vehicles until about half an hour before the official hour, then they file in to start the singing of hymns. The women wear dresses, never pants, but they do not display any special hairstyles or headcoverings (such as the long hair of some Pentecostals or the coverings of Mennonites, Amish, or German Brethren). The men usually wear coats and ties, although younger ones may be more informal, and they too have no special fashions such as the beards and black suits of the German groups; but they would no more come in overalls or jeans than the women in pants or aprons.

The old churches have two doors, ostensibly for the two genders, and the two front sections, for members, are divided according to gender: the section to the preacher's right (when he faces the congregation) for men, and that to his left for women. The two larger sections, in front of the pulpit, or "stand," accommodate visitors as well as members; they are somewhat mixed by gender, insofar as some couples sit together, but these pews tend to be divided in accord with the members' section division—women on the left and men on the right.

The song leader is always a male in these Mountain District Primitive Baptist churches. (Black churches in neighboring associations—in contrast with Mountain District churches, which are white in ethnic composition—sometimes have a female song leader.) The song leader calls out a number, sets the pitch, and starts the song (always unaccompanied; there are no instruments), which the group joins in—powerfully, in straight (no vibrato) mountain-style voices.

Hymnals usually give words only, so the leader must sing out the tune and the congregation must know it. Certain traditional modes of singing, such as by shape notes (a way of indicating pitch by the shape of the notation rather than placement in lines and spaces) and lining out (where the leaders sings each line solo before the congregation repeats it in chorus), are known but not typically practiced in these churches. They go through a half-dozen or so hymns, singing every verse of each.

An elder then takes the stand to give the opening prayer. In preparation, he asks that the congregation join him in a song, which is often a particular one expressing the lowly and humble state in which he and they approach God. He then gets down on his knees, behind the stand, bows his head, and prays a long prayer asking God's forgiveness and support. He does not, however, necessarily ask for God's help in preaching, for usually this elder is not the one who will preach the sermon.

As the praying elder returns to his seat, to the right of the

stand, he shakes hands with the preaching elder who mounts
the stand to deliver his sermon (formally known as "discourse"). This elder begins by reading (or quoting from memory) a passage from scripture. Since the elder has not been
permitted to prepare a sermon in advance, this passage will
be the basis from which he must construct a message while
in the stand. Depending on whether or not he is "blessed"
(that is, inspired by God) he may preach at length—perhaps
an hour—or sit down almost immediately if he finds he has
little to say. If, as in many services, more than one elder is
to preach, the retiring elder may leave the stand saying he will
"get out of the way" of the next elder, so that the next has
ample time.

When the last elder finishes preaching he calls for the singing of a closing hymn. As the congregations sing, they initiate
a distinctive ritual known as "the hand of fellowship." The
elder comes down from the stand and stands, flanked by other
elders and deacons, at the front of the church. Beginning with
the male members, then followed by the rest of the congregation, the people form a line that passes by the elders, then
passes back down the center aisle, so that eventually everyone present shakes hands once (and only once) with everyone else. Many not only shake hands but also embrace, and
many are moved to tears by this extension of the hand of fellowship. As all return to seats they are still singing the hymn.
The elders remain standing in front, and the pastor gives, or
calls on someone to give, a closing prayer. The pastor also issues an invitation to anyone who feels "desire" to become a
member, but this is not dramatized or emphasized as in the
evangelical churches; it is simply stated.

This concludes the Sunday service. On Saturday, the service as such is followed by a business meeting called "conference." This meeting is opened by the pastor asking if there
is peace in the church; once that peace is affirmed, the meeting proceeds.

Needless to say, behind the ritual performances are certain
nuts and bolts. Before communion, the deacon's wife must

prepare unleavened bread, and the deacon ferment or pro-
cure wine. All of the women must cook and pack dishes for
dinner on the grounds. The deacon's wife must wash and iron
towels in preparation for foot washing. Women of the church
host the visiting elders, bidding for the honor of doing so and
relishing their visits because of the chance for contact and
learning. (Mrs. Crouse, who has a guestbook listing elders who
have stayed with her over many years, remarks that she
would rather listen to the elders argue than go to church.) It
is the woman who cooks and serves the table of visiting elders
before they go to church in the morning and after they preach
in the noon and evening, the elders and other male visitors
sitting at the table talking, the woman serving (though usually
assisted by her husband).

The men may not have prepared the food, but they may
have grown it or butchered it. And they have, especially if
they are deacons and clerks, mowed the church lawn, repaired the roof, painted the walls, and turned on the heat.
They have likewise maintained, by their own hand, their own
houses and cars, which are then placed at the service of visiting elders. If they are deacons or clerks, they have helped to
arrange for the visits to occur, having taken charge of inviting
elders to preach and setting dates. Without hired staff of any
kind, all such work, except large-scale construction in some
instances, is carried out by the laymen of the church.

Inasmuch as preparations and maintenance are rendered
as sacred services, they are themselves ritualized. The clarity
and rigidity of division of labor between men and women is
itself of ritual character. Some activities that are "practical"
are also "ritual," such as the cleaning and decorating of cemeteries, undertaken on such special occasions as the annual
communion Sunday, when family members from near and far
gather.

Even the mundane is imbued with ritual. Eating, for example, is done in standard fashion, standing up, at dinner on
the grounds. Menus are standard for Southern Protestant
gatherings everywhere, precisely the same dishes. (Yet some-

thing is made, jokingly, of special dishes—Mrs. Truitt's banana pudding, Mr. Nichols's lemonade.) The shelters for eating at many churches are set near cemeteries, symbolizing a link to tradition and past.

Within the frame of such practical activities as preparing food, cleaning the grounds, repairing the buildings, eating, and transporting, things are done efficiently, without fuss; the Primitive Baptists are practical people. Yet their choice of the frame itself signals the ritual character of these activities. They live, after all, in the secular world. They eat fast foods, live in mobile homes, drive on highways and expressways. They live expertly in this world, too, yet for that practical domain most intimately part of their Primitive Baptist identity, they deliberately choose, for the most part, to maintain what they remember as traditional: the set country menu, log benches and shelters, division of labor between men and women. They are firmly "primitive."

Annual Meetings: Communion
Communions and the association meeting are complementary in that a communion is held during the summer months—June, July, or August—by each church individually, then followed immediately, in the first week of September, by the association meeting, which brings all churches together. The two kinds of meetings differ in that the communion meeting has a more sacred character whereas the association meeting is somewhat secularized, especially in recent times when, owing to limitations of space in certain churches, the association meeting may be held in a school auditorium with dinner in the school lunchroom (the case for the Mountain District Association meetings in 1982 and 1983).

The minutes show the annual schedule of communion meetings; a separate Sunday is assigned to each of the nine churches for communion, beginning with the third Sunday of June and continuing through the fourth Sunday of August. Typically, no two churches schedule communion on the same Sunday, so that a member of the association could conceivably attend all communions of all churches in the association. In fact, some do make a point of attending communions at churches other than their home churches, but this practice seems especially prevalent among the deacons, clerks, and elders, who sometimes reciprocate: If you attend my communion, I'll come to yours. Ordinary members seem on the whole to stick to their home church, but the schedule for the entire association is public knowledge. The practice of designating Sundays by order (first, second, third, fourth) rather than by specific dates means that the formula remains essentially the same year after year, so that people know by memory the communion schedule just as they know the schedule of weekly services. As is typical in ritual cycles, such a formula emphasizes repetition and predictability; perhaps a liking for formulas and formulaics reflects also the Primitive Baptist Calvinistic propensity to rationalize and systematize.

A communion is held following a break after the regular Sunday service; the presiding elder instructs the congregation to return "at the sound of singing." The communion meal is eaten only by members, although a number of visitors are usually present also, seated in non-members' pews. The communion ritual is divided into three parts: the regular service, with hymn singing and preaching; "foot washing," which ends with handshaking, embracing, and weeping, as members experience their fellowship; and communion itself.

A small table below and in front of the stand is covered with a white cloth, on which is placed a tin pitcher, filled with water, beside a tin bowl. Members then take turns washing each other's feet. The washing proceeds in strict spatial order down each pew, such that each person washes his or her neighbor's feet, then the neighbor reciprocates, with no choosing of partners. (This procedure encourages disregard of status or other ways of "respecting person"; we have seen a church leader sharing washing with a retarded man; however, one does not wash the feet of the opposite sex.) Each person removes his or her shoes, and socks or stockings (they joke about the problem this would pose for a woman wearing panty hose), the partner rinses off the person's feet with water from the bowl, and then wipes them with the towel.

The scriptural basis for this practice is the Gospel of John (13. 1-10), which recounts how, during the Last Supper, Christ girded himself with a cloth and washed his disciples' feet.

When the washing is finished, a deacon disposes of the remaining water by throwing it out the open doorway.

The actual communion is centered around the same table as the foot washing. The presiding elder introduces the ritual with some commentary (in those we heard, he explained that some Christians ceased at a certain point to believe in transubstantiation—a word he explicates—but that the Primitive Baptists do follow the scripture which calls for true wine—the "fruit of the vine"). After the sharing of the plate of bread and the cup is complete, a deacon throws out the remaining wine just as he threw out the remaining water.

The deacon's wife is, as noted, responsible for preparing the wine, bread, and the water for the foot washing and communion; the deacon for disposing of the remains at the end.

After the communion, the church holds "dinner on the grounds." Outdoors on long tables the women bring out baskets and coolers of food and drink. The menu is again typical of Southern Protestant reunion meals: fried chicken, roast beef, sausage, congealed salads, cooked vegetables (corn, green beans, sweet potatoes), rolls or white bread, cakes and pies, and iced tea, coffee, or soft drinks. A man says grace, the women prepare and distribute the food, and everyone eats on paper plates, usually standing around in conversational groups. Within an hour the meal is finished, the tables cleared, and people pile into their trucks and cars and leave.

The Association Meeting
Most formal and official of all meetings of the Mountain District Association is the association meeting itself, which is the only meeting reported in printed minutes (see Appendix A); the monthly business meeting of each individual church is re-

ported in handwritten minutes. The heading of the minutes, echoed in the opening statement at the meeting, states how many association meetings have been held before—e.g., the "One Hundred and Eighty-Fifth Annual Session of the Mountain District Primitive Baptist Association"; the place, e.g., "held with Peach Bottom Church, Independence, Virginia"; and the date, "beginning on Friday before the first Sunday in September, 1983." It also announces the time and place of the next meeting. It tells the names, addresses, and telephone numbers of the association officers: moderator, assistant moderator, clerk, and assistant clerk.

The minutes then report the previous year's "Proceedings": that singing had been followed by prayer by a certain elder and an introductory sermon by the moderator based on a certain text (in 1983, Colossians 1. 12-13, pertaining to the topic "Translation"). After intermission with lunch, "the messengers assembled in the meeting house to attend to the business of the association." Following prayer by a certain elder, the clerk had called for, received, and read letters from the churches; officers had been elected for the next year; visitors from "sister associations and sister churches" had been called for and welcomed (these visitors and their associations are listed); minutes had been received from certain associations; committee members had been appointed by the moderator for this session (to committees on preaching, finance, arrangements, and distribution of the minutes). Finally, the association had adjourned until Saturday morning at ten a.m., closed with a prayer by a certain elder.

On Saturday, continue the minutes, the association had opened, following singing, with prayer by a certain elder. The roll of messengers had been called, visitors called, and committees called to report, after which they were discharged. (These reports had announced: decisions about where to meet the next year and how many copies of the minutes to print and distribute; decisions to print memorials and obituaries and to poll churches for building funds; a financial report; and the person selected to preach at this session.)

For each session (Friday afternoon and Friday night, Saturday morning, afternoon, and night, and Sunday morning), the minutes give the roster of preachers, together with the text each had used, and who had prayed the opening and closing prayer.

The clerk had been appointed as treasurer and charged with superintending the printing of the minutes.

"Thus closed the one hundred and eighty-fifth session of the Mountain District Association in peace and fellowship. Each minister who filled the stand was wonderfully blessed to preach the gospel in its purity and love to a large congregation."

These were the formal events, in accurate and precise summary, as reported by the clerk of the association. For a description of informal happenings, compare our observations of this same meeting at the end of chapter six.

Thus goes the year of the Primitive Baptists of the Mountain District Association: the weekly cycle of Saturday and Sunday services; the summer season of communions held at each church individually; and the annual association meeting held the first week of September. This system of cycles frames the lives of the members and especially the elders and other officers. Unlike more hierarchical churches, where the congregation as a whole does not participate in clearly demarcated annual meetings uniting every church, the association meeting for the Primitive Baptist is attended by most of its active members. Each association meeting is well documented by printed minutes, which are distributed annually to some 800 persons and sent for deposit at appropriate archives.

In counterpoint to the monthly and annual cycles, which are regularized according to calendars set in advance, individuals enter and leave the church and assume church offices according to rituals held as occasion demands. Entrance is by the ritual of baptism, exit by exclusion, dismissal, or death. Dismissal is rare (no cases in the Mountain District Association in 1983, the year on which we shall focus in our case study), as is exclusion (two cases in 1983), whereas departure from the church by death is more common: ten persons died in 1983, balancing fourteen received by baptism (and none received by letter or relation). So in practice, baptism and funerals are the common ways of signaling entry and exit. Members assume office by ordination. The other important rite of passage is the wedding.

Unlike the monthly services, of which we attended dozens, the communions, of which we attended several, and the association meetings, of which we attended two, but which are well described in outline in annual minutes, we were limited in our attendance of the occasional rituals—baptism, funeral, ordination, and weddings. Accordingly, we are less confident that in describing these we describe what is "typical" for Mountain District Primitive Baptists. We attended only two baptisms, one ordination, one funeral, and one wedding.

Baptism occurs in a river or other body of water (unlike the majority of Baptist churches, Primitive Baptists do not have baptismal fonts in the building behind the pulpit). Those baptisms we witnessed were in the afternoon. After a prayer, the candidate and the elders (usually one on each side of the candidate) wade out into the river about waist deep, and the elders support the back of the candidate as they submerge him or her, face up, then raise him or her face up. (This face-up posture has many significances, one of which is the look up toward heaven; at a more psychological level, the face-up position suggests a passive, accepting, feminine attitude, as contrasted with the more active posture of a person going under face down with his body in a crouching position to maintain control. Such a face-down posture is imputed to neighboring German Brethren, who are accordingly termed "Dunkards".) After coming up, the newly baptized person looks and describes himself as tremendously happy; people baptized in icy winter waters—sometimes even through holes cut in the ice—describe themselves as warm despite the cold. Just as going under face up, as into the grave, is seen as symbolizing death, so does coming up symbolize rebirth.

Complementing baptism in the river, burial, of course, is in the ground; the two rituals are alike in that in both a person is put under, later to rise again. When a person dies nowadays, the funeral may begin at a funeral home, with the Primitive Baptist ceremony differing from the ceremony of other orders in their exclusion of the taped organ music that some funeral homes play; after all, instrumental music is prohibited in the church. The service begins with singing of Primitive Baptist hymns, both by soloists and congregation, and is followed by prayer and a sermon. Demeanor is reserved, with little show of emotion. Given the Calvinist creed, no promise is given that the deceased will go to heaven—although, in the funeral we attended, the elder stated that the deceased had fine qualities suggesting that she was a "child of God." The sentimental and elaborate eulogy heard in some mainline Baptist services was absent. After the service, the procession went to the graveyard, beside the home church of the deceased, and, after a prayer, lowered her casket into the grave. An obituary was published in the annual minutes (for an example of an obituary see Appendix H).

A Primitive Baptist wedding is similar in format to those of other Protestant denominations, except that instrumental music is not permitted. In the wedding we attended, the wedding march issued from a record player placed in the outer section of the church; also a soloist sang. A visiting elder presided. The bride proceeded down the aisle, in a gown, and was given away by her father to the groom, after which the couple left the church in a shower of rice. A reception was held in the shelter behind the church.

Ordination, like baptism, weddings, and funerals, is a rite of passage, but one undergone only by elders and deacons. Elders and deacons are considered complementary officers; elders are called to preach, deacons to take care of practical matters of the church. Their careers differ but the ritual of ordination is similar. Each is examined by a committee of elders, a presbytery, regarding knowledge of doctrine; then, if found adequate, each is "returned to the church" as ordained elder or deacon. An elder must still await the call from a particular church before he can become a pastor, but a deacon assumes office immediately. The deacon, having been examined by the committee, sits with his wife facing the stand while an elder lectures them on their respective duties, quoting St. Paul regarding the duties of the "Bishop's wife." (In practical terms, the deacon's wife is, as noted, assigned the task of preparing the communion, whereas the elder's wife has no specific assigned duties.) Ordination is incorporated into the regular Sunday service.

Baptism, funeral, ordination, and wedding often assume a sequence in Primitive Baptist life cycle different from that in many Protestant denominations. This is because baptism often occurs very late in the life of the Primitive Baptist—perhaps in middle age or even very old age. Accordingly, one may be married before being baptized. Some persons have been baptized, ordained as deacons, and then buried in close succession, owing to the late age of baptism.

The mountain environment, dispersed settlement pattern, and rather individualistic values of most Mountain District Primitive Baptists encourage independence and solitude. The farmer on his small plots, the hunter in the forest, the stone mason, the housewife, all work alone or with a spouse, child, or partner—but rarely as part of a large organization. Nor, as noted, do most of them live in towns and clustered villages. Nor is the Primitive Baptist church a highly bureaucratic institution. Neither individual churches nor the association sponsor Sunday schools, youth groups, recreational activities, choirs, or social welfare or educational endeavors. They confine themselves to the weekend services, the annual communions and association meeting, life cycle rituals, and special services when visiting elders pass through. The financial investment in these activities is strikingly small: a total of approximately $2000 for the entire association of nine churches, plus contributions to visiting elders and for other needs given quietly at services, sufficed for 1983. There are no financial campaigns, pledges, or even offerings taken at services. Correlatively, there are few officers and committees—little "organization" in the bureaucratic fashion of the mainline churches.

Yet the ritual cycles do frame the lives of the members in a way deeply meaningful to many. Daily lives are incorporated into stable cycles rooted in long histories. Space as well as time is sacralized, in a geometry of well-traveled roads among graveyards, baptismal rivers, and churches. Individualism is subsumed in deeply moving rituals of fellowship and communion, and practical jobs are grounded in carefully conceptualized theologies and cherished aesthetic forms. The association is a true cultural entity, but, in the view of the Primitive Baptists, not just cultural. For them, the association and each church, though fragilely human, are not merely human creations, but the Visible Church—a manifestation on earth, despite all human limitations, of the will of God and of His plan, as best the human intellect can discern it.

Doctrine

The premier doctrine of the Primitive Baptists, the hallmark of their Calvinism, is concisely stated in the third of the association's Articles of Faith: "We believe in the doctrine of eternal and particular election."

This article and others in this credo echo across centuries and continents. In 1647 the Westminster Confession declared in Chapter III, Number 3, "By the decree of God, for the manifestation of His glory, some men and angels are predestined unto everlasting life, and others foreordained to everlasting death." In Chapter IX, Number 3:

> Man, by his fall into a state of sin, hath wholly lost all ability of will to any spiritual good accompanying salvation. So that a natural man, being altogether averse from that of Good, and dead in sin, is not able, by his own strength to convert himself, or to prepare himself thereunto.[1]

Compare Article 10 of the Mountain District Association's Articles of Faith: "We believe in the resurrection of the dead, both of the just and the unjust, and a general judgment and the punishment of the wicked will be everlasting and the joys of the righteous will be eternal." (See Appendix A.)

The Primitive Baptists hold that God decreed, inscrutably, "before the foundations of the world," who will be saved and who will be damned. When this doctrine of prior divine decree is joined with its companion doctrine, stated in the fifth article, the glory and the agony of this Calvinistic cosmos become plain: "We believe in man's impotency to recover himself from the fallen state he is in by nature of his own free will and ability."

As an inheritor of the Calvinism of the sixteenth century, the Primitive Baptist experiences life in ecclesiastical, sociological, and spiritual contexts defined by an election already held on behalf of a human nature constitutionally impotent to improve its lot or even to know that lot, present or future. What light there is in this dark landscape comes from the doctrine, known to Calvinists as "effectual calling," which, in the words of the Westminster Confession, is stated thus:

> All those whom God hath predestinated unto life, and those only, He is pleased in His appointed and accepted time effectually to call, by His word and spirit (out of that state of sin and death, in which they are by nature) . . . taking away their heart of stone, and giving unto them a heart of flesh; renewing their wills, and by His almighty power determining them to that which is good. . . .

These central theological tenets are starkly explicit. In the Mountain District and Senter associations they are spoken with a characteristic "flat out" style, without hint of ambiguity or recognition of paradox. Such tenets are grounded in scripture. Scripture, "if rightly divided," is without contradiction, though more than one text must support an interpretation. Biblical stories are read as allegories of Primitive Baptist doctrines and as proofs against contrary positions. The meaning of human experience, from mundane incidents to dreams and visions, is to be found in the books of scriptures. The Mountain District Association declares in the second article of its Articles of Faith: "We believe that the scripture of the Old and New Testament, as translated in 1611 into the King James Version of the Holy Bible, is the written word of God and the only rule of faith and practice."

Even these doctrines, though born of theological argument and a relentless logic, and documented by scripture, cannot be understood, according to Calvinism, without the enlightening grace of God. But doctrines are abstractions not touching the experience of ordinary persons. The meaning of individual destiny is, as Max Weber writes, "hidden in dark mystery which it would be both impossible to pierce and presumptuous to question."[2] It is one of the paradoxes of Calvinism, plainly evident in the preaching of elders in these associations, that deep mysteries are ordered by a severe theological rationalism. This rationalism is, however, tempered by a sense of history that stands in a tense and ambiguous relation with doctrine.

The Primitive Baptists: A Reflexive History

History and heritage are a prominent part of Primitive Baptist writing and talking, as they reflect on their lives and their destinies. We shall try here not to write an "objective" history of the Primitive Baptists, but rather what might be termed a reflexive history—their history as they see it.

We begin with some documents that characterize what is perhaps the most widely acknowledged element of their heritage: the experiences of the British Baptists.

British Beginnings and Continuities

Here are some comments Elder Evans made to our colleague Daniel Patterson:

. . . I've recently run back to, back to about 1689, when over one hundred churches met in London in I believe in July . . . Drew up what's called . . . the London Confession of Faith, and still stands as the London Confession. Adopted by the Philadelphia in 1742 I believe . . . and down to the Mountain in 1798 (this was the date when the Mountain District Association was founded). Anyway, well, on a sort of a controversial thing of recent date . . . I found reference to where over one hundred churches in England met and adopted on their articles of faith this principle dealing with the state of the souls of men after death and one of their reference scriptures was Luke 16. 23–24, rich man and Lazarus, teaching the state of the soul of men after death, see. I went back and found all this, over 100 churches, Dan, had believed that then, of course known as Strict Baptists of England. Elder C.B. and Sylvester Hassell took the same position, Elder Lee Hanks the same position . . . So I do sometimes go back to those books in dealing with scriptural, doctrinal positions and what have you. I don't preach just because they said it, but I see if what I believe is what they believed. . . .

At the British Museum is preserved the original minutes of the meeting to which Elder Evans referred. In "A Narrative of the Proceedings of the General Assembly of Divers Pastors, Messengers and Ministring [sic] Brethren of the Baptized Churches," dated 1689, it is reported that "the Elders, Messengers, and Ministring Brethren of the Churches met together in their General Assembly in the City of London, September from the 3rd, to the 11th, 1689." The meeting progressed from the Greeting to Listing of Causes of our Decay, appointing a general fast, a "Statement of Principles Agreed upon" and a "List of English and Wales Churches" ("owning the Doctrine of Personal Election and Final Perseverance") that sent either "their Ministers, or Messengers, or otherwise communicated that state in our General Assembly. . . ." More than one hundred "Ministers, or Messengers," were present. (See Appendix B.)

Following are synopses of additional documents preserved at the British Museum.

1772: "The Circular Letter from the Baptist Ministers and

Messengers Assembled at Leicester May 19–20, 1772." Here is reported that the moderator read letters from the churches, then preached a sermon. Thanks are given to a Dr. Stennett. The number of increase (baptized, received by letter), diminished (dismissed, dead, and excluded) are given. Mention is made of John Gill, moderator of the North Hampton Association.

1798: In the minutes of the "Particular Baptists Assembled in Association at Halifax on 30th and 31st of May 1798," the meeting opened at 2:00 p.m.; the sequence was a hymn, a prayer, another hymn, then a sermon. The meeting is described as follows:

> Met at two o'clock on the Wednesday, as usual. A hymn being sung, Mr. Cockin opened the service by solemn prayer, after which Mr. LITTLEWOOD preached, from Isaiah xxxvii 31. The remnant that is escaped of the house of Judah shall again take root downward, and bear fruit upward. J. FAWCETT then read the letter he had prepared, which was approved, and ordered to be printed.

Concerning the "State of the Churches," the following categories are cited:

ADDED
On a profession of faith	52
by letters of recommendation	6
Restored	5

DIMINISHED
By death	12
By dismission	6
By exclusion	14

A third document, published in 1875, is the Articles of Faith and Rules for the Governance of Strict Baptist Churches (London: J. Gadsby, 18 Bouverie Street, 1875). This gives rules of conduct and also doctrine. Among the doctrinal points noted are these:

1. Redemption: "We believe that the eternal redemption which Christ has obtained by the shedding of his blood is special and particular, that it was intentionally designed only for the Elect of God . . . " (Heb. 1 and 12, Rom. 1. 15–16, John 5. 15; 25–28);

2. Communion: that it is only for baptized members;

3. Regeneration: it is the work of God (Psalms 110. 3, Rom. 11. 54; Jer. 20).

Let us move forward another century and visit a service of the mother church of the Strict and Particular Baptists. This is the Gower Street Memorial Chapel in London at 11 a.m. on Sunday, February 26, 1984. A few points to note are these.

The church, quite gray and stark from the outside (incongruous in the midst of pornographic bookstores of the Soho district) is equally plain on the inside. It has no stained-glass windows, no carpet in the aisle, in this plainness resembling Primitive Baptist churches. It differs from these in the arrangement of the pulpits, however. Instead of the simple "stand" of the Primitive Baptist, Gower Chapel has two pulpits, one higher than the other and both higher than the pews. The Bible is the King James. The hymnal is Gadsby's.

The service begins punctually at 11:00 a.m. with singing of hymns (numbers 18, 608, and 955 from Gadsby), followed by a pastoral prayer, then a scripture reading (Acts, chapter 27, read in whole) by the pastor, then the sermon, based on the passage from Matthew concerning the "salt [which] has lost its savor." The sermon is described as a "statement" followed by a "warning." It is quite formal, with only one personal reference: how the pastor's father used to salt beans to preserve them. After his benediction, the pastor strides to the back door to shake hands with departing members. The doors are locked within ten minutes after the service ends at 12:15.

The point in giving these snippets of documentation—some minutes from 1689 and 1798, a statement of rules and doctrines published in 1875, a service witnessed in 1984—is to note continuities over time and between continents. That the basic doctrine is the same is not surprising, for that is the official cornerstone of the denomination. More striking, perhaps, are the continuities of form and practice. We find the same terms: elders, messengers, letters, minutes, exclusion, dismission, etc. The meetings follow the same sequence, as does the service. The minutes are organized in the same format, as in the classifications designated to categorize the "State of the Churches." Many of the names noted in these early reports are still alive in the religious life of the Blue Ridge Primitive Baptists, and are known by all the elders. John Gill's works are read assiduously, while Stennett's hymns are sung; and Elder Evans notes casually that Stennett preached at Gill's funeral (his text: "A great man has fallen this day in Israel"); while Evans has a copy of the same Gadsby that is sung in the Strict and Particular Church in London. Obviously Evans is familiar with the 1689 meeting, though he has not visited the British Museum. The point is that these "historical" events live in the memories and practices of Evans and other Primitive Baptists. Nor is their concern with history antiquarian; it is, as Evans's comment to Patterson suggests, directed, too, at contemporary controversies in which elders like Evans avidly participate.

Ethnohistory of the Primitive Baptists: *History of the Church of God, from the Creation to A.D. 1885; including especially the History of the Kehukee Primitive Baptist Association.*

Unlike in conventional anthropological constructions of non-literate groups, the Primitive Baptists have written voluminously of their own history. And unlike the mythic and ideological accounts that anthropologists are fond of imputing even to literate groups, the Primitive Baptist histories are frequently of high scholarly caliber that compare well with professional historical works, though informed by doctrinal allegiances of the Primitive Baptist writers. Of these histories, perhaps the most definitive, encyclopedic, and widely known is a tome of more than a thousand pages entitled *History of the Church of God, from the Creation to A.D. 1885; including especially the History of the Kehukee Primitive Baptist Association.* Begun by Cushing Biggs Hassell, a merchant in Williamston, North Carolina, and an elder in the church, the work was completed by his son, Sylvester, also an elder. It was published in 1886 by Gilbert Beebe's Sons, Publishers, of Middletown, Orange County, New York, has been repeatedly reprinted, and is on the shelf of virtually every elder or other leader in the Mountain District Association. (We have noted Elder Evans's referring to it, with regard to the 1689 meeting, and Raymond Nichols keeps several copies on hand, one of which he pressed us to borrow.) Although the title may sound evangelical or localized, or both, in fact the work is impressive by any scholarly standards, showing encyclopedic knowledge of European and American religious history as well as of local history, and written in an elegant cogent prose. (The younger author was, incidentally, a graduate of the University of North Carolina at Chapel Hill.) We shall treat the book as an "ethnohistory" in a dual sense. On the one hand, it provides for us a history of the Primitive Baptists that includes much of the information one might expect from an "objecive" historian who, as an outsider, attempts to recount the events leading to the present condition of the order. On the other hand, it projects the Primitive Baptist viewpoint—their construal of their history in terms of their own doctrine and values; this is the "ethno" part of this history.

The first ten chapters are concerned with history and doctrine as given by the Bible, the next five with the history of Christendom down to the Reformation, the next four with the period from the Reformation to the present (which, for the authors, is the late nineteenth century), and the last eight with the history of the Kehukee Baptist Association and other Primitive Baptist associations in Canada and the United States.

We shall take up the story at the time of the Reformation, which the author describes thus:

the century of the dim, early stormy morning, when the true
white light of the unrisen sun shot athwart the medieval night
of Roman Catholic Europe, but was soon greatly, and in Southern Europe almost totally, obscured by the regathered masses
of heavy and tempestuous clouds, reddened by the infernal
glare of the rekindled fires of persecution . . . .[3]

Much of the chapter is a detailed account of the many movements and figures that comprised the Reformation: the Anabaptists, Luther, Calvin, Zwingli, Melanchthon, Knox, and numerous lesser known leaders and movements. The authors'
evaluative comments show clearly their knowledge and iden-
tification with the mainstream line of theological thought represented by Calvin, and before him, Augustine, bishop of
Hippo. They consider that Calvin "recast Augustinianism in
its Protestant form, and handed it to the modern world
stamped with his own name," and they trace the diffusion of
this creed through Europe and Britain, showing the variations
and disputes surrounding the central doctrine of predestination. Here they leave their historical narrative momentarily
to defend the logic of predestination against "Modern Liberal
Philosophy (misnamed religion)."[4] They do not, however, un-
critically accept Calvinism. Their summative evaluation of
Calvin is:

> Calvin had extraordinary light on the doctrine of grace and
> the holy effects of that doctrine in the heart and life; but he
> was in great and lamentable darkness in regard to infant bap-
> tism, indifference of the "form" of baptism, a modified
> sacramentalism, alliance of "Church and State," the civil pun-
> ishment of excommunicated persons, the subjection of the in-
> dividual church to a gradation of higher bodies, and fellow-
> shiping Catholics and all the members of every so-called
> Christian "Church."[5]

On these matters the Primitive Baptists differ from Calvinists.

The seventeenth century is, for the Hassells, highlighted by
the publication in 1611 of the King James Bible; the formation
in England and North America of the Congregationalists,

Quakers, Baptists; the anti-Arminian pronouncements of the Synod of Dort; and the Westminister Confession of Faith (1643–1649). But that period is darkened by deplored missionary activity by the Jesuits in Japan, the Dutch in Ceylon and Java, and John Eliot among North American Indians.

The seventeenth century was also the time of Jacobus Arminius of Holland (1560–1609), "an able, learned and amiable man, . . . a disciple of Theodore Beza, and at first a strict Calvinist . . . ,"[6] but

> through the combined influences of the rationalism of Peter Ramus, the synergism of Philip Melanchthon, the Semi-Pelagianism of Robert Bellarmine, and the liberalism of Theodore Koornhert, he [Arminius] came to believe and advocate that the election of the sinner to eternal life is not absolute, but is conditioned on the sinner's foreseen faith and perseverance.[7]

While the authors agree that Arminius was less Arminian than his followers, still Arminianism is the archenemy of Calvinism. Yet the authors do not condemn it, but only report the anti-Arminian National Synod of Dort, and remark with disapproval the cruel treatment of the Arminians.

The Church of England is considered more harshly, owing to its persecution of the Puritans, the Covenanted Presbyterians, and "most of all against the Baptists and Quakers."[8] Accounts are given of all of these. It is noted that "the last man burned alive in England for his religion was Edward Wightman, a Baptist, April 11, 1612."[9] Especially during the reign of Charles II and James II (1660–1688) the Baptists were persecuted in England,[10] and the story of persecutions is extended to America, including Roger Williams's banishment from Massachusetts in 1635. In 1643 the "Church of England" was established in Virginia, and the governor, Sir William Berkeley, drove out Baptists and Quakers, who found refuge in Albemarle County, North Carolina.[11]

The authors trace the history of the Baptists back to the first English Baptist church, formed in 1608, by refugees in

Amsterdam. This was a General Baptist church, because they were Arminian, believing in general atonement. The first Particular or Calvinistic or Predestinarian English Baptist church was founded in 1633, September 12; it was called Broad Street Church, and was in the parish of Wapping, London.[12] At the close of the seventeenth century, the Hassells estimate, there were about two hundred Baptist churches with about twenty thousand members in England and Wales, and there were sixteen Baptist churches in the United States, the oldest being at Newport, Rhode Island (1638), and Providence, Rhode Island (1639), but several of these were Arminian or General Baptist.

Among the Baptist leaders, John Bunyan is considered the "most gifted preacher of the seventeenth century, and the most wonderfully gifted experimental and spiritual writer since the days of the Apostles,"[13] but other British Baptists— William Kiffin, Benjamin Keach, and Hanserd Knollys—are also cited as revered leaders.

The eighteenth century is considered by the Hassells a low point in religious history, owing to the loss of religious values spurred by such enlightenment figures as the "notorious, ignorant, shallow, conceited, ambitious, avaricious, and licentious infidel, Voltaire," and to many other forces noted; it was an "undoctrinal, indifferent, Arminian, Pelagian, corrupt, antichristian age."[14] But the authors applaud, with mixed doctrinal approval, the spread of basic Christian ideas through the preaching of Whitefield and the Wesleys, "Whitefield being Calvinistic and the Wesleys Arminian"; and they comment on the Moravians, Swedenborgians, Shakers, and Glassites. They note the formation of the London Missionary Society, in 1795, and the creation of Sunday schools; they also note the writing of some English hymns (some of which are still heard among Primitive Baptists): "Rock of Ages, cleft for me; let me hide myself in thee"; "Amazing grace, how sweet the sound"; "Savior, visit Thy plantation"; and "How tedious and tasteless the hours."[15] Considerable attention is

given to John Wesley, though his Arminian theology is criticized; certain hymns of Charles Wesley such as "Come Thou
Almighty King" are praised. Likewise, attention is given to the
congregationalists or Independents, such as Isaac Watts,
whose hymns include "When I survey the wondrous cross,"
"Come, we who love the Lord," and "O God, our help in ages
past."[16]

"Jonathan Edwards (1703–1758), a native of Connecticut,
for depth of religious thought and feeling, was perhaps never
surpassed, if indeed equalled, among uninspired men," say
the Hassells, while they consider that "George Whitefield
(1714–1770), a native of Gloucester, England, was the most
persuasive preacher since the days of the Apostles."[17] The authors acknowledge the revival, from 1734 to 1760, of spiritual
life in the British American colonies, under the leadership of
such men as Edwards and Whitefield, and with it the strength-
ening of predestinarianism; and again the second revival at
the close of the eighteenth century and the beginning of the
nineteenth.

During the first half of the eighteenth century, forty-eight
Baptist churches were founded, the first being Welsh Tract,
New Castle County, Delaware, in 1701,[18] considered the
mother church of American Old School or Primitive Baptists.
Many more were founded in the second half of the century. Locations were throughout the Northeast and Atlantic
Seaboard, down into Virginia and North Carolina, and as
far west as West Virginia and Kentucky. Sixteen Primitive
Baptist associations were founded in the eighteenth century, in North Carolina, Virginia, Ohio, Delaware, Maryland, Kentucky, Pennsylvania, and New York. The oldest
was the Kehukee (1765) and the last the Mountain District
Association (1799). These contained about two hundred
churches and about ten thousand members. But the Baptists were persecuted, in Massachusetts, Virginia, and elsewhere. Nevertheless, the authors believe, they went about
their preaching, in a way remarkably similar to the Acts of
the Apostles.[19]

While there are many indications that, during the nineteenth century, the sun has continued to ascend above the horizon, and while his bright beams have occasionally illuminated some parts of the British Isles and the United States . . .

Thus begins the Hassells' chapter on the nineteenth century, but, they continue, various ungodly schemes and the like "are emitting such volumes of pitchy fumes as to shroud much of the Heavens with clouds of inky blackness, fearfully portending wide-spread visitations of Divine judgements, to startle the nations into thoughts of God."[20]

After quoting C.H. Spurgeon, the London commentator, to the same effect, they trace the frightening trends of the century (for example that European nations spend, on the average, four and a half times more on war than on education). They then take note of religious controversies of the day, ranging from Oxford Tractarianism to the Unitarians to the separation of the Primitive Baptists from the New School Baptists. Considerable attention is given to the Strict Baptists in England, such as William Gadsby and J.C. Philpot, who are said to share many views, such as antiseminary and antimissionary ones, with the Primitive Baptists.

This brings the work finally to the "Old School, or Primitive, or Predestinarian, or Covenanted Baptists of the United States and Canada." These orders the Hassells consider most like the

> models of the apostolic and primitive churches, as described in the New Testament and in Gibbon's *Decline and Fall of the Roman Empire* and in the most reliable Church Histories. At the same time, like the apostolic and primitive churches, they neither are nor claim to be perfect, only in Christ . . . [21]

The Hassells estimate that there were in the late nineteenth-century United States about 1,500 elders, 3,000 churches, 240 associations, and 100,000 members, most in southern and western states. Among the early leaders they mention Shubal Stearns and John Leland, who came down from New England to found churches in the southeastern states

(Stearns is buried in Mt. Airy, North Carolina, according to one of the elders from there), while John Gill, of London, is deemed "the soundest, the most learned, and the most able Baptist theologian since the death of the Apostle John . . . the only man that ever hunted and drove out Arminianism from the explanation of every verse in the Bible. . . ."[22]

The Kehukee Association, described in chapters authored primarily by the elder Hassell, is traced back to the first association of Baptist Churches, the Philadelphia Association, through which it endorsed the 1689 London Articles or Confession of Faith. The Mountain District Association is listed as having twenty churches, 1,193 members, and eight elders, at the time of writing, having been founded, according to the Hassells, in 1799.

Living History

Much of what has been lifted out from Hassell's voluminous history is a story that still lives in the oral and literary tradition of Primitive Baptists today. The writings and language of Calvin and Bunyan, Gadsby, Philpot, Spurgeon, and Gill, the melodies and words of Isaac Watts and John Newton, infuse their services and conversations.

Jeff Weaver, a burly, bearded man in his late twenties, is an elder from Ashe County. He joined the army and is stationed in Washington, D.C., but with frequent overseas assignments. Recently he was in London, riding on the second deck of a bus, when he spotted the collected works of Spurgeon in a secondhand bookstore. He jumped off the bus, bought the volumes, and brought them to his friend Elder Eddie Lyle, who now has them on his shelf in Ashe County.

An elder is seen unpacking volumes of Gill, ordered from England; another subscribes to a journal of the Strict and Particular Baptists in England; and John Bunyan's *Grace Abounding* is reckoned by Elder Evans to be his favorite book after the King James Bible.

Certain dates are cited as crucial: the Welsh Tract Church was founded in 1701, and 1832 is named as the time when the

Primitive Baptists split with the Free Willed Baptists. This was at the Black Rock Convention of Particular Baptist Churches of the Old School, held in Baltimore County, Maryland, in 1832. These particular Baptist churches, later to designate themselves as Primitive Baptists, saw themselves as a minority persecuted by the majority of Baptist churches, which were embracing modern inventions that to this day the Primitive Baptists reject: tract societies, Sunday school societies, Bible societies, missionary societies, denominational colleges and seminaries, and revivals. Such outreach efforts are viewed as vain attempts to gain salvation through works and humanly inspired conversion of nonmembers, thus offending the doctrine of predestination and the sovereignty of divine grace.

After the great ancestral figures and places and dates, which are commonly known, renditions of local history come to vary with the teller. Elder Wilson Thompson or Elder C.W. Mills, or others within living memory of contemporary elders, loom largest in these reminiscences, the style of which, though in speech, is not unlike that of the Hassells. Elder so-and-so is characterized as "one of the ablest men of this century," and a great sermon that he preached or a doctrinal point that he made will be recalled, along with the scriptural passage that was his text.

As a final set of texts, we sample remarks about their history made in conversation by contemporary members of Primitive Baptist associations.

On July 23, 1982, in the home of Elder Eddie Lyle in Ashe County, North Carolina, Lyle and another elder in the St. Claire Bottom Association, Jeff Weaver, are reminiscing about the past of their association and a small, remote church Lyle pastors. Their opening narrative, paraphrased, goes like this: Pond Mountain Church was organized in 1881; 14 members came from Horse Creek Church to form Pond Mountain Church. St. Claire Bottom Association was organized by R.D. Martin, moderator, and Harrison B. Miller, clerk. Miller, who was a member of Horse Creek Church, was Weaver's great-

great-uncle. Elder R.D. Martin's son is the stepfather of the current moderator of St. Claire Bottom Association, Eugene Blevins. The son, who lived to be over 100 years old, is Rob Martin, . . . St. Claire Bottom is one of the younger districts among the Primitive Baptists. St. Claire Bottom Association membership at its constitution was 236. It now has only three churches: Rush Creek, Tumbling Creek, and Pond Mountain. Pond Mountain was originally in the Senter Association, and withdrew in 1961, entering the Roaring River Association. . . .

Here is a certain kind of historical recollection that foreshadows our contemporary case: the entangled kin and associational divisions that are recalled with much precision. As the narrative continues, we will hear about St. Claire Bottom Church being excluded, divisions among the absoluters (those who believed every act is predestined) and others in the late 1920s, the non-resurrectors (those who do not believe the bodies of the elect will be resurrected) versus others, and other doctrinal divisions characteristic of this century; about preaching running in families; and about major figures. We are given a chronology of all the associations from 1707 to 1906; this is similar to that given by Hassell, tracing the Mountain District chronology back to the Philadelphia Association in 1707, which gave rise to the Ketocton (upper Virginia) in 1766, to the Strawberry (Roanoke area) in 1770, to the Yadkin (Valley of Virginia) in 1787, to the Mountain (founded, according to various sources in either 1797, 1798, or 1799). These associations were given off by letter, i.e., amicably, rather than by schisms.

A second conversation is with Clerk Nichols and his wife Nonnie Lee on July 2, 1982, at their home in Baywood, Virginia.

Nichols: Now we had a lot of Absolutism in our church down here.

Tyson: At Cross Roads?

Nichols: At Cross Roads. They didn't insist that their children attend church, they just let them go; [they] said,

"God, if he wanted them to visit the church, he'd grab them by the hair of their heads and set them in there," and that's just not good sense, I don't think. So there wasn't many of our ancestors' children come along and join this church. I think that had a big bearing on the children just not going to church. . . .

Tyson: What kind of dates are we talking about?

Nichols: I'd say, in 1840s to a little after 1900; I could see it come up when I used to attend church, just as a kid, that Absolutism was in there. You see, none of our old elders really preached it, as I remember, the others believed it, you see.

Nichols goes on to recount a 1940s split of the old New River Association, how in the 1950s Senter split off from the Mountain Association, how in 1962 some churches withdrew because they opposed preaching over the radio.

Peacock: Has there ever been a time when church was not at peace and therefore you could not have a communion?

Nichols: Not in my time, no not in my, well say, sixty years that I've been going to church, down there.

On June 24, 1983, at the home of the Nichols, a visiting elder from Georgia, Darrity, is discussing with Beverly Patterson the interlacing of doctrine with the history of hymns:

But when you go far enough back, even like Charles Wesley, even though John Wesley was basically Arminian in a lot of ways, I mean he believed in conditionalism to some degree. But yet the Methodists back then were stronger in grace, far more than they are today. And Charles Wesley's hymns, you could hardly ever find one that's not fully acceptable by Primitive Baptists . . . Isaac Watts . . . even John Leland. He wrote some very deep spiritual songs. And Bunyan, and others. It's just those songs are certainly in harmony with the grace of God, and very true to the experience of a child of God . . . .

The last conversation we recount occurred at a recent point in our fieldwork, on June 30, 1987, and the place this time was where we live rather than in the Mountain District. The Primitive Baptists returned our many visits by visiting us.

During the winter, two elders, Danny Parker and Jeff Patterson, who had many ties with the Mountain District Association but live west of there, in Tennessee, had crossed the mountains in the worst snowstorm of the year, to preach at some churches in the Piedmont, and to pay us a visit. Later, in the spring, they called to ask if we could arrange a place in which they could hold some services to bring together Primitive Baptists from our area, where there is no Primitive Baptist church. They had in mind the possibility of founding a church. Two meetings were held, on the evenings of June 29 and 30, 1987, in the Community Church auditorium in Chapel Hill, North Carolina. These were well attended, drawing Primitive Baptists from more than a hundred miles away, including many of our friends from the Mountain District Association. Following both services we gathered at the home of Dan and Beverly Patterson. The conversation reported here occurred the second evening. Present were the visiting elders, Danny Parker from Tennessee, Lonnie Monzingo from Danville, Virginia (originally Mississippi); us; Nichols; and the younger Truitt, son of the deacon of Cross Roads Church. Conversation turned to the history of the Primitive Baptist church.

Elder Monzingo began by noting that some say that the original Baptist church in America was the one founded by Roger Williams in Providence, Rhode Island, in 1639. They would agree that Williams manifested good Baptist principle in breaking with the Massachusetts Bay Colony theocracy, which identified a faith with the state, in order to find a separate church. But they deny that Williams was properly baptized because it is said that he first baptized himself, then baptized another. On this ground, Williams is not properly ancestral to the Primitive Baptists.

Elder Parker continues that Williams "had some light" just as Luther and Calvin had, but none of them were in an unbroken chain from John the Baptist. Primitive Baptists see themselves as descendants from the original Christian church over nearly 2,000 years of proper baptism by those having authority to baptize. Because Williams is a weak link in this chain, they would trace themselves not back to his church but directly to the Baptist churches in Great Britain, some of which crossed the Atlantic as more or less intact congregations to found the Welsh Tract Church and the London Tract Church in America in the early seventeen hundreds.

Before 1832, they remind us, churches were identified as simply Baptist rather than Primitive Baptist.

They see the early constitutional writers, owing to their deist and Enlightenment beliefs of separation of church and state, as of a mind with the Primitive Baptists. Thus it is said that Patrick Henry was a Primitive Baptist, which means he was of like mind. It is also claimed by some that George Washington was baptized a second time (after his earlier Anglican baptism) by a Primitive Baptist, John Gano, and it is reported that the parents of Abraham Lincoln were Primitive Baptist such that his reading of the Bible by firelight was influenced by that doctrine. Similarly, Jefferson and Madison held views consonant with those of the Primitive Baptists about the need for religious freedom, though their doctrinal grounds were different. Owing to their strong emphasis on separation of state and church, elders fear the Christian right, led by Jerry Falwell, which would dictate to society how to live. One of the elders says, commenting on the evangelists in the news in 1987: "Jimmy and Tammy are a joke; nobody could take them seriously." But he truly fears Jerry Falwell because he would legislate morality. This elder's view on social activism generally is that it is fine to march on Washington, to demonstrate or protest, but the business of the church is to inform people that Christ has died for the elect to save their souls. That is why Elder Parker puts 40,000 miles a year on his car, preaching throughout the country. In this regard, no one disagreed with Roger Williams's refusing to identify Massachusetts Bay Colony with the New Jerusalem; he was right. They thus affirm a doctrine of election with reference to a class of people but not to a nation, so they refuse theological grounds for a Reagan/Falwell "evil empire" ideology that condemns a nation.

The Primitive Baptists, then, have a clearly principled view of history. They trace descent not so much on the ground of contact of persons or the suggestion of influence, but rather on the principle of like doctrine. Roger Williams is excluded from the line because he violated the proper procedure for baptism, while less likely figures such as Patrick Henry might be included because of like-mindedness.

While we are not concerned here to record "the" history of the Primitive Baptists, a comment is perhaps useful about the relationship between the group's own views of its history and parallel accounts by outsiders. (See Appendix I for general historical background.) For North Carolina, the standard history has long been that of Hugh Lefler. Lefler does not contradict Hassell; in fact he cites him as a major professional source concerning the split between the missionary Baptists and the antimissionary Baptists in the 1820s and 1830s.[23] The main difference is that Lefler does not "preach" one side or the other, but simply quotes the two sides; and in his account he goes on to treat developments among the missionary Baptists, such as the establishment of denominational colleges and seminaries. Also he is more ready to speak of the Baptists sociologically, after a fashion. "The rapid growth of the Baptists Church in North Carolina prior to 1860 was little less than a profound social movement,"[24] and its appeal was to "plain folk," to whom he sees "its simple form of service and style of preaching, its emphasis on revivals and emotional religion, and indifference—prior to 1830—to an educated ministry" appealing.[25] Representing the Virginia side, and a more contemporary and hermeneutically sophisticated kind of historical writing, Rhys Isaac in *The Transformation of Virginia 1740–1790*[26] is, again, basically in agreement with Hassell. Both see the Baptists as a reaction (Isaac terms it "counter-culture") against the Anglican hierarchy of Virginia, and dates and persons found in the two accounts overlap. The difference is primarily in style of analysis. Hassell vehemently takes the Baptist side against the Anglican, while Isaac, though perhaps himself identifying with the rebels, provides an elaborated portrayal of both, and is much more circumstantial—more ethnographic—in his efforts at depicting and interpreting the social and cultural worlds of the two groups.

Whatever the viewpoint represented by the Primitive Baptists themselves, it is clear that they place their lives within a richly perceived historical stream, one which is interlaced with doctrinal issues seen as significant not merely in a single time but for the eternal fate of humankind as willed by God. Such is the case even for seemingly trivial and local splittings and reunions, family quarrels and networks, and endless doctrinal debates among the elders. The events that we shall consider are themselves part of this historical stream.

CHAPTER TWO

Orientations

The Sociology of Religion

For almost a century, sociologists and anthropologists of religion have grappled with issues posed by the great founders Emile Durkheim and Max Weber. This is so partly because Durkheim and Weber exemplified, with complementary emphases, major arcs that still define our conceptual framework. Although these complementary emphases are well known, it is useful to begin by outlining them; certain aspects of these complex theories are crucial for our argument. We focus on the two texts most significant here, Durkheim's *The Elementary Forms of Religious Life* and Weber's *The Protestant Ethic and the Spirit of Capitalism*.

Durkheim argued, especially in *The Elementary Forms of Religious Life*, that social experience was the root of religion and, conversely, that religion fortified and sustained society. Together, religion and society constituted a steady, integrated unity—or at least tended to do so, especially in primitive "elementary forms."[1]

Weber argued, especially in *The Protestant Ethic and the Spirit of Capitalism*, but also in his comparative studies, that religion was more an instrument of change than of stability, that religion could create a new social structure and disrupt an old one—the revolution wrought by Protestantism being a case in point.[2]

Behind these rather obviously contrasted views were certain premises. For Durkheim, religion tended to be reduced to social experience (and social experience elevated to a kind of religiosity). For Weber, religion had its own being; it could not be reduced to social life. These premises carried several implications.

Social facts were central in Durkheimian analysis. To grasp the religious experience, one had to comprehend the absolutely compelling force of the group and social norms; these constituted objective social facts as powerful and objective as physical matter. In fact, for Durkheim, society was part of nature and to be understood by a kind of natural science. Society was the highest order of natural phenomena, but still part of that order; and one had to grasp its brute force as it impinged on consciousness, which had reality only in its rootedness in collectivity.

In Weberian analysis, meaning, and therefore subjectivity, is more central than is society; one begins by taking the viewpoint of the actor, or trying to, and one moves to grasp what is meaningful to that actor. This question of meaning moves one rapidly to ask what kinds of symbols and beliefs frame the subjective world of the actor. Like Durkheim, Weber was concerned with the collective, shared meanings that constitute culture; but where Durkheim emphasized the social grounding of that culture, Weber saw the culture—as a complex of meanings—as significant in itself. This Weberian emphasis had two implications. One was that if culture had independent status, transcending any social basis, then culture and society could be discrepant. And if they were discrepant, then change would be inevitable—in either culture or in society, or in both. Hence, humans would be evolving through never-ending struggles to establish meaning by rationalizing their lives at the levels of both culture and society, of ideation and action.

A second implication for the Weberian social scientist was that particularities of cultural definitions, of ideologies, creeds, and beliefs, were of great concern. How can one grasp meanings without serious attention to their content? In Weber, therefore, one finds an emphasis on the particularities of theologies, independent of any immediate social parallels; his tracing of changes in Calvinist theology as a process of working through logical problems is a well-known example. In Durkheim, attention to representations is restricted to those which can be shown to parallel social structures; his studies of totemism are classical examples.

Other strands of Durkheim and Weber require note to moderate this stock contrast. Although Durkheim emphasized the social groundedness of religion and the unity of society and religion, he also recognized that the two aspects tended to differentiate as society evolved from the "elementary" type that was his baseline. And while Weber emphasized the transcendence of religion over society in the Protestant type, he also recognized the unity of the two in traditionalized societies such as classical China and India. In fact, the Weberian analysis of China and India shares with the Durkheimian analysis of the Australian aborigine an emphasis on the social definition of religious value.

But Weber more than Durkheim saw religion as taking the lead over social constraints in motivating change, given such special historical circumstances as those of Reformation Europe. And where Durkheim emphasized the social implications of religion, Weber broadened the scope of investigation to include the most fundamental existential issues confronted by religion: the problem of evil, for example.

Given his sociologism, Durkheim was more apt than Weber to ground his understanding in the total social system. Weber did treat social wholes, as in his studies of India and China, and he elaborated vast sociological schemas, as in his typologies of authority. But in much of his work he was oriented toward the acting subject rather than the social whole, and the social base to which he links the believer is often the social stratum—proletarian, aristocratic, mercantilistic, or artisan—

rather than the whole society. But if Weber short-changes us in attention to the total social system, he repays us by his attention to culture. He demonstrates how the interests of each social group or stratum are not transparent reflections of position but have a determining cultural basis as well: in doctrine, in values, in symbols that define an existential posture, a worldview. In short, again, his sociology is a sociology of meaning.

We do not mean to group the entire field of the history and anthropology of religion within Weberian and Durkheimian emphases, although much can be seen in their terms. But for us, as for many, the juxtaposition and interweaving of these classical texts remain seminal in posing issues for our own ethnographic queries. Here we have the Primitive Baptists of the Mountain District Association—a group, a moral community, a church in Durkheim's definition. Much of their social life, in its conflicts as well as its unities, is comprehensively understandable in Durkheimian terms. But what would the Primitive Baptists themselves say about this view? From a certain standpoint, they are radically anti-Durkheimian. Durkheim identifies society with the sacred. Nothing could be further from the Calvinist persuasion of the Primitive Baptists, who consider nothing human to be sacred. The world is fallen, humans are fallen, while only in God and His Will can one speak of sacrality. Of course, the Primitive Baptists do, in fact, sacralize the social, or tend to on occasion, rather as Durkheim would predict. But for them this is merely a sign of human weakness, of a propensity to idolatry, and they must suspect and fight this tendency, even if they know that, in this fallen world, they will succumb to it.

There is an important difference between a group like the Primitive Baptists, who do indeed, as we shall see, act as Durkheimian social beings, yet elevate a doctrine that at once predicts and despises that tendency, and a group like that described by Durkheim in his *Elementary Forms*, which seemingly sacralizes the social with acceptance and satisfaction. For Durkheim this difference might make no difference.

Weber would alert us to attend sharply to the doctrine and its impact on attitude and action.

Calvinism and Max Weber

Weber is of special pertinence to our study not only because he is concerned with doctrine in social life; beyond that, of all major sociological theorists, Weber is certainly the one who most directly addresses the place of Christianity of the Calvinist type. And, of some historical interest, Weber had a direct link to the geographic/cultural site of our study; he had kinfolk there, whom he visited, and his observations of their religious subculture were woven into his theoretical formulation of the Protestant Ethic, as manifested in the American scene. This remarkable coincidence, that a seminal theoretical source turns out to have a kind of genetic and ethnographic link to the particular site of our study, is suggestive for intellectual history.

What was Weber's view of Calvinism? In sketching his "view" we shall first summarize the major tenets of his argument—briefly, as these are well known. Less noted are the imagery and form by which his view is presented; some attention will be given to these as well.

In *The Protestant Ethic and the Spirit of Capitalism*, Weber's depiction of Calvinism synthesized views of several seventeenth-century Protestant groups, most of which were Anglo-American and not all of which would conventionally be considered "Calvinist." Weber included in his sketch Pietists, Methodists, and Baptists, all of which he contrasted with Catholics and Lutherans. He was concerned not so much with their official creeds as with the psychology of their teachings, he said, but the cornerstone of his argument was a doctrine: predestination. This doctrine, Weber stated, is best represented by the Westminster Confession of 1647, which affirms the Calvinistic view that God has predestined certain persons to be of the elect, enjoying eternal salvation, while others are of the damned, condemned to eternal suffering in hell.[3]

What has been the psychological implication of this doctrine? Weber emphasized the Calvinist's state of terror. Believing that God had determined before the foundation of the world who would be elect and who would be damned to an eternity of suffering in hell, each Calvinist was understandably anxious to know into which category he or she fell. Yet a second tenet was that God's will was absolutely unknowable by humans. A third tenet, corollary to the doctrine of predestination, was that humans could do nothing to alter their destiny and, in fact, Calvinism rejected traditional means of affecting one's chances for salvation. Membership in a church could not help; some congregations were presumed doomed, though even the damned should attend church to glorify God and carry out His commandments. No bond to a priest could help. Sacraments, ceremony, and magic were worse than useless since they promoted false hopes based on idolatry and superstition, and the Calvinist denigration of those elements was crucial in that process of rationalization that Weber termed "disenchantment of the world" (*Entzauberung der Welt*).[4] Friendship, kinship, and other social bonds were suspect since they were of the fallen world. Anything material, sensuous, or human was condemned: idle talk, ornamentation, the arts, sports.

Calvinism, then, would seem to have forced a terrible alienation: an awful loneliness, in that one had to face one's fate without support of other humans; an abstraction from the natural, the sensuous world; and a denial of one's own emotions, for, unlike the Lutheran, the Calvinist could not trust a subjective sign of faith or, indeed, any emotion since it could derive from a fallen human. What was left? How could the Calvinist find meaning in an existence his theology had stripped of meaning? Weber notes that this was not merely a philosophical issue but a problem for "practical pastoral work, which had immediately to deal with all of the suffering caused by the doctrine."[5]

Weber argued that through a paradoxical psychology the Calvinist drew from his pessimism a triumphant and militant optimism, or, at least, a hope. Somehow the "humble sinner" became the "self-confident saint."[6] How could this be? The Calvinist came to believe that he could prove his elect status by his conduct. He could demonstrate his destiny for salvation by acting as though he were destined for salvation. This he would do by acting as a saint, one called to serve God. Only the saints, the elect, would be impelled to serve God, hence to serve God was a sign, if not a proof, that one was of the elect. Good works, stated Weber, "are the technical means, not of purchasing salvation, but of getting rid of the fear of damnation."[7] But as this proof was always subject to doubt, this work for God had to be constant and relentless. Waste of time was the deadliest of sins, and all of one's life—every waking (and even sleeping) moment—had to be harnessed toward one's calling:

> . . . The life of the saint was directed solely toward a transcendental end, salvation. But precisely for that reason it was thoroughly rationalized in this world and dominated entirely by the aim to add to the glory of God on earth. . . . [8]

Weber extended his argument to suggest that the attitude engendered in the religious sphere came to dominate life in every sphere, instilling a sense of calling, of having a duty in the world, and, to carry out that duty, a systematic discipline that, among other things, facilitated productive capitalism. This particular tack, which is widely known as Weber's controversial thesis that Calvinism created the cultural conditions for capitalism, is not of central concern here, nor was it the only concern for Weber. He also noted, for example, the paradox that a theology like Calvinism could be so radically individualistic yet generate a "superior social organization"[9] while never permitting the member to "enter emotionally into" a social organization. For Calvin, social relations were not emotional but instrumental: to serve God was to serve humanity—a somewhat abstracted attitude toward social life.[10] But while Weber did not elaborate a sociology of Calvinism, he was seminal in elucidating its psychology: the dilemma for the individual and the culture, as one confronts the problem of doubt about one's destiny; how, not knowing, one proceeds to organize one's life, to direct one's energies, and to live in a fallen world.[11]

While Weber did not elaborate in detail the denominational variations among Calvinists, he did note some suggestive differences of emphasis. Pietists, Methodists, and Baptists were, in his view, arranged along a continuum with Baptists the most radically Calvinistic and puritanical. The Pietists extended systematic control of conduct beyond Calvinism but, owing to Lutheran influence, were more open to emotion as an element in faith and considered that salvation was possible through forgiveness of sins.[12] Methodists, akin to continental Pietists (after all, Wesley had been influenced directly by Zinzendorf), also accepted emotion, unlike the sterner Calvinists who considered everything emotional to be illusory, the only sure basis being the *certitude salutis* . . . a pure feeling of absolute certainty of forgiveness. Methodists were methodical in organizing conduct but with the end of bringing about an emotional conversion. The Baptists most radically devalued sacraments as a means to salvation, and they were anti-worldly though nonmonastic.

Aside from particular clues about denominational attitudes and doctrines, we draw from Weber an "ideal type" of Calvinism. There is a sense in which Calvin himself was not a Calvinist in terms of Weber's typology, for Weber defines a logical pattern and tendency that no individual theologian or denomination carries out completely. Yet the whole constitutes a coherent pattern. We shall find this a useful clue in treating the Primitive Baptists, for they can be seen as manifesting Weber's Calvinist type. They cite, for example, in their own authoritative writings, precisely the same Westminster Confession that Weber cites, as noted above. Yet Primitive Baptists will deny being "Calvinists." One reason is that they consider that Calvin deviated from strict predestinarianism by suggesting that one could achieve salvation through study of the scripture. In fact, Primitive Baptists will deny that they are even Protestants, on the ground that the Protestants were a reaction against Catholics, and both were mere sects within the Church of Christ, while Primitive Baptists see themselves as continuous with the original and true Church. Nevertheless, it is historically and sociologically helpful to classify Primitive Baptists with other groups that we might term "independent Protestants" (see Appendix I). When we refer to the Primitive Baptists as Calvinist or Protestant we do so in this typological sense employed by Weber.

Weber as Text
How does Weber tell his story? He is a narrator whose characters are of three varieties. First, the ideal types: the Protestant Ethic, the Spirit of Capitalism, and other such constructions of meaning and cultural orientation. These are the *Geist*, the spirit. Second, the historical figures: Dante and Milton; Aquinas, Luther, and Calvin; Franklin and Baxter. Third, the sociological types: traditionalists, peasants, guild members, and the wealthy by inheritance; then the capitalists; and the systems behind these, whether the village, the marketplace, or the "iron cage" of the entire capitalist system.

The ideal types are exemplified by the historical types. Benjamin Franklin is, Weber says, a "document of that spirit."[13] Franklin is not developed as a full biographical or historical actor, but sufficiently to enact the values and attitudes that constitute the Protestant Ethic and the Spirit of Capitalism, as manifested in a certain time and place. But the ideal types are not inert. They are presented dramatically as well as typologically: "The spirit of capitalism had to fight its way to supremacy against a whole world of hostile forces."[14] And the hostile forces are often the sociological types: the peasants, the wealthy, the traditional community, and the status quo.

In this struggle, the historical types occupy an interesting position. While breathing life into sociological and cultural abstractions, they are not real historical actors. Rarely are they themselves seen as part of a struggle; instead, they are primarily cited as sources of texts: it is their writings, their sermons, their opinions and ideas that are presented, not their actions. But then these ideas are themselves actors within the struggle of the rationalizing spirit to gain dominance in the world.

This drama concludes tragically, telling us that we are now trapped in the iron cage of capitalism and that we live in a world stripped of its enchantment through rationalizing Puritanism.

What do we learn from this rhetorical format? In Weber as in much German writing, systematics and history, and types and narrative, are intertwined. Existence and dilemmas of meaning are grounded not solely in social settings but in the flow of history. Any problem and formulation is at once patterned structurally and part of history.

Within anthropology, the concept of "social drama" has developed out of a Durkheimian social anthropology, as anthropologists have sought to capture the dynamism of social life as well as its systematics. A Weberian dimension offers a sense of the historical stream of which a localized conflict and dilemma are part, and a sense of the ideational *Geist* in terms of which this historical-sociological-personal process is posed. As we note above, Weber construes historical figures more as documents of the *Geist* than as actors in social dramas, which a Durkheim-Turner orientation stresses. Our ethnography works from both orientations. We imagine the historical figures in the Primitive Baptist world as active agents of their tradition formed by their reading of texts, reciting of creeds, and preaching and listening to sermons. Our biographies of the protagonists of the case show how the texts of scripture and doctrine are translated into the lives of these believers. In fact, we suppose these lives express and comment on Calvinist doctrine and King James scriptures. In their interaction, thus informed by their reading and listening, by sermon and creed, they compose a social drama within the contexts of the polity, history, and ritual of the Mountain District Association. This drama interweaves texts, doctrines, and cultural histories, their own and those surrounding them, as a minority religious tradition with a distinctive past that reaches from the Blue Ridge of Carolina and Virginia to Britain and Western Europe.

Weber's Blue Ridge Connection
In 1904 Max Weber visited the United States as part of the German delegation to the Louisiana Purchase Exposition, the St. Louis World's Fair. He visited cousins living near Mt. Airy, North Carolina. While there he witnessed a baptism, which he reported in his essay "The Protestant Sects and the Spirit of Capitalism." This essay, which followed *The Protestant Ethic and the Spirit of Capitalism* in its original German publication, located Weber's Protestant/Capitalism argument within the particularities of groups within the United States, several of which he observed during his 1904 trip.[15]

Mr. Julius Miller was a year old when Weber visited the two-story white house outside Mt. Airy in which Mr. Miller still resides. A mile or so from the house is Mt. Carmel Church, near a pond where Weber witnessed the baptism. Mr. Miller told us of the visit as he had heard about it from his father. He said that Weber was picked up in a surrey (by Jeff Miller, Julius's uncle, and probably Jim Miller, Julius's father) at the Mt. Airy train station, and whisked to the Miller home, the surrey almost turning over when it ran into fallen logs in the forest as they passed through in the night. Mr. Miller showed us where Weber slept in a certain bed, spat tobacco in a certain fireplace, and attended a baptism and church services before traveling on west.

What was the connection of Weber to the Millers? A certain Francis Fallenstein von Mueller, the grandfather of Julius, was born in Düsseldorf in 1822. Mueller ran away to sea at the age of fifteen, and left his ship in New York at the age of seventeen, changing his name to Miller. He enlisted in the standing army of the United States and traveled through America, eventually settling in the vicinity of Mt. Airy, where the forest seemed suited to his expertise in woodworking. He married Mary Stoneman, started a family, and was joined by two Fallenstein relatives, one of whom returned to Germany after a certain incident discouraged him, in the Mt. Airy fundamentalist setting, from making wine. Francis became a captain in the Civil War and later was elected sheriff and county commissioner.

Down the road from Mt. Airy is a country store run by a sister of Julius named Helene (the name of Weber's mother), and down the road from the store is a once-imposing house on a ridge, built by a Doctor Branscomb, who was reportedly still practicing just before his death at 106. Branscomb's wife was Francis's sister, and, through her, Branscomb's son has inherited letters and photographs from the Weber family. From this man, Jay Branscomb, as well as other sources including Marianne Weber, Max's wife, one gleans the following genealogy. A Georg Friedrich Fallenstein married Emilie Souchay, who was Max Weber's grandmother. This man also married another woman, and from this line issued the Millers. Fallenstein is thus the grandfather of Julius's father, Jim, whom Weber visited, and also the grandfather of Weber himself.[16]

Owing to this connection, then, Max Weber found himself in 1904 in the same region as our own fieldwork and among his people who were broadly of the same denomination (though apparently they were mainline Baptists and Methodists rather than Primitive Baptists). Weber's observation of a baptism was a preliminary bit of fieldwork in the area. The link between Weber's theories, his visit, and his kinfolk reminds us that his theory is not sui generis but situated. Weberian theory, its predecessors and successors in Western thought, including Calvinism and the Calvinistic doctrine of the Primitive Baptists, the Blue Ridge frontier, and our fieldwork are all part of a common cultural history.

Ethnography

While issues in our study can be framed in terms of the grand
theorists, our exploration of these issues is in terms different
from theirs. Weber and Durkheim, like most other anthropological and sociological theorists of the late nineteenth and
early twentieth century, worked with documents rather than
through fieldwork; although both intensively treated particular cultural traditions, they tended toward comparative and
holistic rather than microscopic analysis of particular groups
and incidents—such as those characterizing some ethnographic (as well as historical and ethno-sociological) work
today. Within ethnography, more than a half-century of development has shifted some of the emphases of early studies.
We shall briefly trace these developments and indicate how
this study reflects some of them.

Among the various strands and tendencies in Anglo-
American ethnography perhaps the most influential are holistic. Simply put, the objective of holistic ethnography is to por-
tray the life of a group as a whole. Earlier, we used the term
synthetic for this type. Emphasis might be placed on the func-
tional interworking of social aspects (as in British social anthropology) or on the configurational integration of cultural
themes (as in American cultural anthropology), but in either
case holistic description is the objective. Economic, political,
religious, familial, and other aspects are depicted not as separate compartments of life but as interwoven threads of a single
fabric. The whole might then be seen as focused around some
central institution, such as the Kula ring of the Trobriand is-
landers[17] or the segmentary kinship system of the Nuer,[18] or
around some set of values, such as the Apollonian or the Dio-
nysian (to evoke Ruth Benedict's comparison of Pueblo and
Plains cultures).[19] Such descriptions are termed constitutive
of the group in question: the Nuer, the Trobrianders, the
Pueblo or Plains.

While these descriptions are in fact more complex than this

simplification suggests, the holistic model was nevertheless found too simplistic for many purposes. Holistic description gave the impression that the group and its culture were isolated, unchanging, and homogeneous. Attention was needed to interplay with outsiders, to historical process, and to variation, conflict, and contradiction.

Many notable ethnographic analyses have treated these matters. Some address the dynamics of entire socio-cultural systems. *Political Systems of Highland Burma* by Sir Edmund Leach[20] remains the classic treatment of the dynamism of a total socio-cultural system that sustains itself while encompassing outsiders, history, and conflict. Another pioneer study, *Lugbara Religion* by John Middleton,[21] provides an exhaustively detailed analysis of conflict and schism expressed through rituals.

A second approach was to turn away from ethnographic description of a social system and to focus on case studies of particular events. Events revolving around a motivating conflictive issue could be described so as to lay bare underlying social and cultural patterns. Developed in social anthropology especially by students of the Manchester school guided by Max Gluckman, the case study approach was elaborated most cogently through the work of Victor Turner in what he termed "social drama."

Turner's "social drama" could be seen as an elaboration of Durkheim's guiding thesis that ritual solidifies society. For Turner, social drama was a ritual set in motion when society was disrupted; the ritual progresses through a set of predictable phases that culminate in the restoration of order.[22] Turner demonstrated such a process through detailed ethnographic description of events ranging from the Ndembu healing of social rifts expressed in individual neurosis[23] to the murder of Thomas Becket.[24] Our choice of a "social drama" as a way to describe and understand salient features of the Mountain District Primitive Baptists is obviously indebted to Turner.

Note again, however, that "social drama" is couched in a

fundamentally Durkheimian mode. It is the social process that determines the unfolding of the ritual; society determines religion. This is not to say that Turner short-changed analysis of religious symbolism; his work stands as an exquisitely penetrating exegesis of religious symbolism. But his model of social drama gave precedence to social determinants over meanings. It is interesting to note that Turner's last writings were breaking out of this social model in at least two directions. On the "material" side, he was exploring the grounding of symbolism in the reptilian mid-brain (but doing so with Jungian inspiration).[25] On the "spiritual" side, he was attempting to incorporate into his social drama model Dilthey's notion of *Erlebnis*: experience, as an imputation of meaning to life.[26] Thus, with an openness rare among social anthropologists, Turner was drawing toward a source similar to those addressed by Weber and other German thinkers.

In the meantime, within American cultural anthropology the Weberian influence was more immediately apparent, reinforcing a long tradition, also essentially of German inspiration, of attending to meaning as independently significant. A signal example was one of the earliest published works by Clifford Geertz,[27] who was to become a leading figure in this trend. This study of a "social drama" was organized quite differently from those of Turner. The event in question was the funeral of a Javanese boy, and the conflict turned around a politico-religious rivalry between his uncle and the burial officials, which caused the officials to refuse to bury him. The result was a quite un-Javanese outbreak of emotion, exemplified by the mother's hysterical kissing of the boy's genitals. Geertz chose to interpret the case not as merely a "social" drama, motivated by conflict between factions, but as a confrontation between two meanings: a traditional expectation that the funeral would bring harmony, and a contradictory urban situation that refuted this expectation, thus inducing confusion of meaning and the resulting hue and cry.

Through such analyses, Geertz came to formulate an approach—which, in fact, many ethnographers were already following—that he termed "cultural interpretation." As he phrased it in his essay on "thick description," the approach is quite similar to Weber's *Verstehen*, except that the context is ethnographic and cultural rather than historical and individual.[28] The objective is to discover when twitches are winks, so to speak, that is, when behaviors are meaningful, and what the meanings are, to the actors, in terms of their shared (and therefore public) cultural frameworks. As Geertz stated and exemplified, the approach does not claim to get inside the skin of the actors, which is impossible, but to grasp their shared meanings through symbolic forms that are public. Through particularized interpretation of this kind one comes to grasp the universally significant.

Owing to the influence of Turner, Geertz, and others, and the traditions in and outside ethnography from which they stem, ethnography has developed a more refined and focused (if not necessarily more powerful) concern with a number of ethnographic issues: with the task of depicting the large through the small; with the role of conflict, variation, and history; and with the place of symbols and language. Examples of such concerns include studies of metaphor and other kinds of tropes;[29] the application of literary types to ethnography;[30] combined historical and structural models, whether in treating the "longue durée"[31] or individual life histories;[32] and recognition of ambiguities of the ritual process.[33] Some of these trends and insights have come from scholars best known for their structuralist and formalist analyses, now discerning also the complexities and ambiguities, as well as human and intangible aspects, of culture.[34] Closer rapprochement with the humanities, especially literary and textual studies, with phenomenology and hermeneutics, and with historical disciplines is apparent in these ethnographic endeavors; at the same time, neighboring disciplines appropriate ethnographic approaches in converging toward the same kinds of emphases (some examples that treat phenomena closely related to our own study include Baumann's study of the Quaker use of language, Sutton's and Titon's studies of Baptists, and Isaac's interpretation of the modes of representation of eighteenth-century Virginian Episcopalians and Baptists).[35]

A related development in ethnographic studies is attention to the ethnographer's role in constructing ethnography.[36] Vincent Crapanzano's *Tuhami* is a portrayal not so much of the Moroccan subject, Tuhami, as of the way this portrayal is a joint product of subject and ethnographer.[37] Jeanne Favret-Saada's ethnography of French peasant witchcraft turns around an elucidation of her own engagement in the suspicion and fear that constitute the network of witches and bewitched.[38] Jane Bachnik's account of the Japanese household is possible only with inclusion of her own evolving grasp of the household in which she lived.[39] These and other studies sometimes termed "new" ethnographies emphasize the point that ethnographers have long realized but not systematically elaborated, that an ethnography is constructed by an ethnographer, hence their relationship must be understood in understanding the ethnography. Among the hermeneutical writings in which these ethnographers look for parallels, the arguments of Hans-Georg Gadamer are exemplary. Gadamer advocates that the analyst approach the object of analysis (read, in our present context, "native culture" or "other") by systematically laying bare the analyst's own preconceptions as he projects these onto the object, in this way coming to understand the object as well as the historical and cultural position and orientation of the analyst.[40]

While we did not design this study to exemplify recent trends in ethnography, we should acknowledge some that it does embody. It follows the ethnographic tradition of depicting the large through the small: in this case, issues of a historical and cultural stream, Protestantism of an American Calvinistic bent, epitomized by a localized group and its particular social drama. Representations—symbols, texts, forms—of the actors themselves are given emphasis, rather than ignored in favor of some social forces or other analytical abstractions. And telling "their" story entails, as Henry James reminds us, some account of "them," as characters who stride across the stage engaging each other as well as us. Differing somewhat in emphasis from those who stress the role of the ethnographer in constructing the ethnography, we are impressed more with the power of the Primitive Baptists' own constructions—their forms of representation, the force with which their own social dramas proceed, the depth and consistency of their worldview. We are intrigued, however, with the interplay between the historical process and the cultural discourse of the Mountain District Primitive Baptists and the historical and cultural streams from which we, as ethnographers and Westerners of Judeo-Christian heritage, stem. This interplay will be apparent; occasionally we shall make it explicit.

The Fieldwork

In 1970, shortly after Peacock returned from a study of the Muhammadijah movement in Indonesia, we met at the house of a mutual friend and fell into arguing a point from Max Weber pertaining to Puritanism and fundamentalism. Tyson approached religious studies from a background in philosophy, theology, and textual analysis, but also (as a former student in the Committee of Social Thought at the University of Chicago) with respect for social anthropology and a craving to get beyond the printed page to direct observation. Peacock's background was anthropological and ethnographic but also (as a former student of Talcott Parsons and of Robert Bellah at Harvard University) in the Weberian theoretical tradition. We decided to explore our issues together through a sort of fieldwork among those some would term "fundamentalists." We simply went to church, first at a Southern Baptist church a few miles out of town, where, as in many similar churches since, we, as strange visitors, were hospitably greeted. We were both reared in the South, as Protestants though not fundamentalists, in small towns and in the country, and we were at home with people like these. Nevertheless, we were strangers, professors from a college town that fundamentalists next door perceived as more distant from their lives than Nazareth or Jerusalem. We positioned ourselves on the back row to hear testimonies and an "invitation" characteristic of evangelical Protestantism, took some notes, afterward, and talked about what we had seen and heard.

Over the years we have made many such visits, at first to Southern Baptist and Missionary Baptist churches, then to Pentecostal churches, finally focusing on the Primitive Baptists beginning in the summer of 1982. Our first formal fieldwork together was in 1977, when we spent the summer systematically visiting all the Pentecostal churches in a nearby town. We then selected one church for intensive study, got permission from the minister, began to establish relations with members of the congregation, and spent the summer of 1978 recording services and interviewing members. During the summer of 1979 (while Peacock was in Indonesia), Tyson, assisted by Mary Steedly, broadened our study of black and white Pentecostal churches by doing fieldwork among Lumbe Indian Pentecostal churches in Robeson County, North Carolina. Owing to the fact that both of us were chairs of our respective academic departments during this period, 1975–1980, we were largely confined to summer work.

In 1981 we teamed up with Daniel Patterson, folklorist, for a larger study funded primarily by the National Endowment for the Humanities. We proposed to explore ethnographically some of the ramifications of the two major theological traditions in American Protestantism—Calvinist and Arminian. The Calvinist considers that one's ultimate destiny is preordained, the Arminian that one must choose whether to be saved or not. The Pentecostals exemplify the Arminian or Wesleyan tradition. Seeking a representative of the Calvinist tradition, we decided to undertake a study of a group with whom Patterson had established contact a decade before, the Primitive Baptists.

Patterson, a scholar of hymnology, had heard a tape of singing by a Primitive Baptist elder from the Blue Ridge Mountains. He had traveled to this elder's church, heard him preach, and shared with him his respect and appreciation of the musical and theological tradition. This elder, Walter Evans, became our first contact with the Mountain District Primitive Baptist Association.

The three of us, joined at certain points by Beverly Patterson, a musicologist, spent the summers of 1982 and 1983 living and working in the territory of the Mountain District Primitive Baptist Association. In this mountain area, spanning one county in North Carolina and two in Virginia, churches and homes of members are widely dispersed, and much of our time was spent driving the mountain roads to attend services, interview members, and sometimes just visit. Owing to the musicological interest of the Pattersons, we devoted considerable effort to recording singing and preaching. We recorded dozens of services and videotaped three. Some of this material is being treated in a separate work (in preparation).

The incident that is the focus of the present analysis began between our two summers of fieldwork and came to a head at the association meeting that ended the second summer. We first heard about it when Peacock drove up to Sparta in May 1983 to launch the summer's work, had breakfast with Elder Evans, and was told the latest. As the summer of 1983 wore on, the affair was a topic of conversation among many of those with whom we talked, primarily about other things, and we sensed a gathering storm. We were at some of the strategic events, notably the 1983 association meeting that resolved the matter for a time. The two of us who were most intrigued, Tyson and Peacock, visited all of the protagonists, even enjoyed a snack of bread and milk with the alleged disturbers of the harmony—those we call Cahooney—at their farm. On subsequent visits during the year, conversations came around to the matter. From these observations and conversations we construct our account.

The Problem and the Case

Working out of a heritage of sociology and anthropology of religion, then, we face several issues that call for explication. Durkheim has posed for us the relationship between religion and social life, and he and his successors have demonstrated the absolute grounding of each in the other. Yet among Calvinists, as among others who reflect the rationalizing spirit of modernity, of the West, of Protestantism and other dynamic religions, this relationship is problematic. To sacralize the social is idolatry, yet without a religious community there can be no religion. Within this skeptical, rationalizing worldview, the creation of community is necessary but hedged with ambiguities.

Weber, addressing the Calvinist as one of the most radically rationalizing and disenchanting streams of modernizing culture, poses the issue more broadly than as a relation between religion and community. For him, the issue is the relation between religion and any kind of action in the world. How can the Calvinist act in the world at all, or why this way instead of that? Not only community but human action itself is without determined meaning in terms of ultimate destiny. The Calvinist does act, and triumphantly, Weber finds. But the driven discipline of the Calvinist does not necessarily eliminate the paradox that is the source of drive, and Weber alerts us to the psychology of this paradox.

We strive in this study to draw from both Durkheim and Weber, not to mention numerous of their heirs in anthropology and religious studies, in exploring through an ethnographic case a particular Calvinistic struggle to sustain religious community.

Tracing of conflict and issue is not the only purpose of our case. Our larger purpose is ethnographic. We endeavor to depict the lives of Primitive Baptists of the Mountain District Association and the meanings these people have given their lives. Analogous to the challenges of fiction, noted earlier, we find it best to do this not as abstracted patterns and functions but through characters and their lives as they develop through episodes.

Meanings of the Primitive Baptist world are not sufficiently captured in this particular case history alone. The case itself, with the theoretical issues of Weber and Durkheim and of Calvinism and community, is the thread in the tapestry that comprises the lives of the Primitive Baptists and, beyond that, their (and to some extent, our) culture and history.

Top: Raymond Nichols, Elder Vass (age 95), and Ruel Tyson. *Bottom:* Green Ward with his herd on the plateau atop his mountain.

Top: Jess Higgins and Walter Evans baptizing in the New River. *Bottom:* Julius Miller and the Miller House that Max Weber visited in 1904.

Top: Old style Primitive Baptist church, showing separate entrances for men and women. *Bottom:* Cross Roads Primitive Baptist Church, showing remodeled entrance.

CHAPTER THREE

Multiplying by Dividing: Trouble at Low Valley

> If the singing has varied as much as some of the brethren that
> have talked to me has, since the divide, of course, it would
> create right much friction between it, probably most of our
> people could tolerate that, but there is an issue of doctrine in
> it. It's almost beyond bridging. And that's conditionalism. We
> refer to it as conditional time salvation. That is, that there's a
> salvation here in time . . . We don't believe that you can
> bring about the blessings of God, upon the merits of man's
> behavior. And right much of that has taken place up there.
>
> Elder Eddie Lyle

"We multiply by dividing." Thus a Primitive Baptist elder
once described his church. This dictum folded into one compact expression the stories we had heard from members of
four or five associations of Old Baptists, about divisions in association histories. Hearing such stories is somewhat like
hearing about the splits and divisions within a large family,
and, indeed, family ties get deeply meshed in associational divisions, as our case will demonstrate. Following is an excerpt
from one interview with a knowledgeable elder, Eddie Lyle,
whose grandfather was a distinguished elder before him, and
leader in an association in which he, the grandson, is no
longer associated. It is important to note that Elder Lyle does
not play a major role in the case we narrate below. Lyle:

> So after the divide, which I believe ended about 1959 or
> 1960, that left three churches in the association, that was

Hopkins View, Rush Creek, and Tumbling Creek. And of course as I said, they excluded the other two churches. And it went along for a few years, and the second difference come in the association over independent churches. I was at the conference when this thing really, blew up, I suppose would be a good word for saying. Before the association, and again the last minutes of the St. Claire Bottom Association, in which Hopkins View was a member church, would bear the record on this. The years, right now, it's somewhere in the mid '60s. But at any rate, Hopkins View Church refused at that time to recognize an independent church as being in order, that's a church that's not affiliated with an association. So Rush Creek and Tumbling Creek churches both wanted to recognize the independent churches, because we were recognizing them individually anyway through our correspondence. But the other church wouldn't, so the two churches, Rush Creek and Tumbling Creek, refused to send letters to the St. Claire Bottom Association that year. And the St. Claire Bottom Association was held with one church. And of course at the next session they dissolved the St. Claire Bottom Association. Two years later, Rush Creek and Tumbling Creek started the association back. Now whether it was legally dissolved or not, you know, that would be a matter of opinion. But they started the association back and then a year or two later Pond Mountain joined. And we've had an extremely successful time, I would say, between them and the Mountain now, there is no bars of fellowship between the St. Claire Bottom and the Mountain Association. And should their elders visit our association, I feel confident that they would be used. There is tension, that's quite true, but as far as having bars against the Mountain people, we don't have. There's been some visitation among members, but as far as the elders visiting I'm probably the only one that has visited the Mountain, and I have, since we have been part of the Mountain Association. I've been to Union Church and to Antioch Church. And of course some of their elders have been invited to our association. Now the difference between the two originally, this thing flared up on us back in the early '60s. We left the Senter Association, my home church (Pine Mountain) in 1862 [*sic*: 1962] and we pulled out of the association at the associational meeting at Roan's Creek Church. And it wasn't a divide or anything, we just decided to be independent of the association that year.

The examples Elder Lyle gives are typical, if not routine, and routinely regretted by Primitive Baptists. Inside these commonplaces repeated by many Old Baptists is condensed a complex social history energized by Calvinistic doctrine, ties to land and kin, strong leaders, and what we have distilled as "the problem and the case." This social history is the account of the interplay between the "hard doctrine" of predestination and the possibility of community within the religious ideology and practice of Primitive Baptists. How do quiet religious affections, strongly preached doctrine, and religious polity relate to each other in the social history of these Baptists? These men and women are reticent about the religious life, candid about conflict, strict about doctrine, and stirred to eloquence about the beauties of "the visible church," an "evidence" that they may be included in the predestinated group who will populate heaven at the judgment. Their belief is that the cosmos is ordered by a great divide, a cosmic division, ordained from the "foundations of the world." Believing this doctrine of supreme difference and division, how do they manage differences and divisions among themselves? This is the problem we bring to this case; this is the question the case elicits from us. These reflections, of course, are not exclusively our own. They include the Old Baptists themselves, who are prone, as we have seen, to meditate on the character of their lives and their social history.

The Affair at Low Valley Church

The incident took place at a church we are calling Low Valley, located in the Blue Ridge area of southwestern Virginia, to the northwest of the Mountain District Association and northeast of the Senter Association.[1] Named by an Englishman, who established it in 1775, some twenty-three years before the founding of the Mountain District Association, this church has taken on for those outside its membership the double drama of legend. On the one side, it is romanticized as once a Beulah Land, a happy house of God, full of joyful people, attracting even the young, and giving "good liberty" to the preachers, who recall being especially blessed when taking the stand there. On the other side, it is described by some as a hotbed of intrigue, destroyed by family quarrels and the pride of men.

These double features in the imaginations of many Primitive Baptists about Low Valley Church, which no doubt are based in fact, also represent a structural ambiguity with additional roots. These dual features may have a theological root in competing images of the alternatives spelled out in the doctrine of predestination. Another root may be social. The split described for Low Valley may be a reading of the history of that church as a history of all Primitive Baptist churches, all born of a split from "the moderns" in 1832 and subsequently dividing and recombining throughout their history.

Three brothers, whom we name Cahooney, have come to dominate Low Valley Church. Sons of that church's deceased and widely respected elder, they are themselves elders, and are said by some to have assumed too much authority. The majority of the congregation are reported to be their kinfolk. They keep fellowship with two other churches near them, and off and on with Cross Roads Church in the Mountain District Association to the east. Low Valley is an independent church, belonging currently to no association, though once it was a leading member of an association that bears its name and still thrives today.

One of the members of Low Valley Church, a deacon whom we shall name Redd, was employed by the Virginia Highway Department. After an accident he retired, supported by disability payments from the state. Some allege that his accident was a fraud, that he staged a fall from a truck and pretended to be hurt in order to get the disability. In any case, one of the three Cahooney brothers spotted him at work on his roof (some say on the roof, others say merely holding a ladder for someone else). This brother considered it suspicious that a disabled man could do manual labor and brought the matter before the congregation. The Cahooneys moved, and the congregation voted to exclude Redd. (While the ostensible ground for Redd's exclusion was his immoral conduct, it is also said that there had been bad blood between Redd and the Cahooneys before that, even going back to Redd's father; one of his relatives had been excluded by them after getting pregnant before getting married.)

"Excluded," as noted before, is the Primitive Baptist term for "excommunication" and it means that the individual is cast out of the church. An excluded member cannot vote or take communion at that church or any other Primitive Baptist church. Such a person cannot move his/her membership to another Primitive Baptist church, since to do so requires "a letter of dismissal," which excluded status does not permit. Only members in good standing are voted letters of dismissal. The only way back into the church is through an action of the same church that excluded the person.

After Redd was excluded, the Cahooneys then moved to exclude, one by one, every member who had associated with him, sat with him in a pew, ridden with him in a car, until, finally, they had excluded thirty-seven members of the Low Valley Church, a majority of the congregation.

The affair at Low Valley Church does not itself concern us, nor can we vouch for the details of the dispute except that it became an affair of the Mountain District Association and the Senter Association. Several representatives of these associations went to Low Valley and tried to intervene. According to the representatives from the Mountain District Association, the excluded members sent the "Macedonian call" for help (the allusion is to St. Paul being called by a troubled church in Macedonia). In response arrived a delegation from the Senter Association led by the recently elected moderator, young Elder Yates. This delegation attended services at Low Valley, only to be reviled by the brothers Cahooney, who called them "fools and wolves," scriptural terms of abuse. The older Cahooney brother opened the abusive response during his pastoral prayer, and the second brother continued it during his sermon. The delegation from Senter, sitting at the back of the church, did not wait to shake hands in the closing ritual of fellowship, but walked out and went home. This was late in 1982. Unlike the second delegation, to be described shortly, the first went with the authorization of the home association (Senter) in its annual meeting.[2]

Several months later, in February 1983, a second delegation went to Low Valley, led by Elder Evans, moderator of the Mountain District Association. This delegation included Yates and another elder from the Senter Association who had been members of the first delegation, and several elders from Virginia, West Virginia, and Georgia.

Coincidentally, one month prior to the second delegation's visit, Elder Evans had agreed to a request, relayed by Redd, the excluded member from Low Valley, to preach the funeral of an eighty-four-year-old sister, a member of the Low Valley Church. Redd fetched Evans in a four-wheel drive vehicle and drove him to and from Low Valley in a snow and ice storm. The funeral was not held at Low Valley Church but at a funeral home in a nearby town.

Prior to the departure of the second delegation, Moderator Evans of the Mountain District Association sent letters by certified mail to the Cahooney brothers, inviting them to meet and discuss the quarrel. Receiving no reply, he and Yates and the other elders arranged to meet the excluded members at the home of an excluded female member of Low Valley Church.

Evans, in a letter to our colleague Daniel Patterson dated January 1983, describes the incident:

> I did sit in an assembly or council of elders in a [discussion] of the situation. There was seven of us. We recognized the excluded element being the church in order. The three [Cahooney] brothers had excluded 37 up till the third Saturday in

November, and one or two since; leaves them less than 20 members left. We had the church records to go by. I advised the brethren to invite the three elders and the two deacons to the Council by certified mail but none of them attended. So it showed the more that they were in the wrong and could not stand against us and defend what they had done . . . Well, this is not all that interesting to you.

After hours of deliberation, dutifully recorded in typed minutes circulated to members of the delegation and some of their home churches, the delegation declared the excluded members to be "the orderly element" in the church, implying that those who had excluded them, the Cahooneys, were out of order. The orderly element, then and there, set up another church with a new name, elected a moderator and clerk, and called a pastor.

When news of these actions reached members in the Mountain District Association, some considered the action of the second delegation premature, if not entirely unjustified. This faction, unevenly distributed across the association, was especially concentrated in the Cross Roads Church in Virginia, where Nichols, the clerk of the Mountain District Association, holds membership. Nichols was the clerk of Cross Roads Church as well as of the Mountain District Association in which his church is one of the larger members. Cross Roads's pastor, Elder Reed, also took the same position. They said the church at Low Valley was having a family quarrel and had not been given due time to settle their differences without the intervention of outsiders. In any event, the church was independent and could not be dominated by elders from other associations, especially from associations that Low Valley church did not recognize. Moreover, objected Nichols, Moderator Evans had gone without any authorization from his association, the Mountain District. Reed argued further that the elders on the committee were from outside the Mountain District Association altogether and, he added, one of them was notoriously unable to keep order even in his own church, while the representative from the Senter Association was too young and inexperienced. The newly formed "orderly" church had no status, he said, since they could not present a letter of dismissal from their home church. These members could not be accepted into any church, because they were excluded. So various parties disagreed on various grounds with the action of the Mountain District/Senter delegation. While Nichols and Reed held one view, one could hear support, too, for Evans's and Yates's visit to Low Valley. Certain laymen and laywomen who had always thought well of Evans (one being his deacon) saw nothing wrong with his trying to make peace. There was disagreement, then, about the wisdom of the response to the Macedonian call.

Yet no one disagreed that the actions of the Cahooneys were at best abrupt and ill-considered, especially, said Nichols, since the matter had to do with a dispute between Redd and the state of Virginia and was no concern of the church. Nichols, as a retired section head of the Virginia Highway Department, had actually sat on the panel that reviewed Redd's disability claim.

Between February 1983, the date of the second delegation's visit, and the summer of that year, the action of Evans and his fellow elders in connection with Low Valley was much discussed, evoking many stories of the doings at Low Valley over the years. During this period, several incidents occurred, keeping the topic alive.

On July 30, 1983, a wedding of the daughter of Reed to a nephew of one of the deacons in one of Evans's churches in North Carolina occurred at Cross Roads Church in Virginia. Reed, in addition to being pastor at Cross Roads, where Nichols is clerk, was, in 1983, assistant moderator of the Mountain District Association. Following the wedding, Clerk Nichols invited the Cahooneys to his house for supper, together with an elder from the South Carolina low country, a special friend of Reed's, who had performed the wedding ceremony at the bride's request. Also present were: Reeves Douglas, the groom's uncle and fifty-year member of Evans's North Carolina church, and, like Nichols and Evans, a longtime friend of the Cahooney brothers' father, who had been a highly touted preacher among Primitive Baptists; Nichols's son and his wife and daughters; and ourselves. Before and after supper on Nichols's front porch, the elders and deacons traded stories and "talked scripture" while the children played in the yard and the women worked in the kitchen. More than one story about the father of the Cahooney brothers was told with fond recollections.

Later that Saturday evening there was a regular church service at the Cross Roads Church. Near the end of the service, which featured the South Carolina elder as preacher, Nichols, sitting in his usual place on the front row of the men's side of the church, audibly proposed to Pastor Reed that the Cahooneys be invited to come from the back pew where they had been sitting in exile from the elders' benches, even from the members' benches, and join with the elders in the hand of fellowship, to form a receiving line with them. Pastor Reed did this and the Cahooneys were enthusiastically received. Reeves Douglas, the elderly song leader and stalwart member of Evans's home church, crossed lines, so to speak, and gave the largest Cahooney a bear hug in the line of fellowship. Mrs. Nichols said that old J.T. (a resident of Baywood and father of a deacon of Cross Roads) looked, when he saw the Cahooneys, as if he were "seeing lost sons." Someone else said, "My old mother got out of her seat and with her cane walked all the way to the back to greet them." In short, there was both enthusiasm and a kind of sentimentalization, perhaps drawing on the imagery of the return of the prodigal son(s), of the reunion with the Cahooneys. Finally Reed remarked that they did not want to sustain conflict but to regain peace. He asked one of the Cahooneys to give the prayer of dismissal, which he did. This reunion between Cross Roads and the Cahooneys occurred within a group of men who formed a bastion of support for Cross Roads Church and for Pastor Reed. In the front row were Reed and his friend from South Carolina, the guest Elder deLoach; in the second row were the song leader and cousin of Nichols, Deacon Truitt, and the other pastor at this church, Sparks; in the third row, Nichols and Elder Higgins; on the fourth row, John Anders, supporter of Reed, and Reeves Douglas, song leader for Evans but grandfather of Reed's son-in-law. In the first row of the women's section were Mrs. Nichols and the deacon's wife, Mrs. Truitt.

Elder Reed and Clerk Nichols later confirmed that this action signaled that Cross Roads Church and Low Valley Church were in fellowship, despite the exclusion of the many members at that church.

The relationship, publicly cemented, was one of church to church and elders to elders. Elder Reed of Cross Roads, we learned later, had recently preached at Low Valley, and young, recently ordained Deacon Truitt of Cross Roads had attended a service there. Presumably Nichols had invited the Cahooney brothers in advance to attend church and have supper. These actions, culminating in the public acceptance of the Elders Cahooney, was a statement by the Cross Roads Church on the actions of Moderator Evans and the delegation, and served to override and oppose the rift between the Mountain District Association and the Low Valley Church partially created by the action of Evans.

A few days later Evans approached Clerk Nichols after a service at one of the North Carolina churches that Evans pastors and offered to discuss the Low Valley affair with him. Evans invited Nichols to come to his house alone to discuss the issues. The annual meeting of the Mountain District Association was only a few weeks away. Nichols said to Evans that he and the majority of the association disagreed with his actions. On the night of the second service, Nichols and Mrs. Nichols stopped by the house of Deacon Reeves Douglas for ice cream and cake. They were advised not to meet privately with Evans at his home, and Nichols declined Evans's invitation. Instead, Nichols planned to introduce the matter at a scheduled meeting of the association Building Committee on which he, Evans, Evans's son-in-law, and a distant relation of Nichols from another Virginia church had sat as appointed members at the 1982 association meeting. Nichols's wife told us that Nichols's son had a plan to propose, perhaps at the association meeting, a plan similar to one the church at Cross Roads had used in relation to a conflict at another independent Primitive Baptist church in Virginia a few years before. She invited us, "You all ought to slip by here later and find out what happened." The matter, however, was not discussed at the meeting of the building committee, leaving the matter still not discussed among Evans and his critics in the association.

Now the prospect loomed of debating the matter at the annual meeting of the Mountain District Association, held according to custom "beginning on Friday before the first Sunday in September." Elder Yates's Peach Bottom Church in Virginia, a few miles west of Cross Roads Church, was to be site of the first session.

Of immediate issue was the disagreement between Moderator Evans and Clerk Nichols and a faction allied with Nichols, which included pastors and deacons from two strong Virginia churches in the Mountain District Association. The dispute could be discussed in open session as a matter of new business and/or the matter could be addressed through the election of a moderator, the first act of business for the association. The defeat of Evans as moderator for another year could be the means for registering protest over his actions in relation to Low Valley.

The Two Factions

Mountain District Association is composed of four churches on the North Carolina side of the state line and five on the Virginia side. Stereotypes contrasting the two states are rife in the Piedmont. Virginia is seen as the aristocratic planter state that produced the fathers of the country, North Carolina as the small farmer and businessman state of little historic renown. North Carolina is called the "valley of humility between two mountains of conceit" (Virginia and South Carolina, both with planter and aristocratic heritage). Virginia was the home of generals and the site of battles during the Civil War, while North Carolina contributed more men killed. Virginia is seen as being in the tradition of the English squire, North Carolina of the Scottish highlanders or Scotch-Irish; Virginia as a seat of Episcopalians, North Carolina of Presbyterians.

Considering how salient these stereotypes are in dominant Southern culture, it is remarkable how little distinction the Primitive Baptists of Mountain District Association draw between the two states. Little stereotyping, prejudice, or even distinction in terms of state affiliation can be discerned, and the unity of the association appears to prevail. This could be explained in part by geography: the mountain region does not accommodate the state identity found in the lowlands, which, after all, are the site of the planter-based society of Virginia heritage. "First an Appalachian, then a North Carolinian," one elder put it, and in the mountain regions a similar sentiment obtains for many Virginians. But Primitive Baptist allegiance comes before both, and this allegiance has seen the association through its nearly two hundred years.

Despite this unity, the churches do tend to divide along state lines. Consider again the map and chart in chapter one. With the one exception of Cross Roads Church, each Primitive Baptist church meets only one weekend each month, hence a member who wants to attend every week must circulate among several churches. Every week, one or more Virginia churches meet, and one North Carolina church meets. Accordingly, Virginia members, if they choose, can circulate among the Virginia churches only. Likewise, a North Carolina member can circulate only among the North Carolina churches. Attendance does, in fact, tend to follow this bistate pattern. The map shows the convenience of this arrangement in that the North Carolina churches are closer to each other than to most of the Virginia churches, and vice versa. Churches on both sides of the line do "turn out" for each others' annual communion days, certain elders serve churches on both sides of the line, and certain members attend churches on both sides. Nevertheless, the Mountain District Association, formally unified, is divided geographically into two clusters. The two clusters are separated by the Virginia/ North Carolina line, marked by a wide river, across which a bridge was not built until 1927.

Moderator Evans is associated with the North Carolina cluster, in which are his home church and the two other churches he pastors, while Clerk Nichols is associated with the Virginia cluster, in which is his home church, Cross Roads.

The home church of Nichols and the cluster of churches pastored by Evans differ in settlement pattern. Nichols's church is in a village of small frame houses with yards and gardens where Nichols himself lives. Evans's three churches, including his home church, are distributed at distances of two to eight miles from his home, which is not in a village, but, like two of his churches, isolated among fields and hills. Nichols's milieu, then, is communal, while the settlement pattern of Evans and the North Carolina churches is dispersed.

What is said of Nichols's setting holds generally for the Virginia faction in this dispute, which includes all officers of Mountain District Association except Evans: that is to say Clerk Nichols, Assistant Moderator Reed, and Nichols's son, the assistant clerk. All these are associated with the communal village of Baywood and the church there, Cross Roads. The leadership of the nine-church association is thus localized at one church. This church, Cross Roads, is buttressed by communal and kinship ties among members as well as by a bureaucratic layer of clerk, deacons, and pastor.

Cross Roads gains support and resources, too, from several members of its congregation who were born in Baywood and continue to worship at Cross Roads, but who have prospered by moving a few miles down the highway to Galax and succeeding in business. The sometime song leader, Nichols's cousin, who is an executive in one of the furniture factories, is an example. This cousin's wife, however, attends a downtown church of another order. A town-living but Cross Roads-affiliated family is that of the new deacon, Roy Truitt. The Truitts live in a suburban neighborhood on the west side of Galax, only five minutes from Baywood by car. The family runs a downtown jewelry store.

The houses of many of Evans's supporters are quite substantial: large, old-fashioned, two-story white houses, or newer, one-story, brick ranch-style houses, with considerable land for this area—several hundred acres. And they are often inhabited by substantial people, who nonetheless usually do physical labor, as in running farms, rather than white-collar work. Their children are often white-collar; the daughter of one, for example, is assistant to the governor of Alaska (who happens to be from North Carolina). But whether major landowners or smaller holders, they live dispersed, unlike those who live in the communal coziness of Baywood.

Arole Choate, for example, is a deacon in Elder Evans's Antioch Church. He lives out in the country in North Carolina and attends four churches: Elk Creek, Antioch, Union, and Little River, all of which happen to be in North Carolina. He considers Evans to be the greatest elder his home church ever had. His attitude toward dispersal is suggested by the following: he says he grew up in sight of Evans, still owns land near him. But he wants to sell it. He may want to build a house some day, and he wouldn't want to live in sight of a preacher (he pokes us and laughs when he says this).

To the communal Baywood/Cross Roads pattern, Evans's churches, too, stand in contrast. They are not only dispersed, but also not so highly organized, populous, or well attended as Cross Roads. Most have lost members (see Appendix E, which shows that Union Church, for example, has dropped from sixty-nine in 1970 to six in 1986). Even their songs express in music and word a kind of anti-organizational resignation, the heightened Primitive Baptist sense of tragic yet stoic individualism, opposing bureaucracy—since the doctrine of predestination deems the feeble organizational efforts of man folly compared to the power of God: "Guide me O Thy Great Jehovah, I am weak and thou art strong" is a favorite hymn of Evans, which he recalls singing while plowing as a lad behind a team of oxen.

What, then, gives force to these North Carolina churches, seemingly feeble? Is it Evans the gifted preacher, he who, as the Primitive Baptist hymn puts it, is one of those "old professors tall as cedar," here towering over the bureaucratic wall at Cross Roads?

CHAPTER FOUR

Interlude: Doctrine, Polity, History, and Form

Before we reply to the question we posed at the end of the previous chapter, we interrupt the narrative of our case to describe what the case idiom cannot supply. The actions we have organized into our version of the case occurred within a rich medium of local history, the long history of this group and the longer history of Calvinistic sects from Europe to the New River area of the Blue Ridge Mountains. The medium of the case, however, is richer than the roots and extensions of Primitive Baptist histories. For what animates that history and informs the consciousness of Old Baptists are the doctrines that distinguish this group from other Protestant Christian bodies, namely, the doctrine of particular election and predestination, and other allied articles of belief. The case, then, is not merely the actions of individuals acting out their convictions. It is a drama of doctrine as much as it is a clash of wills and passions, however present these are, if understated, in the public manners of Old Baptists. Or, to offer another formulation, the clash of wills and passions lacks meaning without their doctrinal rationales. As Henry James said, "What a man thinks and what he feels are the history and character of what he does. . . ." While our attention is arrested by the dramatic gesture, or the decisive act, understanding requires knowledge of the ideas, theories, or doctrines that inform it. This is particularly true of Old Baptists who are to doctrine bred and by scriptures fed. Their discursiveness about doctrinal matters is only exceeded by their taciturnity about religious experiences.

Just as we would not want to separate thought from action, we would not wish to isolate Primitive Baptist doctrine from history. It is appropriate here, before turning directly to their doctrine, to sketch their view of history. But to do this we cannot avoid beginning with doctrine since it is doctrine that stipulates the status of history.

Doctrine and History

Doctrine is found in their name, "The Primitives," as they are sometimes called.[1] How do they understand this word in their name? Primitive: first, earliest, original, simple, primary. As so often for Primitive Baptists, who frequently prize grammatical analysis of words over rhetoric or dialectic, the term is first doctrinally understood:

> For whom he did foreknow, he also did predestinate to be conformed to the image of his Son, that he might be the first born among many brethren. Moreover whom he did predestinate, them he also called, them he also justified: and whom he justified, them he also glorified.

This favorite passage, according to Primitive Baptist reading, sets forth the doctrine of election, predestination, and effectual calling. But it is superceded in its favored status by another passage (Ephesians 1. 4) that opens the way for setting forth the first meaning of "primitive": "According as he hath chosen us in him before the foundation of the world, that we should be holy and without blame before him in love." The cardinal doctrine of the Primitive Baptists designates as the most important event in the cosmos the electing of a group of persons and "predestinating" of that group to one of two destinations, heaven or hell. Primitive Baptist religion is a religion of the a priori. The most decisive event of all was God's before the creation of world, nature, and time. That is the purest meaning of primitive. This view implicates a view of history that does not impute to any historical event constitutive meanings or purposes of salvation. Human history is the history of human will, intention, action, mistakes, sin, and carnality. A great divide is set between the world of history and the sacred world of divine action.

What about the life and times of Jesus? readers may ask. The life and times of Jesus, and the early church, foreshadowed in Moses and the Exodus, are a part of "scripture," the Old Baptist shorthand for the sacred world—somehow "in" history yet "above" it. There is the strong presumption that all that is recounted in the Bible, Old and New Testaments, was itself predestinated. The biblical accounts in all their various genres are unfoldings of the a priori plan of the inscrutable deity. The knowledge of deity is strictly limited to what of His Word breaks forth in the readings of scripture; and that breaking forth into human understanding itself is an evidence of being *called*, the illuminating of dark human understanding by the electing Spirit of God. The way scripture is understood, the transforming of human speech, under the impress of scriptural reading, and the turning of listening into the blessings of God, all are the works of God's free and unmerited grace. For Old Baptists grace is manifested most impressively in the calling of individuals through giving them a sign or "impression," *possible* evidences of their election—"if they be not deceived"—and through movements of mind and heart that motivate them "rightly to divide the Word of God." Grace, like "the wind that bloweth where it listeth," is given freely but according to no moral, social, or churchly scale of good works. Doing one's duty or performing good acts is seldom considered a work of grace in practice, though in theory, that is to say, in doctrine, all good works, whether in the realm of social and personal life, or in religious action and understanding, are "motivated" by God's electing grace.

Primitive then refers to God's action in the "time" before creation: the purity and mystery of divine election, predestination, and calling. Before everything began, the plot had been preordained, but from the human point of view, the lines of that plot development, the events in its history (except those recorded in scripture), and those in the human race to be included, are all unknown, first and finally only known to God.

There are no golden moments in history for the Primitive Baptists. There is a strict separation between the worlds of "scripture" and "history." We never heard any Primitive Baptist express strong interest in visiting biblical sites. For them, a little bottle of water from the River Jordan would hold no sacred aura or magical status.

The grand division between history and the sacred is most frequently evident in the careful distinctions the elders observe in their preaching, particularly when they engage in quoting. They will pause before or after quoting "an old poet" (which usually means a hymn writer) and say, "now I am not quoting scripture." This means that sources from poets' songs or the historians' records carry no authority. Only scripture carries authority. When Elder Evans preaches on one of his favorite themes, pilgrimage, and if he has occasion to refer to the landing at Plymouth Rock, he will say, "now I'm not quoting scripture."

A large number of implications flow from this distinction between history and scripture. Their own history as Primitive Baptists carries no authority—at least, according to the logical implications of their doctrine. When Elder Danny Parker, during his visit to Chapel Hill to which we have referred, talked to us and our students about Calvinism and Calvinists, he was most insistent that Primitive Baptists were not Calvinists. He gave doctrinal reasons, differences between the doctrines of Old Baptists (for example on baptism) and Calvin. But there was a deeper reason: Primitives cannot align themselves with any historical group that has come into existence after the events recounted in sacred scripture. For the second meaning of primitive refers to their conviction that they practice the rituals and hold the beliefs of the "church" as they read it in the New Testament. This conviction is most evident in the things elders say and the scriptures they read during their annual communion and foot washing service. At the end of one such service, Elder Reed, pastor of Cross Roads Primitive Baptist Church, founded "on the fourth Saturday in June, 1845," told the congregation "to go forth just as Jesus and his disciples departed outside the room where the Last Supper was held, going out into the garden and mountains." Local "gardens and mountains" get their meaning from those that Jesus occupied. In this religion of primitive norms all meaning is displaced from the present (and history) to the sacred past as represented in holy scripture.

The doctrinal denial of any salvational meaning to history means that major events like the Protestant Reformation and, for that matter, the great synods of Dordrecht and Westminster, hold no doctrinal normative standing. This includes, of course, the major event in the Old Baptists' struggle against the Missionary Baptists, the meeting at the Black Rock Church in 1832. Yet their own account of their history is crucial to their sense of themselves, to their collective identity. As we have described, the large volume by the Hassells, father and son, holds a central place in their reading of themselves, and this is a work that recounts, rather in the genre of Sir Walter Raleigh's *History of the World*, the history of Primitive Baptists from the Creation through the formation of the Kehukee Association.

We are sure that one reason our presence was welcomed in general, and why in particular our request to have copies made of a number of local churches' minute books was accepted so readily, resides in the interest Primitive Baptists have in making their history known to a larger public: they immediately understood the importance of archives and libraries in this way.

We arrive here at a paradox, not the first or the last in our account of Old Baptists. On the one hand, they consistently affirm a doctrine that places all the meaning of history in divine acts prior to history; on the other, they prize their own memories of the past as well as admire the work of the historians and theologians who have kept them in touch with a past beyond their memory. Their identity as a group of believers in primitive doctrines of election and predestination and effectual calling gains no authenticity or authority from those doctrines if they are applied to history. On the contrary, doctrine erodes history of significance, except, of course, its significance as a vale of tears or as a city that does not abide.

To grasp how unusual this view is, note what this denial of history implies ecclesiastically or theologicaly. There is no teaching among Primitive Baptists that there is, even hidden to the human eye, a sacred strand amid the secular city of man throughout human history. There is no teaching of the two cities doctrine in the Augustinian tradition. One consequence of this view is particularly striking in the American context. Primitive Baptists, like Roger Williams before them, do not identify *any* group, region, city, nation, continent, or civilization as selected by divine favor and set on a course of manifest destiny. They do not see any "city set upon a hill." All of us weep by the walls of Babylon, without exception. God's electing grace is not confined to one order or to one religion, according to Primitive Baptists. By the same doctrine, human designation of nations as "evil empires" would be doctrinally ruled out for Old Baptists, or further evidence of human pride and presumption: Judge not, that ye be judged.

If there is no sacred strand in human history and no divinely elected group (as far as human perception and judgment is able to discern), there is no anticipation that the future will hold special dispensations in human history for the elect. Old Baptists do not look forward in time to a millennial reign of Jesus. They do look for the return of Jesus, who, significantly, will never set foot on earth again, but who will return in the air to call the elect home to heaven from their sleep in the kingdom beneath the sod. The rest will be dispatched to eternal damnation.

We do not pause here to spell out the political and cultural implications of these theological doctrines except to note that Old Baptists do not engage in any form of "civil religion."

They are not religious nationalists, and they do not accord special status to the political state of Israel as a sign of the end of the world.

We cannot pause either to note the psychological and cultural implications of these doctrines with the thoroughness they demand. But the following invite further work of inference by the reader.

There is no nostalgia for the lost moment of fullness in some prior place and in some prior time. There is no anticipation of some special dispensation when Old Baptists will enjoy power and security in this world, thanks to their conversion and good works. There is simply no compensation in this world. They do look for signs of the end of time, but they do not translate these signs into political or social imagery expressive of desires for power and prestige they presently lack. No one can accuse Primitive Baptists of projecting their minority social status or ritual ceremonies of humility into majority rule under some future divine order in the world. Theories of relative deprivation will not work in their case.

There is a leveling primitive equality in human existence itself that is not to be changed in this world. This world is to be left twice: first, in death; second, when Jesus comes in the air to judge the elect and the damned, calling the quick and the dead to this final judgment. The translation to heaven—a favored sermon topic for Elder Evans, including the sermon he preached at the opening of the annual association meeting that we recount in chapter six—is the eschatological equivalent of baptism in this life, both a dying and a rising to new life in hope, to be confirmed or not at the final judgment when one's destiny will be known. By the same token, the gift of a home in heaven is the eschatological equivalent of the Lord's Supper observed annually by each Primitive Baptist church. But neither of these two sacraments are sacramental as this would be understood by Roman Catholics, Lutherans, Calvinists, or Anglicans. They have only memorial, not ontological, status.

As for history itself, "life here in time," the apt symbol—or, better expressed in their own idiom, the apt emblem—is the dead body decaying in the grave sites that usually adjoin each Old Baptist meeting house.

The world is entirely disenchanted for Primitive Baptists. Its only magic is the magic of snare and delusion, the magic of attachment, the spell that teaches falsely that this world is home. Vital energies, natural beauties, striking human achievements are not understood as signals of transcendences or glimpses of divine light breaking into this dark life except, and this is a major exception, when they speak of the doctrine of "the visible" or "organic" church. Their aesthetic of simplicity is theologically grounded in the belief that the world is disenchanted. The display of the dead body, the candor about human mortality, their quick reference to every death in their midst as the sign of their own mortal flesh, their precision about the length—in years, months, and days—of a person's life in the official obituaries that are found in their annual minute books, are all reminders that this life is under the sign of the skull. Unlike evangelical groups, they cannot use the presence of the dead body as a striking exhibition of the imperative: "Believe before it is too late," and convert to Jesus. Primitive Baptists cannot convert or believe of their own free will. Only the effectual operations of grace can incline the mind and heart to these dispositions. So the dead body is a reminder of the unknown destiny that awaits all souls asleep in the mouldy places beneath the ground.

The paradox generated by the doctrinal denial of the significance of human history for salvation and the need for history, particularly history of the church and the authority as well as the identity it provides, may be seen in the opening passages of a short treatise Elder Evans published in June 1968, entitled *The General Judgment*,[2] which may be understood as a translation of the doctrine of predestination for Old Baptist understanding of the end of time.

Evans says he has been requested to write on the subject

and has hesitated to undertake the task since it is controversial. Yet he feels obligated to do it since "I am the one who subscribed to a general judgment in my ordination, being called upon to answer, 'Do you or do you not believe in the resurrection of the dead, both of the just and the unjust, and a general judgment and that the joys of the righteous and the punishment of the wicked will be eternal?' [Articles of Faith, Number 10, Mountain District Association]."[3] He writes that he replied "Yes to this article." He also says that this was one of the several articles of faith or principles upon which the church (Primitive Baptists) had been organized.

"This was by a church that had been organized upon several articles of faith or principles, this being one of them." It is singular that a doctrinal basis is given for the church, not an event like the Incarnation or the reception of tradition or creeds, but principles. We will speak in what follows of the doctrinal rationalism of Old Baptists, the problems this causes for polity and authority; here we are addressing the tension or paradox between doctrine and history as the foundation or organizing matrix of this group of Calvinists.

Elder Evans then, in a characteristic Primitive Baptist commonplace, confesses: "I realize my weakness and inability and don't feel qualified to deal at length on any subject in the Bible, much less a subject of this depth. But it's either a Bible doctrine or it isn't. I believe it is."

Two things are pertinent here: humility before deep mysteries of doctrine, and the phrase "a Bible doctrine." Evans proceeds to examine twenty-eight passages of scripture dealing with judgment. They are all gathered up to prove the article of faith that teaches or declares a general and a particular judgment at the end of history. The majority of the space of this short work is devoted to reading scriptural passages doctrinally interpreted. The majority of his writing consists in expounding these texts. But before he proceeds to the central argument he mentions the 1689 meeting noted earlier:

Before I go farther, I want to refer to some old churches or
associations or groups of churches. In July 1689 ministers
and messengers of more than a hundred churches in England
and Wales met in London. They drew up and adopted several
articles of faith, among them the doctrine of the resurrection
of the dead, both of the just and the unjust, and a general or
last judgment with the joys of the righteous to be eternal and
eternal damnation for the reprobates who are the wicked.
(Elder Lee Hanks's History, pages 28 and 29.) This principle
was adopted by Kehukee Association in 1777—article 14: "We
believe in the resurrection of the dead, both of the just and
the unjust, and a general judgment" (Hassell's History: page
700); and the Mountain District Association of Primitive Baptists organized in 1799—article 10: "We believe in the resurrection of the dead, both of the just and the unjust, and a
general *judgment*, and the punishment of the wicked will be
everlasting and the joys of the righteous will be eternal," the
latter of which I am a member. I could go on and mention
many others, but I don't think it necessary since Primitive
Baptists in general know it is an article of faith. I have only
mentioned these to show that this has been a concern of
Primitive Baptists in the past who surely must have given it
much thought and prayerful study.

The attentive reader will notice that there is no appeal to
church history as authority for the doctrine in question.
Evans's purpose here was "to show that this has been a concern of Primitive Baptists in the past. . . ." So there is no
resting of the argument on church history or the actions of
synods, at least not normatively. Yet it was important for
Evans to cite the historical precedents, particularly those of
Hanks and Hassell. Yet again, Hanks and Hassell, like the old
song writers elders like to quote in their sermons, are not
scripture but history.

Doctrine denies history. Collective sentiment and rhetorical requirements bring history back in, working effectively in
the group's procedures for self-definition and intragroup advocacy. The paradox of history and its doctrinal denial is, as we
have said, only the first of such abiding tensions in the personal and collective lives of Old Baptists.

Polity

The mixed structure of the Primitive Baptist polity, working unsteadily between local autonomy and associational union, houses a rationalism that places strains on the capacity of the structure to maintain "inviolably a chain of communion among the churches," to quote from Article 15 of the Mountain District Association Constitution. This rationalism rules out any official recognition of custom or tradition as authorities for the polity and exposes every adopted practice to normative criticism as not conforming to doctrine, whether that doctrine is theological or constitutional.

The rhetoric of scripture shaped to express doctrinal positions is the customary language for disputes about the polity and much else in the lives of Primitive Baptists. Yet in spite of the priority of doctrine over practice, Primitive Baptists are not close-order drilled in theological rationalism. For a much prized part of their personal and common lives is the experience of "fellowship" among members in individual churches and among sister churches. Laity in particular accuse elders of disturbing "the peace and fellowship" of the churches by their doctrinal disputations, preferring the sweetness of fellowship to divisiveness born of a theological controversy.

The Primitive Baptists are beholden, then, to twin modes of expression that resonate throughout their church life and provide the inherent tensions that make this group so distinctive. On the one hand, there is the ruthless logic of doctrine—what Max Weber called "its magnificent consistency"[4]—and on the other hand, there is the mysticism of fellowship, the feelings of the "heart of flesh," in "sweet fellowship." A kind of grace in the sense of experience of fulfillment, not in the sense of salvation or favor, presumably can come through both modes for the Primitive Baptist; there is a recurrent possibility, frequently realized, that the logic of the preached word is *experienced* differently from that of the spirit in the embrace and handshake of fellowship. Every repetition of Primitive Baptist ritual, with its preaching and praying divided from singing and communing, presents the possibility of incompatibility between doctrine and experience; yet, according to the doctrine, only doctrine is competent to govern experience. Theologically, insofar as worship may encourage magical and sacramental forces, the very source of "signs," "impressions," and "evidences" of grace and effectual calling is suspect, as the sensuous source of potential deception and presumption. Given the predispositions of fallen nature, where the greatest good may be, there the greatest deception is likely to be.

When members present themselves for membership, sometimes after many years of introspection as well as regular attendance at church services—as in the case of Clerk Nichols, as we describe below—they do not typically recite their considered beliefs or report conversion experiences in the sense that evangelical groups understand conversion. Instead, they render brief accounts of their "impressions," as evidences in experience for their "hope that they are called children of grace." But all their assertions about their experience are made with the tacit, if not outright, assertion of the formula, "If I am not deceived." For older members there is a striking disproportion between the firmness of doctrinal assertions and the provisional, tentative quality in their accounts of religious experiences.

These contending features of the religious life of Primitive Baptists may be best imagined by considering a notable feature of their church government, where experience and doctrine meet for the individual member.

Any local church may decide, following attempts at reconciliation or amendment, to declare, by majority vote, that a member is "excluded." This action may be taken for unorthodox beliefs or improper behavior. Any individual church may by vote sever ties of fellowship with another church or with an association of churches. In the individual case, exclusion means that the member cannot vote or participate in the annual communion services, though he/she can attend services.

Such acts of exclusion are not just acts of polity alone. Remember the overarching "hard doctrine" of this Calvinist tradition that teaches a grand exclusion between the sheep and the goats, the awful division between the righteous "whose joy will be eternal" and the wicked who will be "punished everlastingly." So the sublime division at the heart of Primitive Baptist/Calvinist theology is echoed in a church's decision to exclude a member or to sever fellowship with another church or association over some violation in practice or doctrine.

There is a consistent logic of purity and contamination: if a member has been excluded from one church "of our faith and order," that member may not be received by any other Primitive Baptist church without a letter of "dismission," and such a letter will not be granted until the excluded member is restored to fellowship. By the same token, if an elder preaches at one church that is not in fellowship with another church, that other church will not invite him to preach in its services. Since most decisions about which elders are invited to preach are made by the local pastor, elders have the major role in maintaining patterns of reciprocity and exclusion among the churches. There is the constant play of a changing pattern of recognition and rejection with respect to individual members, including elders, and the several churches.

Splitting, division, exclusion, and judgment are potent terms and actions implicating cosmic as well as local aspects of the Primitive Baptist world. Yet again, the other aspect of this view of the world, which may get underestimated in studies that highlight conflict and drama, is the Primitive Baptist doctrine and experience of the church as a visible fellowship, a garden or a ship, a haven against the briars and rocky hollows of this world. An elder preaching to a congregation tells them, "You are a garden of beautiful flowers," and at Cross Roads Church in Virginia, a favorite hymn of Clerk Nichols goes like this:

> Love is the sweetest bud that blows,
> Its beauty never dies;
> On earth among the saints it grows,
> And ripens in the skies.
> (Hymn 249, Goble)

If the doctrine of election makes a member's status uncertain, the experience of spiritual fellowship, a collective experience by and with the members, and not some privately held sense that the Kingdom of God is within each individual, makes a member's sense of being called less problematic. The power of this corporate experience and identity is a stay against the darkness of the hard doctrine that also accounts for the terror of exclusion.

This corporate dimension of the Primitive Baptist world throws into sharp relief a mood in the inner life of Calvinists that Max Weber noted as an implication of the doctrine of election: "In its extreme inhumanity, this doctrine must above all have had [*has!*] one consequence for the life of a generation which surrendered to its magnificent consistency. That was a feeling of an unprecedented inner loneliness of the single individual."[5] The sketch of the life and experiences of Elder Evans in our study will confirm this description for contemporary Calvinists like the Primitive Baptists of the Mountain District Association. The inner loneliness of the single individual has received expression in the genre of spiritual autobiography, which the Primitive Baptists continue in the Puritan tradition, and has been confirmed for us in interviews with elders and laity, and in accounts prospective members presented to the churches when presenting themselves for membership. This inner loneliness, born of the profound uncertainties about the individual's ultimate state taught by Calvinist doctrine, gains in poignancy and relief when appreciated against the fellowship part of the public rituals of worship, just as the action of exclusion gains in importance when seen against the doctrine of election at the center of Primitive Baptist doctrine.

If theological doctrine presents excruciating problems about the meaning of life and destiny for Primitive Baptists, the polity of their church does not offer a stable arena in which to meditate upon the alternatives of "the punishment of the wicked and the joys of the righteous." (Articles of Faith, Mountain District Association; see Appendix A.) If their theology is a mixture of doom and hope, their polity is, as noted, a mixture of Baptist and Presbyterian forms and procedures that often invites conflict. This polity is set within a worldview without geographical, organizational, or symbolic centers. There is no sacred place, or founding site; typically "1832" is mentioned more frequently than "Black Rock Church in Maryland" as the time of the splitting off from "the missionaries," rather than the place where this occurred. There are no churchwide meetings or pilgrimages. There is no towering denominational leader, past or present, who is exemplary for Primitive Baptists. There is no central bureaucracy.

There is a shifting constellation of relationships among individual churches and associations. Some churches, like Low Valley and Woodruff churches in the case that follows, are not members of any association, though they may be "in fellowship" with a number of associational and nonassociational churches. The local church has authority to receive and examine prospective members. If a member, like Elder Evans did, presents himself for membership from another "faith and order," such a person must be baptized into the Primitive Baptist church. The local church also has the right to exclude individual members. Such an event initiated the conflict in the study we present. The local church, on the other hand, may call a man to the ministry, but it must turn that person over to a convened presbytery of elders from other churches for examination and ordination before receiving him back as an elder. If a local church is a member of an association, then associational rules may apply to local churches that compose the association. The interplay between local autonomy and

associational governance may be understood in its ambiguity
from the following sections of the Mountain District Association Constitution:

1. The Association shall be composed of members chosen by
    the different churches in our union, and duly sent to rep-
    resent them in the Association who shall be members
    whom they judge best qualified for that purpose, and pro-
    ducing letters from their respective churches, certifying
    their appointment, shall be entitled to a seat.
2. The members thus chosen and convened shall have no
    power to lord it over God's heritage, nor shall they have any
    ecclesiastical power over the churches, nor shall they in-
    fringe on any of the internal rights of any church into the
    union.

One of the questions presented by the case study is this:
If an association, like Mountain District, cannot "lord it over"
a local church *in the association*, can its elected moderator,
along with a fellow moderator of the Senter Association, and
other elders from several local churches beyond the two associations, act with authority toward a church like Low Valley,
which is not a member of either association and is independent of all associations? Did Low Valley suffer an infringe-
ment upon its internal rights by the intervention of the two
delegations to it and to its excluded members?

Each association has officers elected as the first order of
business at the first session of the annual meetings of the association. In the Mountain District Association there is a debate
about the status of the moderator *between* the annual sessions. Reed of the Virginia faction thinks that the moderator
has no power to act between sessions of the annual meeting
unless expressly authorized to do so by vote of the association
during its session. Evans, the moderator of the Mountain District Association and leader of the North Carolina faction,
clearly takes another view since he led a delegation to the
Low Valley church upon call of some of its excluded members. On the other hand, the Senter Association authorized

its moderator, Yates, a protégé of Evans's, to labor with the Low Valley Church in its time of troubles. It was this action by the Senter Association that caused one and perhaps two of its own member churches to become disaffected from the Senter Association. Here associational majority vote on so volatile an issue was not binding upon those member churches who did not agree with the action.

The problem of order within a mixed polity is intensified for Primitive Baptists by their relentless insistence on purity of doctrine and the firm conviction that principles should dictate practice. Fellowship within the churches is made problematic by doctrinal convictions, and fellowship among the churches is made unsteady by the practice of a theological rationalism within a mixed polity. These combinations of forces, along with a history of doctrinal controversy resulting in the disappearance of some associations and the appearance of new ones, conspire to preoccupy Primitive Baptists with their internal affairs, whether these affairs be spiritual or ecclesiastical. Circumstances conspire to support this internal emphasis.

Social, Economic, and Environmental Circumstances

The church has no organizational life beyond the monthly business conference and the annual meetings of associations; its focus is on the rituals of singing, preaching, and fellowship. Prohibiting Sunday schools and choirs, and not requiring paid ministers or staffs, the church does not provide auxiliary groups for youths or singles, discussion groups, or the like. Nor does it extend itself into the community through bake sales, bingo, car washes, pageants, demonstrations, cooperatives, or like events of which mainline and evangelical churches boast.

The church is somewhat family oriented, in that family reunions are planned around the annual communion weekends the various churches hold during the summer. These weekends include cleaning and decorating the family burial grounds near the churches and dinner on the grounds. One can trace long genealogies of Primitive Baptist memberships within families, and the kin networks within certain churches are strong. However, there is a notable lack of attendance of children with parents at the churches. Since members are prevented on theological grounds from engaging in evangelizing, presumably this doctrine prohibits urging their own children into the Primitive Baptist church. The lack of activities for children and the young causes some to go to the mainline churches that have such activities. Whatever the reason, it is rare to see more than a few persons below the age of twenty-five at a Primitive Baptist church service. On the other hand, perhaps because Primitive Baptists live long, it is customary to see numerous people in their seventies, eighties, and a few even more than one hundred years old.

The Primitive Baptist church explicitly prohibits its members from joining any secret fraternal organization such as the Masons. Members are not prohibited from participation in politics, and some are involved in each party, though none from the Mountain District is at present in a major position such as congressman or mayor. (However, the current governor of Alabama is a Primitive Baptist elder.) Primitive Baptists seem, on the whole, not especially active in social clubs. Age may be a factor for some, and occupation and residence for many. Most of the Primitive Baptists in the Mountain District Association live, as noted, outside the towns. Most own their land and do some farming, though many are also wage-earning artisans, mechanics, carpenters, and the like. Only a few are businessmen, but this is changing for the younger generation; however, many of the young who leave the land to go into business and move to town, or far away, also leave the Primitive Baptist church, at least during their youth. (Among children of the Blue Ridge Primitive Baptists are, for example, a top executive in a large chemical company and a soloist with one of the world's leading baroque singing groups; these live in metropolitan New York City and presumably are not active in the Primitive Baptist church there, although they retain ties to the Blue Ridge area.) When the older Primitive Baptists were young, schooling in this mountain area was limited to the elementary level for most. Despite their limited formal education, or because of it, the intellectual prowess of these elders is impressive; they deploy remarkable powers of memory, eloquence, and acuity of logic in debate and discourse. They are self-schooled in the King James language and the theological literary traditions of the seventeenth and eighteenth centuries. Impressive as their self-taught intellectual culture is, however, it does not translate into the conventional credentials of the contemporary white-collar world: teaching certificates, CPA exams, or even high school diplomas. Consequently, they tend not to move in white-collar circles.

Valleys, rivers, and mountains enforce their own limits, physical and mental, and breed their own kind of intensity of inner life and corporate fellowship. The "hard doctrine" that is preached finds a material analogy in rocky briar patches on steep mountain slopes; and the "sweet fellowship" in the roses and lilies near a mountain spring. In the phrase from one of the elders' favorite books in the Old Testament, the church is like "the lily among the thorns" (Song of Solomon 2.2). With hope and trepidation they sing of the church in the present age: ". . . a garden walled around/Chosen and made peculiar ground/A little spot enclosed by grace/Out of the world's wide wilderness" (Hymn 57, Goble).

When the various socioeconomic features of the Primitive Baptists are summed—their rural residences in rugged country, their non-white-collar jobs, their age, their limited conventional education—one can see a tendency toward exclusion from the middle-class, town-based society that also goes with membership in the mainline churches. This vacuum is filled, in part, by rural networks of kin and neighbors, though these networks are dispersed through hills and coves, and by the church, though the church is limited in its organizational activities. The remaining social vacuum encourages, perhaps, concentration of energies and concerns into that sphere which is salient within the church: politically and religiously charged fellowship. This fellowship exists at several levels. Most immediately, it is the congregation that attends each service and is embodied in the hand of fellowship; most distally, it is the association of churches, and the relations among associations. These relationships, binding lifelong friends (and adversaries), elders, and others, are charged with meaning and, sometimes, tension. As Elder Evans says, in our climactic scene below, "This association does mean something to me."

Environment, doctrine, and relations with the outside world, as well as fellowship within the church and association, together with an unsteady polity, shape the context and generate the preexisting forces that the affair at Low Valley renewed.

Space, Architecture, and Kinesics

Most of the churches visited during this study were built in the early years of the nineteenth century, although the oldest church in the Mountain District Association was built before 1798, the year the association itself was founded by Primitive Baptists from Pike County, Kentucky. The structures are rectangular, small, usually built of wood painted white, though some later ones are red brick. Windows are normally plain glass. Roofs lack steeples. The only exterior marking is a small sign giving the name of the church and its date of building: "Union Primitive Baptist Church, 1843." Most churches have cultivated lawns in their immediate vicinity, separating them from the slopes against which they are nestled or the ridges on which they perch. Most have their own grave sites adjacent, with plain tomb stones (unlike the elaborately carved ones of the German churches—Lutheran or Brethren—in the vicinity). Beside the churches are sturdy shelters that are used once a year for the communion dinner or on special occasions. Sometimes there are still log benches under the trees, where once members sat to listen to preaching in the arbor.

Interior walls are white or paneled and plain. There is no cross or other religious insignia on the walls, nor is there a flag, national or state. Nor are there banners given by a confirmation class or Bible school class, or any other insignia of organizations within the church or denomination. There are no signs with numerals indicating selections of hymns or amount of offering. The only interruptions to the bare walls are pegs where the elders hang their hats.

No shrines, cubicles, or other areas separate from the preaching area of the church divert attention from that place. Nor is this area divided into altar, pulpit, and choir loft. This area consists simply of the stand or "book board," on which is placed a Bible and behind which the elder stands, some chairs in which elders sit while not preaching, and a table in front of the stand on which is placed a pitcher of water. The stand, table, and chairs are all plain. They are not carved, and their finish is clear varnish. The chairs are not padded. There is no cross or sculpture of Christ on the table, though some tables have carved on them the words "In remembrance of me."

The stand is intersected by a wide center aisle that runs directly from this elevated stage to the double doors at the back of the church. On either side of the stand is a small number of pews in which members sit, men to the right of the elder as he faces the congregation, women to the left. Deacons, visiting elders, and the clerk sit on the front benches while their wives are similarly situated across from them on the opposite side. At right angles to these members' benches facing the stand from the left and from the right are two sections of pews for the congregation at large, one on the left and one on the right of the center aisle; these face the stand and the elder. Thus, members, deacons, and visiting elders look at the elder from the sides and behind, in a supportive and sanctioning position, in accord with their occasional supportive utterances of "Amen," while the congregation at large face him as audience. The pews are straightback, wooden, and unadorned, as well as uncluttered with any paraphernalia such as kneeling benches or membership pads; they do hold small hymnals, which have, in most of the Mountain District Association churches, words only, without notes, for three hundred twenty-one hymns.

Undistracted by paintings, photographs, sculpture, or auxiliary structures and units, the attention of the congregation is centered on the stand. At this focal point are the Bible and the elder, with him delivering what he terms his "discourse." The congregation's attention is avid. Seldom do they look to either side. Very rarely do they whisper to a neighbor, though the wives of deacons and clerks will occasionally signal their husbands to attend to some detail during the service. There are distinct spaces between the members as they sit together on the benches. No one places an arm along the top of the pew behind a neighbor's shoulders even when the neighbor is spouse or kin. Attention is focused and steady during the sermons. Some older members quietly dramatize or assist their attention with cupped hand behind an ear. Until the fellowship ritual that concludes the service, members commune with each other by attending to the voice and words of the preacher. They attend to his gestures, too, but these are not flamboyant like those of evangelical preachers. The gestures of the preacher—wearing a plain suit, often dark—are firm and emphatic: downward chops to emphasize points, spreading of hands to invite communion; but the chops do not become pounding of fists, and the spreading of arms is not to full span. The eye is level and straight.

What we have described is the pervasive pattern in the nine churches of the Mountain District Association as well as in other Primitive Baptist churches in the vicinity. Deviations from the pattern are small and to the outsider insignificant. But within the tightly disciplined, if tacit, aesthetic norms of the Primitive Baptists, they may be significant. Most notable are the developments at Cross Roads reflecting its vitality and "bureaucratization." Led by Clerk Nichols, Cross Roads has modernized its decor. The pews are still plain, but they are now padded. Each pew has a small brass nameplate giving the name of the donor. At the back of the church, beside the restrooms (which are also unusual; many rural, older churches have latrines in the woods), is a larger plaque listing the names of all donors. The table at Cross Roads bears the carved words "In remembrance of me." Outside the church, Cross Roads has built a ramp for the handicapped and a new shelter for dinners on the grounds.

The Visible Church

Those powerful images in the Song of Solomon, drenched in sensuousness and the security of a sacred enclosure, are interpreted doctrinally as "the visible church," sometimes referred to as the doctrine of the organic church. As a remedy against the anxiety of profound uncertainty about a member's predestination, cosmically speaking, the fellowship inside the Old Baptist church becomes precious, intrinsically as present experience of the sacred, and extrinsically as a foretaste of heaven. Thus the doctrine of the visible church endorses the experiences of solidarity and collective effervescence evident enough in theory and practice of Old Baptists to please the most strict Durkheimian. This doctrine, along with the doctrine of effectual calling, which endorses "signs," "evidence," and "impressions" as marks of election, never certain, mutually support each other: experience of "a sweet meeting," or "a good meeting," is both a sign of possible election and an experience of fellowship whose doctrinal equivalent is the visible or organic church.

But these formulations cannot stand as if they were on the plus side of a set of parallel columns contrasting the hardness and the sweetness of Primitive Baptist doctrine and sentiment. Here we challenge the Durkheimian reading of this match between ritual structure and doctrine. In fact, both Old Baptists and Max Weber would agree that the Durkheimian interpretation is incomplete and not sufficiently dialectical.

The doctrine of the visible church (which, incidentally, opposes the individualistic Protestant view that founds the church within the consciousness of each believer) is in a paradoxical tension with the ingrained suspiciousness of all sensuous experience as media for divine grace, and this same consciousness with its skepticism and doubt affects the understanding of the experience of signs as taught by the doctrine of effectual calling. Again, the meaning of fellowship in the collective sense and calling with respect to the individual's life history is displaced into doctrine that erodes its substantial status and points beyond to possible transcendental intimations. Every taste is crossed by a prefatory qualification, which is at the same time a mitigation. Every taste is only a foretaste, *if* it is a genuine taste at all.

Both the doctrine of the effectual calling of God and the doctrine of the visible church become visible to members of the Primitive Baptist churches first in the preaching of the elders and then in the experience of the members in song and fellowship. We quote two passages from a sermon by Elder Lassere Bradley, Jr., quite possibly the best-known and most closely followed elder among Primitive Baptists, north and south, coast to coast. The sermon was preached in Antioch Church, a member of the Mountain District Association, one of the several churches pastored by Elder Walter Evans, who, when Elder Bradley finished, said: "I believe every bit of it." The date of the sermon was one month prior to the annual association meeting for 1983, and most of the active members of the Mountain District Association of churches were present that warm August evening to hear the famous elder.

The first passage is cast in an autobiographical mode in which Elder Bradley uses his own experience of coming into the Primitive Baptist church as an allegory of the meaning of effectual calling, an experience which contrasts starkly with that of Elder Evans's struggle with the doctrine of predestination as light to dark, ease to struggle.

> The first time I ever attended a Primitive Baptist church I heard this man preach. And he preached on the subject of the effectual calling. Now I'd been struggling to try to preach the doctrine of grace for some little period of time at that point. And I'd found people being very upset and very unhappy with it. I had had very few people ever come around and shake my hand, or certainly hadn't had any ever hug my neck and say, "I sure loved that." It was an amazing sight to me, to go to that little church up in the state of West Virginia, hear this man get up and preach, and he started out in the beginning talking on the call of the spirit. And I thought to myself, "Well, I've heard some others say they were going to preach on the call of the spirit and before they were done they had messed it up, and it'll be interesting to hear what he does." About the middle of the discourse I thought, "Well he's still hanging in there with it, he hadn't kicked out of the traces yet, he's still preaching that it's the call of the spirit and that it's not dependent upon man's free will or any effort of man's part." And he got clear down to the end of the discourse, and he never [claps] did take it back, preached that it was the effectual call of the spirit, stuck with it clear to the end, and what's more, there wasn't anybody trying to run him off. When he was finished preaching, why some of them walked clear up to the stand, hugged his neck before he could sit down, and the whole congregation came by and shook his hand, began to hug his neck. I said, "That sure looks good to me, nobody ever treated me that way for preaching that doctrine." I found out I was preaching it in the wrong place, wasn't enough people where I was that loved it and appreciated it. Oh, my friends, how wonderful that doctrine of the effectual calling is.

The art of this preacher is impressive as is his capacity to fold into a single sermon all the central doctrines of the Primitive Baptist, as he did on this occasion in a sermon of a little less than an hour. The gestures of neck hugging and hand-shaking enact the exclamations of wonder. In his account, doctrine and narrated incident work in conjunction, both having foreshadowed what followed in the fellowship ritual at

Antioch Church on that evening. But before that closing segment occurred, the elder finished his sermon with the doctrine of heaven, itself made visible, in his account of what the visible church is in practice.

> Oh, my friends, sometimes we've sung songs here that've lifted us up. I can think of times I've heard singing in this part of the country, that sounded to me more beautiful surely than anything the angels must have ever sung. I can hear God's people blend their voice, and sing of their experience, and you could hear them, as though they were mourners of Zion indeed, and they were the pilgrims plodding on the pathway to Zion down here in the world. But I want to tell you, according to this text, there's a glory yet to come. Beyond the little foretastes of experience now, ah, in heaven's pure world today there are angels that sing, yet, they sing before the throne of God, and they praise his wonderful name. Isaiah saw that angelic host, and I want to tell you, when at last our savior comes back, and he resurrects the bodies of these little children, them that are planted in weakness raised in power, some raised in glory. Now predestination is fulfilled and realized, they're made like Jesus Christ, and I believe then that the angels of heaven will have to cease their song, because there'll be a song sung that they've never been able to sing, they could never sing the song of redemption, and because they never have gone down to the depths that we've gone, been plucked up from the awful wretches of humanity and there to bask in the sunlight of the savior's love and to stand in the glory of Jesus, that shine more gloriously than the stars in the sky. . . .

This is rhetorical art of a high order. These are affecting scenes in the discourse that were realized in the rituals of singing and fellowship that bracketed the sermon. But the reader needs to know that all these elevated images and fervent sentiments were prefaced with another order of discourse, with a difference.

The text for this sermon was Ephesians 1. 1-6. As we have reported, this passage is a cardinal text for all Old Baptists in their scriptural proofs for the doctrine of election and predestination.

> According as he hath chosen us in him before the foundation
> of the world, that we should be holy and without blame before
> him in love: [v. 4]. Having predestinated us unto the adoption
> of children by Jesus Christ to himself, according to the good
> pleasure of his will [v. 5].

This text, with "by Jesus Christ" shortened to "in Christ," was
Elder Bradley's choice the evening of August 2, 1983. Here
is how he begins to work on his text, a text from which he
will during his discourse generate five doctrines: election, predestination, redemption, effectual calling, and heaven.

> If anyone is in Christ, they are marvelously blessed. Everything
> they need for time and eternity is attended to, in Christ. I'm
> sure that if that question were to be posed to each of us person-
> ally tonight, as to whether we are in Christ, it is a question of
> greatest concern. A question of constant interest to us, we
> sometimes look for those evidences to try to determine whether
> we are in Christ. In moments of doubt and fear, when we ques-
> tion that we have ever had such an experience, it brings about
> great anxiety, because we know that it is only in Christ that
> these wonderful benefits can be ours.

How much is poised on so small a word: "if." This preacher,
true to Old Baptist plain speaking, names the human condition interdicted by the logic and psychology of election and
predestination, and that term is "anxiety," to which he adds
"doubt and fear." He also names a habit, if not a preoccupation: ". . . we question that we have ever had such an experience." We do not know if Elder Bradley has ever read chapter four of Max Weber's *Protestant Ethic and the Spirit of
Capitalism*. Even if he did, it would only be in the category
of "history," lacking the authority of scripture. (Perhaps Elder
Bradley would suggest to us that Weber's work seems to have
for us as students of social thought the status of "scripture"!)
The elder in one sense has no need to read Weber as far as
his description of the consciousness of the Calvinist goes. But
Weber, if we may so imagine, could learn something from
Elder Bradley and Elder Evans about the role of the doctrine

of the visible church as this translates into the ritual practices
of singing, communal listening, and fellowship as doctrinal
and ritual means for living with the stringencies of the prior
doctrines of election and predestination. While Weber had a
good appreciation for the logic of the doctrine of effectual calling within the practical conduct of Calvinists and their successors, he overlooked the church as fellowship, sentiment,
collective and individual—the church in fellowship, including the fellowship engendered by holding in common such
doctrines as predestination and effectual calling, as Elder
Bradley's sermon demonstrates in its personal and collective
effects. There is for these Old Baptists a theological aesthetic
practiced in sermon, song, and gestures that runs counterpoint to the asceticism of worldly conduct and the austerities
of doubt, fear, and anxiety exacted on consciousness by the
doctrines of election and predestination. Had Weber been
able and inclined to remain for a longer period among his kin
around Mt. Airy, North Carolina, he would have ethnographic
evidences requiring him to question at least some of his own
theory.

But this does not mean that Durkheim in his study would
be better at understanding the Old Baptists. He would miss
their peculiar bind: loving the fellowship and finding the Old
Baptist church beautiful, a foretaste of heaven, Old Baptists'
doctrine undercuts the psychology and aesthetic of solidarity with cosmic questioning: all joining and reunion for the
pilgrim is under the sign of another world making this one a
temporary dwelling for resident aliens. The tie that binds is
also the tie that loosens. A foretaste does not assure entrance
to the full feast.

Singing

> Guide me O Thy great Jehovah
> Pilgrim through this barren land
> I am weak but thou art mighty

Hold me with thy pow'rful hand.
(Hymn 179, Goble)

This song, it will be noted, was sung by Elder Evans as he followed the plow in his youth. It expresses a sense of the absolute sovereignty of God as he guides puny humans through
their lonely sojourn on this earth toward their destinies. Such
a text is acceptable to Primitive Baptist doctrine. Some hymn
texts are unacceptable to them and, after careful examination, are rejected owing to their doctrinal error. "Wayfaring
Stranger" for example is unacceptable; it says "I'm going
there," which promises too much assurance of heaven, and
it sinks into fleshly emotion in lines such as "I'll see my
mother." "Blessed Assurance, Jesus is Mine" would not be acceptable for Calvinistic faithful who distinguish between hope
and assurance; to claim assurance is exceedingly presumptuous. Themes more compatible with Primitive Baptist belief
would be in lines like these: "God moves in a mysterious way,
His wonders to perform"; "Amazing Grace . . . that saved a
wretch like me"; ". . . pilgrim in this barren land"; and
"Dark and thorny is the desert. . . ." "In Sharon's lovely
Rose . . ." gives a hope of entering the garden that is God's
grace but does not claim assurance that one will do so.
"Hymns are small sermons," remarked one elder. We have
noted earlier that the hymns composed by seventeenth- and
eighteenth-century English writers are still favorites; from the
Calvinist Protestants, especially Baptist and Presbyterian,
these hymns have stood the test of centuries of reflection as
well as performance.[6]

If the texts are of a distinct doctrinal content,[7] the Primitive
Baptist form of singing is distinctive as well. The fast-paced,
accompanied gospel singing of Pentecostals and other evangelical fundamentalist Protestants is alien to the Primitive
Baptist. After the tradition of the dissenting wing of the Reformation, Primitive Baptists (except those of the so-called progressive type) forbid instrumental accompaniment—whether

with organ, guitar, or any other instrument—and they tend, especially in the mountains, to favor a slow and sedate style. The Primitive Baptists sing many verses of a hymn, often every verse; this practice reinforces their close attention to words and their meanings, whether doctrinal or inspirational. Where the Pentecostal, drawing inspiration from black tradition, sings with emotional fervor and dramatic climax, heightened by solo song leaders and choirs who elicit group response, the Primitive Baptist appears detached; eschewing both solo or choir singing and group response, he/she sings as part of a unified congregation, but like the older singers of the unaccompanied ballads, Primitive Baptists perform with little eye contact and minimal vibrato, ornamentation, or change of tempo or volume to express emotion. This is not to say the Primitive Baptist feels no emotion. The Primitive Baptists stand and sing in their "flat out" straight voices, but the tears running down their cheeks confirm their admission of being deeply moved by their singing. The Primitive Baptist, with dignity and detachment, describes the human condition in this fallen world stoically, without using the music to overstate the emotion of hope.

This sparse, stoic view is expressed further, perhaps, by the absence of musical instruments to accompany the singing— no full and melodious organ—and by other features of the musical form: preference for minor rather than major keys among at least some influential singers, such as Elder Evans; harmonizing in fourths and fifths, rather than in thirds as in many mainline churches and in much popular and classical music; and the straight-out, as opposed to vibrato or bel canto or crooning, vocal production. The more traditional congregations in the mountains also slow the rhythm, so that melodies are so drawn out as to be almost unrecognizable to the stranger, but give a sense of sturdy constancy. On first hearing, the straight, loud, ponderously slow, repetitive singing with minor-sounding tunes and spare, open harmonies may sound strange and depressing, but later this congregational singing can be appreciated as expressing a mood of dignity and strength in the face of unknown destinies.

Reflecting the congregational autonomy of the Primitive Baptists, there is no national or denominational hymnal such as is used by the Methodists or Presbyterians. Each church chooses its own hymnal. The most popular one in the Mountain District is *The Primitive Baptist Hymn Book*, compiled by D.H. Goble and published in 1887, but some congregations, such as Cross Roads, are choosing other hymnals.

While adherence to the doctrine, as expressed in the words, seems strong, in the musical form—the choice of hymnal, kind of harmony, structure of the scales—change and division are apparent in this district. The basic change is away from the distinctive features mentioned: the minor key giving way to major, the distinctive harmonies to the more conventional ones of the mainline Protestants, including the less Calvinistic Baptists. Such a trend is apparent in the singing at Cross Roads Church, reflecting a shift—imperceptible to the casual listener—toward the musical pattern of the mainline Protestant denominations. An example is in the choice of hymnal at Cross Roads. This congregation has replaced the old style hymnal, exemplified by Goble, which has words but no music, with a hymnal that has music. Whereas congregations choose melodies and interpret harmonies according to their own preferences when they sing by ear, when they sing by note they tend to conform to the choices made by their hymn book publishers. The new song leader at Cross Roads reads music. In this way Cross Roads would appear to be moving away from the distinctive musical tradition of the Primitive Baptists and toward the conventions of the Protestant majority.

A more dramatic though perhaps atypical enactment of such changes was apparent in the incident mentioned earlier: the wedding of the daughter of Elder Reed, held at Cross Roads, where Mendelssohn's wedding march was played on a phonograph located in the foyer of the church: a compromise between the Primitive Baptist taboo on instrumental music and the mainline Protestant custom regarding wedding music.

Preaching

> Moreover he said unto me, Son of Man, eat that thou findest; eat this roll, and go speak unto the house of Israel. So I opened my mouth, and he caused me to eat that roll . . . and it was in my mouth as honey for sweetness.
>
> Ezekiel 3. 1-3

The great divide between the sacred cosmos of scripture and the carnal world of history can only be bridged by the work of the Spirit, "a spirit that bloweth where it listeth." Old Baptists say you can get a blessing in the singing and the fellowship, or alone while working or meditating. The kind of work many Blue Ridge Old Baptists do allows meditation along with it. One elder we know takes his Bible to work in a pipe factory so he can argue scripture with "the missionaries" during break times. One cannot predict or control where or when one "can get an impression" of divine favor, but Old Baptists listen to the sermon as the most favored means for receiving a blessing or feeling a touch of the Spirit.

More time in services is given to preaching than other forms, and more time in conversation is perhaps given to discussing preaching and preachers than other religious topics. Elders are the focus of much attention by other elders surely, but also by the laity.

It is through the preaching of the elders that the great divide is crossed. Their words become the media for hearing the Living Word. Speaking and listening are the two primary modes of contact with Spirit. Both are under the discipline of scripture itself governed in its reading by the doctrines of election and predestination. The space of the Old Baptist meeting house, as we have described it in the preceding section, is auditory space.

Old Baptists distinguish three kinds of preaching, all types, of course, authorized by scripture, explicitly in its teachings or implicitly by examples. Doctrinal preaching predominates in the four associations we have visited. "Experimental" (their seventeenth-century term that we might call experiential) preaching focuses on the spiritual experience of biblical characters, usually coupled with similar experiences of the preacher and those known to him. Duty preaching, the third type, stresses obligations to the Church more than proper actions in the world at large. It is characteristic that Elder Evans of the North Carolina group of churches in the Mountain District Association preaches doctrine, much more than he preaches duty, while Elder Reed of the Virginia group of churches in the same association preaches duty. While both are reticent to invoke their own experiences, Evans is more prone to do so, at least during his later years, than Reed.

Aside from personal gifts and individual temperaments there is a strong doctrinal reason why both duty preaching and experimental sermons are problematical. Both run the risk of falling under the theologically impermissible category of "good works." Doing one's duty as church member or citizen has absolutely nothing to do with one's election, though observing laws and carrying out church ordinance may affect a member's standing with his or her local church. For example, one of the submerged theological issues behind the exclusion of a large number of members at the Low Valley Church is a difference of judgment about observing duties as a citizen and the ramifications of that status with respect to good standing in the local church at Low Valley.

Experimental preaching runs a risk of according religious experiences some role in a person's salvation. The denial that "conversion experiences," crusades, and other activities associated with the evangelical religion of "the missionaries" affect salvation is important in Primitive Baptist self-identification. On the other hand, some recognition of "signs" or "evidences" is necessary to the Primitive Baptist, though,

as Elder Bradley's sermon which we quoted above makes
clear, there is no certainty attached to such experiences. Just
as the doctrines of election and predestination make appeals
to good behavior and religious experience problematical, so
the doctrine of effectual calling makes some appeal to the experiences giving signs of election necessary—"If I be not deceived."

The three kinds of preaching are loosely related to the three
kinds of contemporary Primitive Baptist churches as classi-
fied by some of our informants among the Old Baptists of the
Blue Ridge. The three types of churches are "absoluters,"
"progressives," and "old regulars." (See Appendix I.) It is important to note that this classification was made by elders who
are without doubt that they and their churches are among the
"old regular" group. All types could agree on the doctrine of
election, namely, that there is a class of persons, elected to
salvation, another elected to damnation, and still disagree on
the implication of the doctrine of predestination. In their understanding of the doctrine of predestination, "Absoluters"
believe that everything in time and nature is predetermined.
They are strict logicians and are called "fatalists." It is not difficult to see that the preaching in this group would be primarily doctrinal, and secondarily experimental, and difficult to
see how any "duty" preaching could be sustained.

"Progressives" have in fact become "Arminian," with their
Sunday schools, musical instruments, and accommodating
ways to the world, according to the regulars. As one elder expressed it, "progressives are no longer strangers and pilgrims,
they are at home in the world." There is no strict reason why
this group should favor one kind of preaching over another,
though the preferences probably run toward a combination
of experimental and duty.

"Old Regulars" like to say they steer a middle course between the fatalism and passivity of the "Absoluters" and the
proto-missionary accommodations of the "Progressives." An
example may show how "experimental preaching" can serve
the dominant purpose of doctrine. Again, we quote from the

sermon Elder Bradley preached a month prior to the Mountain District Association meeting, at Antioch in North Carolina:

I had been taught from earliest childhood and believed in all sincerity that a person had to hear the gospel preached, and upon hearing it if they would repent of their sins and believe in Jesus they'd become a child of God. And as I felt burdened to preach, and began to try to preach what I then understood to be the gospel, I felt that it was my responsibility to try to labor with perishing sinners and persuade them before it was too late to make this necessary decision. And I was busy, I was laboring at it, I was traveling about preaching everywhere any opportunity could be given to me . . . Picked up all kinds of rough characters hitchhiking along the highways, cause I thought if I pass them up and don't preach to them and they die and go to hell it's my fault. Many a time by the time I got out to my appointment on the weekend I'd have my car full of people I was preaching to. I'll tell you it was a big relief to find out that saving souls wasn't my business, that was in the Lord's hands. But when I first saw this first chapter of the Book of Ephesians, of course I'd read it prior to the time that it began to mean something to me, and I would see that here was a contradiction with what I was preaching. And so to try to explain it, I thought about it, tried to pray about it. Finally had an idea that I'd decided must be surely the Lord showing me what it was. And that taught me a lesson that every time you feel inspired, it didn't necessarily come from the Lord. But I said well I know what that means when it says that as God has chosen us in him before the foundation of the world, since God knows everything he just looked down through time and saw who would have the gospel, and who would repent and who would accept Christ, and so he elected them, but the whole thing was based on what they were going to do anyway. And I felt good again, because I said my theology is still intact, I don't have to change anything, see, I can believe this and believe the other, all at the same time. Problem with that was, I had a man-made explanation but it didn't fit, it wasn't in harmony with the word of God. In time I came to see that not only was this doctrine of election taught in the Book of Ephesians, I found it in the book of Romans, I found it all through the New Testament, and then I began to see it in the Old Testament. Saw the sovereignty of God, in deter-

mining the salvation of his people, and by this time the whole
foundation was crumbling on everything that I had believed and
everything that I had tried to preach. And it's upsetting enough
if you have believed something and this is what you have trea-
sured all your life, but when you've not only believed it but
you've tried to preach it to somebody else, and you've taught
other people this, well that's indeed a disturbing situation. After
going through a great, great deal of turmoil about it, I finally was
trying my best I knew how to pray, "Lord, if you'll just show
me I know there's something there, I know I can't put all this
together right now, but if you'll just show me what it is, and give
me the grace I'll try to preach it." Finally came to the conclusion that this which I'd been taught, that salvation was depen-
dent upon man hearing the gospel, repenting of his sins and believing on Jesus, that God was using this the preacher to reach
the dead sinner, that this was totally contrary to that which was
taught in the word of God, but that this salvation depended
upon God's own sovereign pleasure and that he made choice of
a people in a covenant before time began. And, oh what a
joyful sound it was, and how beautiful it was for me then to
see things in that order! To see that God planned this salvation, and if God planned something you can rest assured it's
not going to come to naught. That which God has planned
will be executed. God declared this salvation before man ever
had being in himself.

Elder Bradley said, "And that taught me a lesson that every
time you feel inspired, it didn't necessarily come from the
Lord." This habitual suspicion of the human mind is characteristic of Old Baptist psychology, which they exercise as
much on themselves as on others. This places the preacher
in a position of extreme equivocality. If preaching is the main
bridge between the world of scripture and the world of history, spirit and flesh, then anyone occupying the role of
preacher both experiences the terror of history and tastes the
honey of the Spirit.

No preacher can preach unless he is blessed to do so. Preparations in the form of notes, outlines, manuscripts are not allowed. Such would be an insult to the Spirit which bloweth
where it listeth. A preacher does prepare his own heart, to

use the great Puritan phrase, by reading scriptures and through meditations upon them. For example, one elder introduced his sermon with the following remark:

> I want to read some scripture that will be found in the second chapter of Ephesians. This scripture seems to linger on my mind. I hope it's of the Lord.

The last sentence is as doctrinally charged a statement as it is a heartfelt one. Hope is the chief theological virtue of pre-destinarian Baptists. If all human affection is tainted with silent and discernible depravity, and if the human mind is profoundly inclined to idolatry, then knowledge and proper behavior are not to be expected when things of the Spirit matter the most. When Old Baptists offer themselves to a local church for membership, they are asked to "give some evidences of your hope."

> If I can't feel that power, I ain't preaching the gospel. I may stand up there and quote scripture and so on, but it ain't the gospel. That power comes down from heaven that enables me to preach the gospel.

This elder's remark, and the typical passive mood of "enables me," underscore the ambiguity that attends any effort to preach.

You cannot preach, they say, unless you are blessed. Elders will stand behind the book board, read a passage of scripture, and begin what they call "the preliminaries." By rising to preach the elder engages in an action of hope. If he is "taken up on the mountain," that is, if he is blessed, his hope is confirmed. If not, he is not surprised. One young elder told us that when he is not blessed to preach, it reminds him that what he is trying to do is something real, and beyond his power to effect.

Elders are not ordained until they have demonstrated that they "have the gift" of preaching. If clerk and deacons judge a person in their midst a promising candidate, they will vote him license to exercise his gift. If for a number of years (the periods vary) he has shown that he has the gift, he is ordained by representative elders of several churches; thus there is a check on any local church's judgment about a person's fitness for ordination.

Older members then have become qualified judges, like Clerk Nichols of Cross Roads Church, and their motions express a judgment about the fitness of a person to preach. Paralleling the lay judgment here is usually an apprenticeship relation between a young elder and his "father in the ministry." Ask an elder how he learned to preach, and he will reply in traditional craft fashion, "it just rubbed off." These mentorships can be seen in our own case. Elder Yates is a protégé of Elder Evans; Clerk Nichols nominated both Elders Reed and Sparks to the congregation at Cross Roads as trial preachers, and after moved their ordination.

The participation of both laity and older elders in the fashioning of younger elders is important to our case with its several overlapping networks and loyalties. Many of these attachments and differences rise out of the earlier history of relations between laity and elders and between mentors and apprentices.

Our Old Baptist readers would stop us here and point out that we have moved from a doctrinal account of preaching to an anthropological account. In doing so, they would detect one of the patterns in our portrayal of the Blue Ridge Baptists. We return to the doctrinal account.

Elders commonly speak of modes of the Word of God, and all of them are woven and interwoven in the act of preaching. Pride of place goes to the written work of God, namely scripture. But scripture as written words in a book, like the normal speech of the elder, are not modes of God's word. Hear Elder Evans on this point at a pitch of passionate utterance:

> . . . by the word of God. Somebody said, "that's the Bible."
> Well, let's see if it is. "By the word of God, which liveth and
> abideth forever." See, that got the Bible along the way, didn't

it? This is not alive [holds up Bible]; they've got out now what they call "the living Bible" . . . Ain't no way in the world that a Bible could be a "living Bible." That is—this is—a dead letter. It speaks of Him that hath "power to give life, that has given life, that gave the first man life."

The written word only becomes the living word through the divinely inspired spirit which gives life to the letter. It is characteristic of these Calvinists to distinguish between written and spoken words and their divine meaning; that is, only after these media have been displaced by and toward the Spirit is the living word of God preached and heard.

Just as laity is judge of a man's gift, so are elders judges with respect to a person's ordination. Again, hear Elder Evans:

> I refuse to lay my hands on any other man that I've not heard preach the gospel. And I'm not talking about making a speech. The gospel is the power of God, it's not learned in the school of men.

What the power of the gospel is and how it is recognized varies, particularly between elders and laity. For Evans, doctrinal purity would be a key; the laity would say that they recognize their experience in what the preacher preaches. A faithful layman, Mr. Green Ward, told us as we hiked on top of a mountain where his cattle graze, speaking of a particular elder on a special occasion, "I recognized myself in what he said."

Elders do have measure they use to judge whether they are being blessed.

> You can feel, you are the first one knows if God's blessing you to preach. And you can see the people . . . if they are looking out the window and all, you're not blessed, you're just up there talking. But when there's interest showed, and there's a quietness in the church and all, you can feel it, the Lord's with you.

In this remark, Elder Roten, a contemporary of Evans who accompanied him on preaching trips in their younger years, also mentions that weeping by members is a sign of blessing, that the Living Word is being preached. When members and elders are in accord, feeling mutually blessed, and tell about it later, they will say, "we had a sweet meeting." It is important to note that they do not separate their feelings from the doctrine. They use powerful aesthetic terms like "beautiful," "wonderful," and "marvelous" about the doctrine preached that belief and feeling are in concord. It is with respect to such experiences that the biblical phrase "from breast to breast" is used to describe the sense of communion and affectionate solidarity. Such experience, as described in an earlier quotation from Elder Bradley's sermon, undoubtedly gives an experiential backing to such doctrines as effectual calling and the visible church, the sweet counter to the bitter doctrines of election and predestination. Primitive Baptists practice a bitter-sweet religion, poised as they are between anxiety and hope.

The elder occupies a major role in this religion. To anticipate the theme, indeed the preoccupation, of Elder Evans's association sermon, they are both translators and translated. If blessed they are translated into other speech than their own; God speaks through them. This blessing of preaching the gospel enables them to translate the Word of God to the listeners, attentive in their concentration on his words.

Translation here carries more than one meaning: it is linguistic and interpretive; it denotes a change in the congregation's relation to the elder and to itself, thanks to the gifts of words and feelings, flowing "from breast to breast." The sheep are fed. The children of Israel in their exodus receive mana in the wilderness of this world within the space of the Old Baptist meetinghouse. Text is liberated into holy words through the nourishment of the oral art of Primitive Baptist elders. The meeting space is translated into a garden of flowers.

Events and Characters

We have interrupted our narrative to fill in two kinds of contexts: on one hand, the political and social organization of the Primitive Baptists and its doctrinal basis as embodied in such concepts as the Visible Church; on the other hand, the immediate sensory forms through which the Primitive Baptist experience is communicated: music, architecture, and the verbal aspects of preaching. History, for the Primitive Baptists and for us, is a mediating construct which unites, though problematically, a range of such contexts, to each other and to the events that unfold in terms of them.

To grasp the full significance of our narrative our reader must understand these contexts. Stated generally, the point is obvious. Yet, in practice we are prone to forget one or another context. An example will remind us of the point.

The Primitive Baptist elders are often powerful personalities as well as powerful preachers. Elder Evans is a gifted, scintillating poetic weaver of images and a profound analyst of meaning. Elder Yates is jut-jawed, with bull-like shoulders, resonant voice, and strong convictions. Elder Bradley is a cogent systematist of doctrine. Each of these three men impresses the observer on first hearing.

Elder Reed does not make so overwhelming an impression to the outsider as a preacher. He is soft-spoken, and he seems less eloquent and charismatic. Yet Elder Reed was ordained without question; he has been called to pastor several churches; and he was elected assistant moderator. He is a respected leader of the association.

To understand the place of Reed, we must broaden our gaze beyond surface impression. We must consider also the social and political network and doctrinal convictions of the congregation, and, anticipating our next chapter, we must consider the autobiography of Reed.

Elder Reed was suffering from a blood disease when he was called. This was after twenty years of having refused to accept the call. He rose from his bed, seemingly cured, and began years of devoted pastoral service and preaching. Through his work he has risen to his position in the association. His pastorate includes the most vigorous church, Cross Roads, and the most viable social networks within the association, centered around Baywood and Galax.

Reed's hearers know his life, they know him, they know the social and political network and his place in it. Accordingly, when they hear his sermons they hear not just his words, which we record on our tapes; they hear him, bringing with him these personal and social meanings. And, of course, they hear him in a setting, visual, musical, and scriptural, that is rich with associations. Even more, when people hear Reed, they hear that wider cosmic reality that he represents and in which they, as believers, participate, but in which we, as outsiders, do not.

The Calvinist doctrine itself encourages listening beyond sounds and words, looking behind surfaces and appearances. The cautionary phrase "If I am not deceived" reflects an epistemology skeptical of the apparent, and the interpretative schemes of types and shadows elaborate a framework for penetrating to deeper meanings.

Events in history, whether they be sermons heard on a Sunday or the machinations of the Cahooneys, may fascinate, but they do not, in terms of Primitive Baptist worldview, carry ultimate significance. Events yield meaning only when framed. Such framing by the Primitive Baptist is, of course, much richer than what an outsider can suggest. Our frames are blunter and more explicit in some areas, such as the sociological, more schematic and summative in others, such as the theological. But we try, here and all along, to identify the kinds of patterns within which the events of our story make sense to them as well as to us.

CHAPTER FIVE

Parallel Lives

Elder Evans and Clerk Nichols

The personal qualities of the two leaders, Moderator Evans and Clerk Nichols, reflect the contrast between the North Carolina and Virginia groups. Yet the two men share many traits. Both are around seventy years old (Nichols is seventy, Evans nearly seventy-four, at the time of these events in 1983): both are of the mountains, both born and raised in "this country," as they say, where they still live. Both have spent their lives doing manual labor; both are retired. Most important, both are devout Primitive Baptists.

In appearance and demeanor they contrast. Nichols is short, squat, powerfully built, with thick hands. Evans is taller, also very strong, but slender of hand for one who spent his life at hard labor. Nichols speaks deliberately and slowly in a resonant voice of steady timbre. Evans speaks rapidly, with striking fluency and variation in timbre, facial expression, and gesture. Nichols spent his life working with the Virginia Highway Commission, rising to supervisor after years of running heavy machinery, and retiring with a pension. Evans never had any corporate job, but spent his life at many independent jobs: stone mason, farm worker, plowing, dairying. Nichols has one son, who serves with him as a deacon in his church and assistant clerk of the association. Evans has three daughters and two sons (one deceased), none of whom hold office in the association.

Evans's spiritual autobiography, written several years before our interviews, is a complex and rich history of experience, action, and interpretation. This text will serve as a focus of our analysis; comments by Nichols and the other protagonists, who have not written autobiographies, will give comparative perspective. One experience that Evans describes in his autobiography later becomes especially significant in the unfolding of our case. This experience he terms "translation"; he explores the meaning of this term in a sermon. His account has three points: first, he notes that translation, as in translation of the Bible from Hebrew to English, includes two elements: words, the passive element, and a translator, the active element. "Words don't translate themselves," he says. Second, he makes an analogy to the biblical event of Elijah being "translated" from earth to heaven, here too requiring the passive and active elements (2 Kings 2). The passive is Elijah and the active is God. God took Elijah up, not Elijah himself. Finally, in his autobiography Evans describes an experience that he considers parallel to the "translation" of Elijah and a turning point in his own life. This experience must be considered in the context of his autobiography.

The Life and Experience of Elder Walter Evans

Elder Evans begins by stating that some of his brethren have requested that he write a "sketch of my life and experiences." He continues that "having a sense of my unworthiness and realizing the fallibility of man, a fear arrests my heart, that after I have written, my life and labors and experiences are not worthy of consideration. . . ." Yet, he concludes, "I have a deep conviction that the Lord has motivated some of my activities, if I have not been deceived." In the beginning, then, he affirms the Primitive Baptist sense of human unworthiness and mistrust of human observation, but he also affirms the

Primitive Baptist sense of divine motivation or effectual calling, the life guided by God.

"I was born in Alleghany County, North Carolina, December 23, 1909, the oldest son of John H. and Annice (Warren)
Evans, poor but honest and upright parents, who lived in a
small two-room house covered with boards riven from the forest." He continues this classic portrait of the hard but good
life, stating that on their eighty-eight-acre farm "we labored
hard but with pleasure" to subsist, getting about on foot or
sometimes horse and buggy.

As a child he learned to walk, then was struck by a disease
so severe that he had to learn to walk again, then by diphtheria, a disease that "killed most every one that took it."
Diphtheria forced him to learn to walk a third time. His
mother told him about those illnesses and also told him that
his grandmother had said to her, when Walter was still a small
baby in arms: "Annice, that boy will make a preacher."
"This," Evans says, "I didn't know until I was exercising
[preaching] in public." Here he alludes to things to come, reflecting that even at this early time God had set His hand upon
his life. By locating a sense of destiny within the mind of a
third person—the grandmother—Evans underlines how unaware he was of his calling.

His next scene is of his youth; he recounts that in his early
teens, as he "followed a yoke of oxen to a plow or harrow, I
would sing some of the old songs of Zion. . . ."

> Guide me, O' Thou great Jehovah!
>   Pilgrim through this barren land
> I am weak, but Thou are mighty,
>   Hold me with thy powerful hand.

He introduces here an image that he will explicate a half-
century later; he is the pilgrim, the lonely sojourner, traveling
through life guided by Jehovah. He reflects, "As I would sing
these old hymns, a sad lonely feeling would come over me
that someday I would have to preach, but when or how I

didn't know." Again, he remembers a sense of destiny, evidence of calling.

He tells of attending schools six months in the year until he had finished the seventh grade, at which point he stopped (as was typical of that region and period). He tells also of attending schools organized at that time throughout the region to teach shape-note singing, for seven weeks at different times. He showed talent and had a strong, clear voice. As we visited the site of that school (Union Church), he recounted how the teacher, Paul B. Collins, had singled him out:

> Oh my voice was just strong in them days, I didn't have to strain. You know, it was just natural. And he spotted me singing, he called me out, said, you back there (he didn't know my name), says, you back there singing with that strong voice, says, come up here a minute . . . you lead. . . .

"I thought then I would make a singing teacher, but gave up, and went to rambling and sowing wild oats, which in time I had to reap."

Exactly what the wild oats were, Evans does not say here, though elsewhere he alludes to playing fiddle, dancing, and courting girls. The point of interest is his style of referring forward, reflectively; what would happen was set.

We note here a contrast between Evans's mood, as he recollects in his writing and as we visited the sites mentioned in the autobiography. In the writings, he reads back into his early life a sense of gloom and foreboding; he recalls maturing as he sensed his destiny without yet grasping it. In the visit, as to the singing school, the sight of the place seemed to remove him from interpretive theology, and he emphasized the lively experience of the time. Similarly, when we visited his old school, he told us animatedly how he once spelled down the teacher himself. Having defeated all the pupils, he challenged the teacher too: "Come on up here!" he cried, and, when the teacher mounted the stage, Evans defeated him. Across the road from the school he showed us the field where he played baseball; he was, of course, the pitcher, and he says he threw a hard ball.

"Prior to this, perhaps twelve or thirteen years old, I had two experiences in dreams." These occurred when he was living with his family in the house of his grandparents, a larger house than the cabin where he was born. In the first dream, he was pursued through the forest by a snake about twenty feet long. (A hoop snake, he told us, which rolls in a hoop and stings you with its tail; this creature is pervasive in mountain folklore.) After running and running, he was about to be caught, and gave up. "But just before he took hold of me, there was an unseen power raised me from the earth up among the tops of the trees, without any effort on my part, completely out of reach of the great monster. I was made very happy and thought the good Lord had saved me from death." (Here is a theme repeated later on Sheep Pen Ridge, where he exhausted his own resources, then was saved by God.) In the second dream he found himself walking on "mountains of gold somewhere above the world . . . I can almost see the glorious radiance of that golden country as the light of the sun was shining to reflect the wondrous beauty of those golden mountains. . . ." He explains that he tells these things to show how, even as a small lad, he had "thoughts and convictions of a supernatural power, and that I was made to believe that God could perform these things without the assistance of any." He does not offer any specific interpretation of these symbols, such as of the snake, but just points to an early sense of the godly power that works without human contribution.

> In the latter part of my twentieth year, in November before I was twenty-one in December 1930—when I cared nothing for God nor his people, satisfied with my big times attending places of worldly pleasures—my father insisted strongly [that I] attend a meeting being held by people of the Regular Baptist denomination, of which he and Mother were members (sometimes they were called Union Baptist). I finally agreed

to go; however, my purpose in going was to walk home with
some of the girls from the meeting.

It was on Tuesday night of this week while standing in the
back of the house [behind the last pews], a strong power arrested my heart and soul to the extent my body trembled
under the weight like a leaf on a tree shaken by a mighty
wind. A voice from somewhere, a still voice taut with power
said, "You are lost without God or hope in the world."

He felt himself a sinner "by nature . . . doomed without
God's mercy." At the close of the service, he answered the
call by kneeling at the altar, or "mourner's bench," and
"begged God for mercy and pardon of [my] sins." "I was in
desperate need of something to give me relief from this awful
feeling of condemnation. They prayed and sang but I grew no
better but worse . . . This was a day when men and women,
even fathers and mothers, were calling mightily on the Lord—
not only in the meetinghouse; you could hear their mourning
cries as they walked the road to and from the church
house. . . ." After he left the meetinghouse and went home,
nothing could bring relief.

Prayers of Dad and Mother, preachers, nor no one else could
reach my case. After I would blow out the little kerosene
lamp, I would bow on my knees beside my bed and pour out
my heart and soul to God, but he would not hear, that is, he
would not deliver.

This continued two days and three nights until, at the end
of his strength, lying on the floor, relief came. "A still voice
said, 'Your sins are all forgiven.'" He was raised to his feet
"one happy man" and joined the congregation singing (he was
apparently at church): "Christ will bear the Christian higher.
When the last trumpet shall sound!" His voice rang out above
the congregation (as it still can do). "Before the song was
ended, a call or strong impression came to me . . . Oh, how
I desired to tell what the Lord had done for me. I was in a
new world. . . ." He was baptized Sunday, November 16,
1930.

This meeting was moved to another church, some three or four miles away, and during this meeting he offered his first public prayer, in the home of friends. Moved by the groans of "boys and girls, even fathers and mothers, begging God for his mercy," he was "given liberty" and "the room was filled with His sweet and delightful presence." Next night, at church, he was asked by the preacher to pray and, though "a trembling fear came over me," he was again given liberty and found "sweet relief." For four years he led public prayers, while "my burden to preach grew heavier."

A dream ended his prayer in public for awhile.

> I was standing on the outside of this old church building where the meeting had closed. It was dark and I stood alone. I walked up the steps and opened the door. When I walked inside, something different than I had ever seen—a light of its own reflection, no electric lights, the little kerosene lamps were not burning around the wall. It was so bright and clear that I believe I could have seen a pin on the floor. As I walked up the aisle, I looked to my right and then to my left. I saw dark faces that continued on until I was about three fourths the way to the stand, and then they were white the rest of the way. They all seemed to be clean. Just as I walked in front of the pulpit there was a casket in front, gray in color. I stopped direct in front of the casket and stood still. A sadness came in my soul. Oh! how sad I felt. I looked toward the stand. I saw no preacher. A voice then spoke to me and said, "Go in the stand and preach to this people." I turned left, walked around the casket into the pulpit, and in front of the book board there stood a stool with three legs. The top was round and about fifteen inches in diameter. Again a voice spoke to me and said, "Get on this stool and preach to this people." I immediately was standing on the stool about fifteen or eighteen inches high. I started preaching and was soon carried so high in my feelings that I lost sight completely of the congregation. When I came to myself and realized where I was, the congregation was all white. I looked down to see where the casket and corpse was. It had disappeared. My sad feeling was gone and I stood rejoicing in hope of the glory of God, then awoke from my dream much disturbed and troubled.

Elder Evans interpreted the dream as Satan telling him that he was trying to "climb too high," that this experience of exaltation was illusion, since no such stool existed, and that God was warning him not to preach. Accepting the warning, Evans began refusing to pray publicly, and he stopped coming to church altogether. During months of conflict, "I roamed the mountains and rock cliffs, begging the good Lord to show me what to do. I could not understand my dream and I was in deep trouble. . . ." He mentions, incidentally, that he had married in February 1931, and now his first son was about two years old. He felt so sure he would die that he told his wife he had just three weeks to live.

As the days passed, he roamed the hills and prayed with his wife at home, but he became more and more distressed.

> Again, one lonely evening, I wanted to try to pray once more, so I told my companion [his wife] I was going out to see the corn, and did walk through the field. I shall never forget this experience. As I walked through the field of corn, it appeared to be mourning with its blades bending toward the earth.

He climbed the mountain, passing grazing cattle who also appeared to be mourning. He reached the top of the mountain, Sheep Pen Ridge:

> As I stood there alone, Oh! So dark and gloomy, late in the evening. I turned down on the other side. This side of the mountain was a wooded area, so I roamed among the trees, trying to find some place to pray . . . such a burden I was carrying. . . .

He prayed, determined to find relief, but he failed, and finally he said, "Amen." But "this time I thought it was to my own condemnation—that I had been deceived in it all." He climbed back to the top of the mountain:

> . . . suddenly there shined a light around me, a complete circle fifteen feet in diameter, or more, the resemblance of a rainbow's many colors but brighter. Such as this I had never

seen nor felt. Every doubt and fear left me as quick as a flash. I felt so light in my feelings. I actually thought I was going to be taken from the earth . . . I started singing:

> I thank you Lord, for every blessing
> That thou sendeth from above,
> For life and strength that I'm possessing,
> And the wonders of Thy love.

This experience he would later term "translation," when, as a passive agency, having exhausted his own capabilities, he was lifted up and translated by God into a higher realm, as Elijah had been translated by God and taken up to heaven. He walked down the mountain, now preaching out loud "to the birds, trees, to myself. . . ." The cattle now appeared ready to shout. He tried to get in the house without showing his wife the difference in himself, but she saw it, and he took his little boy on his knee and sang, "Children of the heav'nly King."

After "constant research and review," he reinterpreted the dream he had previously attributed to Satan. The darkness outside he saw as his state before he began preaching. The light inside the meeting house was God's grace, the light of Zion. The dark faces inside the house had been blinded by the world, the light faces had seen the truth. The casket represented his sadness before preaching. The stool was the three persons of the Trinity, which is the foundation of doctrine. He saw his being carried above and the banishment of the casket as signifying the power to preach, given him by God; the loss of his sadness was from taking up this task. In short, he reinterpreted the dream as a calling to preach rather than a warning against it.

The dream did not immediately bring him to preach, however. His narrative returns to hard facts of life. He was a tenant on a mountainous farm owned by an elderly man. The work was hard, entailing cutting and carrying rails, cutting and bundling and carrying grain, all by hand and over steep terrain. The old man even resented his stopping for a drink

of water, and paid him only sixty cents a day. Finally, one
Sunday, Evans had borrowed a neighbor's automobile and
was leaving to visit his wife's parents, taking with them their
second born. On the way, he asked the owner to pay him what
he owed him so he could get gasoline. When the owner made
excuses:

> I almost lost control of myself. I opened the car door and
> stepped out in front of him. I spoke quick and sharp. I said,
> "I moved here to treat you like a man. I've done that and you
> know it, and if nothing else will do you but trouble, you've
> got it right here and now."

His wife intervened, and Evans finally got in the car, angrily,
got the gas on credit, and went on the trip. After a few days,
he felt

> condemned over getting so angry, it caused me to repent and
> ask the Lord to forgive, and tried to pray for the man that
> had done me wrong. I didn't strike this elderly man, but got
> close to it. I think yet he should have paid me, which he
> never did, but I shouldn't have gotten so angry.

After gathering the corn that fall, he moved to another farm
with similar work but better pay (ten cents per hour raise).
This incident is simply told; it returns us to material conditions, reminding us that he hardly lived in a spiritual world.
No allegorical or spiritual interpretation is given of it. Fifty
years later, discussing it he still flashes angry, describing
himself as strong and fit then, able to sling two-hundred-
pound sacks onto wagons, and barely escaping injuring the
old man.

He returns to spiritual narration. "My burden to go
tell what I felt the Lord had done for me grew heavier."
He could see his grave at night, feeling sure he would soon
be in it. He also dreamed of preaching, keeping a text in his
mind for days, ruminating on it. He kept all this from his
wife, who had said she would never marry a doctor or a
preacher.

As Evans became more depressed, he felt he would die, and one rainy morning:

> [I] climbed to the top of a mountain to try to pray one more time. I came to a place where two trees had fallen, one across the other crosswise, and in a briar thicket. I parted my way through the briars until I came to where the trees had crossed. Between these two trees and in the briar patch is where I promised the good Lord that I would go and stand before His people if He would give me grace, wisdom, and power to speak of the wonders of his grace and love toward the children of men.

He had made and broken many vows, he says, and he brought up many excuses to break this promise—that he was poor, that he lacked education, that he had been playing violin and guitar all over the country for dances and was a dancer himself—but with "all these promises made and broken . . . in this briar patch is one I made and kept by God's grace and mercy. The church liberated me to exercise a public gift April 13, 1935." From the winter briar patch, he moved to spring liberation.

After he was liberated, Evans made his "first attempt to speak in the name of Him that had done so much for me." He tells how he was introduced by an old preacher [this was probably his mentor, Elder Kirby, the only preacher, other than Elder Roten, with whom he was to serve a church jointly]:

> I arose to my feet, my body trembling like a tree shaken by a mighty wind. My text was one so often used or quoted in preaching, St. John, 3rd chapter and verse 16: "For God so loved the world that he gave his only begotten Son, that whosoever believeth in Him should not perish, but have everlasting life." My mind was exercised far beyond what I ever expected. I set forth with all the power of my being and under the weight of God's powerful hand, that God sent forth His Son into the world to save poor helpless and ruined sinner . . . I didn't hunt for words. They were given to me. They seemed to just flow out, and oh how sweet the taste. My heavy weight was removed and

sweet peace came into my soul . . . Many tears were shed during this exercise. . . .

In the years since, he says, when he would feel that he had been "deceived," never called to preach, and feel "destitute," he would recall this first experience and gain courage and trust "in the God of all grace to deliver again and again."

He then reports his second effort at preaching, which was at an association meeting. Again he was blessed and had a "sweet peace." But this was not, to use modern psychological language, simply a "peak experience" offering "personal fulfillment"; this was "evidence" of being called. Convinced that he was, he plunged in Bible study day and night. His father became uneasy and told some of the neighbors "I was going to lose my mind" (the fevered search of the eager young man contrasted with the fearful conservatism of the old man, who is not called). "But I had entered into a great work and I must know what the Bible taught."

The week before the meeting time at the church he had joined, he was forced to move because he refused to vote for a certain candidate for public office whom his landlord supported. (Here we glimpse Evans's somewhat precarious position in his society.) He and his father built a small two-room cabin on their old farm, to which Evans and his family moved. He mentions this move only briefly to go on to another spiritual experience; in that cabin he began to read his grandfather's Bible. In Genesis, chapter 24, 58th verse, he read of Rebekah saying, "I will go." Instead of sleeping, he had "wonderful meditations and revelations." These were not interpreted psychologically, as relating to his move, but instead on a scriptural and political point, how Rebekah, going to become the wife of Isaac, brought forth two nations from her womb. Again, it is the theological and biblical, rather than personal, world to which he moves.

". . . Sad hours and conflicts awaited me." The Saturday and Sunday following was the meeting time for his home church, and he went, eagerly prepared to preach about his visions and meditations. His wife had not been present on his first two "attempts at preaching," but she was on this occasion, and he wanted to prove himself to her. "I was sure if I made a failure she would say, 'What's all this noise about preaching? If I couldn't beat that, I think I'd be quiet if I were you.'" He relates every step of the service, to the point where he was called to the stand. He spoke for three or four minutes, then came to the verses: "I will go." He was ready to really preach, "but alas, sudden darkness intervened. I forgot my beautiful text and everything else." He sat down, terribly abashed, and did not even go home but "went home with a man in the lower part of the county." After a sleepless night, he realized that God must bless a man to preach, that he could not do so by his own power. In the morning, he tried to pray on a large stone in a river, which he saw as representing perhaps Christ the Rock, "the Stone that became the head of the corner, or the Stone that was laid in Zion." But his prayer, he felt, was unheard, for he had sinned too greatly. As he stood on the bank of the river, watching a baptism, he felt totally detached: "Beholding the scene, I could see no real reason for the action that was underway . . . as for me, I got nothing out of it."

Next day at the service, he got relief. He heard a "still small voice say, 'I'll not leave you comfortless.'" After the prayer, he rose quickly to preach, told what had happened the day before, what he had heard, and he related this to the scripture, too. "David anciently said, 'Will the Lord cast me off forever? And be favorable no more?'" Evans says he was "given comfort," that he preached well. Later he saw his wife and his aunt coming down the path. Expecting her to taunt him about his failure the day before, he said to her, "Go ahead and say it. It's all right anyway." She just looked and smiled and "never said what I knew she would."

On August 8, 1932, Evans was ordained as elder "by a presbytery of elders and deacons of the aforementioned denomination (Regular or Union Baptists), having been called for by the church of which I was a member." He described the ser-

vice at which he preached (on Isaiah 28. 16) and the procedure of the ordination, quoting the first epistle of Paul the
Apostle to Timothy as he lays down the requirements for a
church officer, and the nine Articles of Faith of the Union
Baptist. Following this procedure, he recounts, "I was then
delivered back to the church an ordained orthodox minister."
He explains that he quotes these Articles of Faith to show that
they contain that doctrine which, following his ordination, he
defended, but which defense resulted in his eventually leaving
the church. This doctrine is that of election by God's free and
sovereign grace, irrespective of individual will or choice.

After his ordination, he was "called" as pastor of his home
church and others. He served them for more than fifteen
years. But he preached the doctrine of what he would later
term "strict and particular election," so he was branded a
hard-shelled "Old Baptist." "My persecutions grew more severe when brethren began to denounce this truth." The brethren maintained that salvation was open to all men "if the man
would only yield himself to Christ after being convicted of his
sin . . . I contended that this work of grace was not the sinner's choice, nor his will, but according to God's sovereign
will. . . ."

Evans contends that he didn't want to be an Old Baptist.
"I undertook to read the Old Baptist out, but instead, I read
myself in." That is, through his own study of the Bible, he
concluded that the Old Baptists were correct. Still, he undertook to preach their doctrine in his church, rather than join
theirs. Some of his members, even those who had ordained
him "took a firm stand against me, because of what I was
preaching."

The conflict came to a head in the following incident. Elder
Evans had long reflected on the scripture, Second Thessalonians, chapter 2, verses 13-14, which he now believed taught
predestination, that God had elected the saved before the
foundation of the world: ". . . God hath from the beginning
chosen you to salvation. . . ." For two monthly church
meetings, Evans had suffered, "condemned in my heart," for

not proclaiming this message. A few days before the next meeting time, he had this dream:

> I was on my way again to this same church. I was walking a highway that I thought led to the church, which was some twelve or fifteen miles . . . my attention was attracted by two white she bears, that were walking on the left side of the highway on a bank or rise some fifteen feet above the road level. Traveling the same direction, they both turned their heads and looked at me for a few moments. I wondered if they would attack me and perhaps destroy my life, but they turned a little from me and set their faces an air-line direction toward this church, and I was made to wonder what meaneth this. I saw them no more. When I had reached the Church and had entered the door, the Congregation had gathered. As I walked up the aisle, two preachers were sitting in the stand on the left side, sitting very close together. I knew them very well, had been with them many times and knew that they both denied that God chose his people from the beginning. I looked to the left side where the sisters always sit, and there sat the wife of one of these preachers. She was a good humble woman in heart, I feel sure. I walked into the stand . . . I rose to my feet and announced the text I had run from twice before. I was carried completely above everything that pertains to this world. Just as I closed my discourse, the chill of death struck me in my feet and began to come up my legs and over my body. When it had enveloped me completely, I fell dead.
> . . . I awoke from this dream speechless and couldn't move even my fingers. My eyes were opened, and I couldn't close them. I thought I was dying and tried to speak to my wife and could not speak. . . .

When Evans regained his movement, he vowed that he would affirm predestination at the next meeting, to which, in a few days, he started on foot.

"My dream was before my face all the way. I thought 'Oh my God, must I die in defense of the gospel?'" He reached the church. "No tongue could possibly express the burden of my heart as I walked up to open the door . . . As I walked up the aisle, I looked directly at the pulpit to see if my dream was true." Everything was exactly as in the dream. He was invited to the stand, so he went, fearfully: "Everything pointed directly to death." He began: "I've carried the weight of a scripture three months," then he read the text, and he began to preach predestination: "I delivered this message with all the power of my being. I still thought this was my last and final message. I was carried above every trouble, every fear in this world."

As he closed, the two white she bears "came before me. Well, everything happened that I saw, except I didn't fall dead naturally, but I guess I died to their fellowship and love."

In Elder Evans's reading of the dream and his experience, a psychological slant is not entirely absent; note his remark, "I did not die, I died to their fellowship." But, as usual, propensity is toward the scriptural. What did the she bears mean? He describes how the she bear is vicious, but he refuses any suggestion that they might have symbolized persecutors. He alludes to close friends, to relatives who were in the church, but his narration of events omits them and focuses on the scriptural symbols of the dream.

On this occasion he was in his thirties. He continued to preach in the Union Baptist church until 1951, when he was in his early forties. Throughout this time he faced, as he recounts it, a crisis in theology—not in career, or lifestyle, or place to live, or marriage, but in theology. As he continued to preach the doctrine of predestination, he faced other challenges, such as this one:

When I arrived on the ground, I noticed a small group here and there. I knew there was something wrong. I could feel a bad spirit was present. We went in the house and began singing or trying to sing. It's not pleasant to mention, perhaps not expedient, but the spirit of Satan was so strong in some of these men, that I could feel my life was almost at stake, as well as the life of others. The church had four deacons. Two of them reminded me that it was time to go to the stand. The other two asked me with sharp words not to go in the stand. I looked over the congregation and I saw danger, so I didn't know what to do. One deacon repeated and said, "Brother

Walter, it's time for preaching." I looked toward a friend of
mine. He shook his head. He also had discerned the spirit
present. I said, "Let's sing another song." We did. The tension
lessened just enough that I thought I could go to the stand
without causing serious trouble. I felt like I could get them to
reason it all out, but failed to do so. The deacons that forbade
me to go to the stand, after I had lined and sung a hymn and
offered prayer and rose to my feet and read my text, came in
the stand. One took hold of one arm and the other, and said
"Come down." I walked slowly with them to the edge of the
stand and stopped. Their arms and hands seemed to weaken
to the extent that they seemed to fall from me. I said, Brethren, you can see what I'm up against. I'll decline the idea of
trying to preach under such pressure. I didn't know it at the
time that one man had his knife out, cutting on the bench.
He also said to me to come down. An old brother with mus-
tache came to his feet with tears in his eyes and began to beg
for peace, and said, "Let's all pray. We are in the wrong
spirit." When he concluded, I said, Brethren, we can't do
church work this way. You are all dismissed to some future
date. A brother brought me home. I shall never forget what
he said: "Brother Walt, the Lord may never be with you anymore, but he was today." During all of this, I never was a bit
angry. I know these things are not pleasant memories. I have
made mention of them to show how the Lord has preserved
me and led me on.

He felt bound by fellowship to his congregation, "some of
whom were my own flesh and blood." (The Old Salem Union
Baptist was his father's and mother's church, also his wife's
church; his sister, father, mother, and son are buried at this
church and the grave site of his wife and himself is here.) He
felt that

> . . . these were God's sheep and that Christ had died for them
> . . . but I also could see a great flock of sheep when I would
> again look toward the Primitive Baptists, and yet these two bod-
> ies of people had no direct fellowship, that is, no church fel-
> lowship. Here I stood between—couldn't go and couldn't stay
> —and yet I had to make a decision between these two bodies of
> people.

As was his wont, he sought resolution through doctrine and scripture; at least that is how he describes it. He reasoned that he was baptized already in the Union Baptist, and that was it: "One Lord, one faith, one baptism. I could see no way to make two out of one. . . ." He argued the issue for nine years, finally deciding that if the first baptism were unscriptural, owing to the unscriptural doctrine of those who had baptized him, then a second baptism was permissible. "And another experience had helped me very much to decide my course." He was husking corn in the fall and heard "or it appeared that I heard" voices singing that were Old Baptist. Then suddenly he thought of a "sketch of history concerning George Washington, who was General Washington at this time during the Revolutionary War." Washington had been reared Episcopalian, but when he saw a chaplain John Gano baptizing some soldiers, he asked that Gano baptize him, "for he felt he had never been scripturally baptized." Gano, Evans knew, was an Old Baptist, "member at Hopewell Primitive Baptist Church in New Jersey, organized April 23, 1715. . . ." "Washington's expression I've never been scripturally baptized was the thought that caught my mind, and I too felt I had never been scripturally baptized. This impression never left me, not for long. . . ."

On the third Saturday of November 1951, Evans was baptized, and on the third Saturday in December 1951, he was ordained in the Primitive Baptist church. His account states little about these momentous events; he elaborates in an interview:

> After a long hesitation then came on down to the house,
> walked that evening to New Salem. Two sisters I'd baptized,
> my neighbors, just a little while before that, a few months,
> mother and her daughter. They stopped and, me and my
> wife, and my wife said I hope you haven't made a mistake
> today. I said I feel O.K. about it, just as calm as I am now.
> Left a lot of good friends, lot of good people, good people. Had
> over a hundred members up here at old New Salem then, now

they're almost gone, almost gone. The morning that I was to
go to Little River, Saturday morning, third Saturday morning.
Woke up Saturday morning, it was windy, snowing, cold.
Awful cold. My wife said it's snowing this morning, said I
guess this'll try your faith. I said let her snow, I've got it. I
never will forget that. I was baptized that evening [afternoon].
But when I went, went to the church, took my clothes, I
might have to bring them back dry and not get them wet. I
didn't know whether they'd take me for certain or not, I was
hoping they would, as unworthy as I was. Brother C.B. Kilby
was pastor then, moderator certainly of that meeting. Brother
Edd Douglas, I'd seen him in a funeral, at a funeral that week
before, I mean during that week. Between the time I'd called
for a letter and the time I'd united with the Primitive Baptists. I said, "Brother Edd, can you come to Little River next
Saturday?" He said, "Well I could, far as I know, if it's important or need to be." "Well," I said, "I plan to offer myself to
the church there next Saturday and I want you to help baptize me. If they receive me." He said, "I'll be there." So he
was there, preached that day. But Brother Kilby moderated
the meeting, which was of course right and custom. Church
doors of course were publicly open as it always is at the close
of the service. So I went, my mind's done made up, I'd done
fought it nine years. So my mind was made up, that day.
Snow or no snow, cold or hot, that wasn't going to faze me no
further. So I walked on down the aisle. I wrote a song about
that, "the Lonely Sparrow." You know, when I was on the
house top I could hear them singing but the door wasn't so
clear. How to get in it, that's what had me see. Door, that's in
a poem I wrote or a song actually. And old Brother Charlie
Kilby of course they just broke down. And of course there
was a larger crowd at that point, there wasn't too many members at Little River, had some, few years of decline, and
there's still church all right. But they'd heard of what I'd
done, and a lot of Union Baptists or Regular Baptists at that
time, and of course some Union Baptists heard about it, and
of course they was there to see the show, you know. See what
went on, really, what's gone wrong with Walt Evans, you
know. Gone to the Hard Shells. Well, the house was, wasn't
maybe not full but it was pretty well, more than we have now
on Saturdays, and more than they was having then on Saturday for that matter, particularly that day. And so my neigh-

bors, particularly one sister, very precious sister, known her all the time, baptized her later in the Old Baptist church. But she told my wife she said I'm going to be there, and can get there I'm going to see that, with my own eyes. And she told me on Wednesday evening, or Wednesday morning, between the two weeks, weekends, she walked right through the field over here, come in and said Walt, said I ain't slept a wink, said for about two nights, said I'd rather put you in the grave up there and bury you as see you left us like you did Saturday. Well I said, "Sister Dorothy, I'm sorry you feel that way about it." She said, "I've always believed the Lord called you to establish New Salem church in the doctrine of salvation by grace. . . ."

Anyway, back to the church, Saturday. Brother C.B. Kilby said Brother Walt he said, of course he and I had talked and I had asked him questions. Brother Charlie Kilby said, "Brother Evans," said, "anything you want to tell us?" I said, "well, I never even told my experience. I reckon it's been so, well maybe not like nobody else's anyway. I says well there's two things I want to say, Brother Charlie. There's two things I don't believe, in the absolute, what's known as the absolute predestination of all things, I denounce and deny. I do not believe the theory of James Arminius, I'm not an Arminian. I do believe salvation's by the grace of God. That's about all I want to say, I'd like to have a home with you." I never even told my experience, but they made a move to receive me as a candidate for baptism. I was baptized, they wanted to know when I wanted to be baptized, I said this evening. That evening. Had me right down too. They made a move among our people, among old Baptists, like this: that we liberate him to exercise the public gift it being effective after he's baptized.

. . . Here come Sister Douglas, Reeves Douglas's wife Laura, she thought I was going to freeze to death you know, here she come with a coat you know just to wrap me up. And as Job said, as God is my witness, my record on high about what I'm saying, I wasn't even cold. And it was a cold day. And you say now Walt that ain't so, but it is. I wasn't even cold. And it was a cold day. I still never took her overcoat, or whatever she had. I went on up there and changed clothes, I was still warm about that thing, inside and out, far as I know, I couldn't tell it was cold or hot, I didn't mind. That's how I went to the Old Baptists. I've had a lot of battles since, and a lot of joy since. But I believe the church of God.

With his baptism, Evans brings his written account to a close. He concludes by briefly summarizing the history of his home church, the doctrine of the Primitive Baptist church, and his career as a Primitive Baptist elder, stating only that he has now preached twenty-nine years, in eighteen states, and at hundreds of funerals, as a Primitive Baptist, while his total years of preaching have been forty-five. His last sentence is that the Primitive Baptists have no "mourning bench but sometimes many mourning hearts."

During the weeks of the Cahooney controversy, it was not the events in Elder Evans's later life that he recollected; rather it was the turning points in his early life, leading to his becoming a Primitive Baptist. The subject of "translation" was on his mind. He discussed it privately, he preached it, and, as we shall see, he alluded to it in his opening remarks at the association meeting when at risk of being deposed as moderator. This translation experience resonates with his own experiences on Sheep Pen Ridge fifty years before. Convicted by his feelings of sinfulness to the point of despair, he vowed to pray to God until he wrested an answer from him; he struggled to do this near the ridge, but failed. In a wretched state, he went on to the top, hopeless. In this state of receptivity, he was "translated" by God to a state of spiritual ecstasy. Among other themes, this experience alludes to man's utter passivity in the divine work of regeneration and, it seems clear, to Evans's own impending death. We shall see, also, an analogy to the she bear dream, as Evans faced, once again, a potentially hostile congregation.

Nichols

Nichols reports no effervescent spiritual experience, but one remarkable fact that attests to his sturdy integrity; he attended Cross Roads Church weekly for thirty years before finally consenting to join. He explains simply that he did not consider himself worthy. Clerk Nichols does not preach nor pray publicly. He confines himself to clerical and construction work for the association and leading the singing at the Cross Roads Church services. But he has played an important administrative and social role as well. As a lay leader, he is a councilor in resolving disputes, and he speaks out at business meetings and in church when it is necessary to pass motions or take action. It was Nichols who, as clerk both of Cross Roads and of the association, brought Reed before the church to be ordained. He says the church (Peach Bottom) that wanted Reed as pastor came to him, as clerk of Reed's home church, Cross Roads, and that Cross Roads, as Reed's home church, should "give him liberty" to preach. So he brought Reed before the church, Cross Roads, at a conference.

When he got up to speak, he thought of Elmer Sparks, too, who had been given liberty within Cross Roads a long time:

> It come to me that I was sure that Brother Sparks had a gift. But what kind of a gift I didn't know, whether it was one talent or two talent or fifteen, whatever. And I just felt like that if the church hid that talent there . . . we would suffer for it. So I, just as free as I've ever done anything, I asked for the church to set him aside too.

Notably, Nichols, who claims no "liberty" of one called to preach, reports a kind of liberty or inspiration in an administrative action: that, not preaching, is his calling.

Nichols is a craftsman. His autobiography is best represented not in words but in construction, of the Cross Roads Church, which he has repaired and remodeled, of his home, of his mountain cabin, tight as a ship's cabin with rough exterior but beautiful paneling inside. Nichols tells us plank by plank about the building of the Cross Roads Church, the cutting of the back door, about how in sawing through timber in the wall of the church they hit a nail and kept on going. He tells us about the age of the roof, the age of the building, the number of remodelings. He shows us each new pew, on which is indicated in a brass plaque the name of each donor. He tells us how he and his son built the outside pavilion, where they now hold dinner on the ground—about the wood they saw-milled themselves, yellow locust, cut on his own property.

He tells us and shows us about the building of his house in Baywood. Which rooms came first, which were added. He tells us how he built a corner cupboard, to match precisely a 100-year-old cupboard he had inherited. He explains how his house began as a small one; he added three bedrooms upstairs, two downstairs. In the bedrooms are double beds with quilts by Nonnie Lee, with purple rows down the middle.

He then shows us the grounds. In back of the house is a grove of piney trees, shielding the house from the wind; a shed; a garden, covered with shavings, eliminating the need to plow each year, and showing no weeds at all; fine crops of tomatoes, rhubarb, lettuce. There is a concord grape arbor; in a corner are swings and seats.

As with the church, this house and the hand of Nichols are in the service of the Lord. These are the bedrooms in which the elders sleep when they come to preach (remember the story of Cahooney and Evans), this is the porch where they sit, and the living room and den. In fact, as usual, we ourselves are now at a social gathering here. Here are four elders with us in the breakfast room: Higgins, Reed, Stevenson (a visiting elder from the Piedmont), Sparks. Women are in the living room: Mrs. Stevenson, Mrs. Reed, Mrs. Truitt, and Beverly Patterson.

Food is arranged on the counter, progressing from mashed potatoes, gravy, and biscuits to meat; then turkey; sweetened apples, congealed salads, and then cakes and pies. Raymond Nichols helps Nonnie Lee serve.

The elders sit around the table talking. Dan remarks on the good biscuits; Elder Sparks—resonant voice, shambling gait, large, brown hands, reddish hair, ruddy complexion: "Something happened to mine." The conversation turns to the Absoluters and their doctrinal fallacies.

A visit to Evans's house contrasts sharply. His wife, not a Primitive Baptist, is incapacitated, and no elders are gathered here to sleep and share a meal; we go out to a town restaurant to eat. Our conversations, wonderfully alive through his own genius, are in his living room, as he sits beside his picture window and stove, looking out over a vista of mountains. Like Nichols, he was a handworker, a stone mason, but his house is not by his hand, and he displays to us nothing of his handiwork. The Nichols house unites man and wife in creating a gathering place for elders. Their home is a location of their work and calling.

Yates

Yates is a powerfully built man in his early thirties whose rough and ready demeanor reflects his physique and physiognomy—his face is ruddy of an English cast, but with the extremely prominent jaw sometimes seen in mountain men. His speech is peppered with old-fashioned words; so and so is "quare" (queer), while he himself is "stout" (strong). He is open and friendly, but direct and challenging.

Abandoned by his father, Yates says he raised himself, living in an abandoned automobile on a nearby mountain where the foliage was so dense the sun never penetrated. He also lived with his mother, washing dishes at the school for his lunches.

He was "point man" for his combat squad in Vietnam, and now works in the shipping department of the local pipe factory where he carries on scriptural arguments with some of his co-workers who are "Missionaries" or "Free-Wills." After his factory shift is over, he works in construction, often putting in a sixteen-hour work day at the two jobs. This incessant labor has allowed him to acquire a six-room brick home, and a large sedan and big-wheel truck that he likes to drive at high speeds along the mountain roads. His family room is adorned with hunting trophies, and the rustic coffee table there displays a large collection of cassette tapes of sermons, his own and those of other elders he admires. His main recreation is deer hunting with a bow, and he tells proudly of killing a

400-pound buck that he had to drag out of the woods by himself.

Billy Yates converted to Primitive Baptists after returning from the war. He, like his mentor Elder Evans, had been a Union Baptist. He became an elder in the Senter Association. Preaching in a forceful style, he has a resonant chanting voice. He is, in 1983, beginning to be in demand as a preacher beyond his four churches. Three of these churches are in the Senter Association, while one—Peach Bottom Primitive Baptist Church in Virginia—is in the Mountain District Association. From his first years in the ministry, Yates has enjoyed the mentorship of both Evans, moderator of the Mountain District Association, and Elder Dewey Roten of the Senter Association, whom he succeeded as moderator in 1982.

Reed

Joseph Reed tells that the Lord called him when he was nineteen, but he did not start preaching until he was thirty-nine. During those twenty years, he recounts, he resisted the call, feeling uneducated and unable. All those years he felt burdened, that the Lord would not let him go.

He had first been called after being in a car wreck. He was in the hospital. He had a broken back and broken legs and was paralyzed. He felt the Lord called him in the hospital, but being a young man, he got out and learned to walk, and so put off answering the call. Twenty years later, he had been virtually bedridden for three years with a blood disease when he felt called again. When he finally accepted the call, the disease went away.

During the years of resistance he had perceived many signs of his being called. Once he was driving a truck filled with sand. He crossed a mountain unconscious of what he was doing, then suddenly awoke at a stoplight in Galax. He couldn't tell his wife of such experiences, but finally he did tell her he had to preach. Usually she encouraged him, but she did not believe he should preach.

He joined the church anyway, then immediately asked for liberty to preach. The church at Peach Bottom asked him to serve them and asked Cross Roads to ordain him. After he recovered from his illness and began preaching, he cleared the land on which his house and farm stand, and built this farm starting with a few cattle and some horses. But he says he wants to sell his horses and travel, taking preaching appointments, even though they don't pay anything.

Reed has just expanded his house to hold social gatherings, including hosting visiting elders. His oldest daughter had just married the grandson of the leading deacon in Evans's church, and he is the pastor of Cross Roads, as well as one other church (Rock Creek) on the Virginia side and one in North Carolina (Elk Creek). He is assistant moderator of the association (later to be elected moderator). He seems solidly part of the leading element within the association.

Yates Again

Yates identifies his first call as in December 1971 at Fort McClellan, Alabama.

> . . . I was out on OP, which is Observation Position, in other words you observe, and I was by myself and had an M-16 across my lap. Ever since I was a kid, you know I always had a desire to preach . . . I couldn't raise the weapon off of my lap, which is strange. I told the Lord then, I says, "Well if this is what you want I'll go and do it." But immediately, you know, I could lift the weapon . . . A scripture kept coming to my mind "Try the spirits whether they be of God or something else, or the devil" (1 John 4. 1).

About two years later he was at his mother's place, about three in the morning, and heard a small voice say "Go and preach thy word." He heard it three times. "Why I just laid there and cried . . . It was one of the greatest desires I ever had, yet it was one of the greatest fears I ever had. So I belonged with another order of people, Union Baptists, at the time."

When he began to preach predestination with the Union Baptists, women began to complain that his doctrine was "too hard," and he challenged them with the Bible. Then he went to hear Evans and Roten, and then

> eventually, I just, first thing I knowed I just joined them . . . it's been almost twelve years. So it's been a while. I've learned a whole lot, and yet I don't know nothing (chuckles) . . . But I've come a long way in my life. I lived up here in Bullhead Mountain, didn't know my father till I was twenty-one years old, he and my mother had separated . . . I was raised pretty hard. In fact, I've raised myself since I was nine years old.

He says he had a hope as long as he could remember but is not going to recount his personal life: "Tell me about your alls experience. I'm going to put you all on the defensive for a while" (chuckles).

Peacock: That's fair enough. Of course neither of us has joined the Primitive Baptist church.

Yates: That doesn't keep you from being a child of God.

Tyson: That's right, I've learned that since I've been down here.

Yates: Do you think, since you've been with us, that we're the people that actually hold to the truth? (Our response to this question is not memorable.)

Yates tells us about his preaching schedule as we try to calculate the services we can attend this weekend. It comes out that Reed is preaching at a church that Evans left, and Yates won't go there; while Yates is preaching at a church that Reed left because of Yates being there.

He tells us about the times he has had liberty and says he enjoys preaching more than anything he has ever done in his life.

But in a later visit, when we spent the night, Yates talked about the stress of preaching four times a weekend, driving

back late on a Sunday night, then needing the rest of the
work week to get over it, coupled with playing softball two
nights a week—formerly shortstop, now in the outfield. He
says people think he is strong and "stout" but "I get awful
tired sometimes." He tells of staying with Elder Parks (a huge
old man with an amazingly powerful voice) for an association
meeting. He left all the other elders talking, went to bed in
a dark room, woke up thinking it was still night, went down,
and the others were already at breakfast. He seems to interpret this oversleeping as a sign of exhaustion, remarking that
this was just on a Thursday night, and they had the rest of
the weekend of the association meeting to go.

Reed, Yates, and the Two Wives Controversy.

The rivalry between Yates and Reed has been alluded to already, by Yates, and will be elucidated further. Why don't
they get along? Their obvious differences in personality are
sufficient to explain their incompatibility. One might add to
that the mentorship of Yates by Evans, contrasted to that of
Reed by Nichols—two senior figures who, as we have seen,
while not unfriendly, are of different outlooks and opinions.
But, as is usual in Primitive Baptist interpretation, a psychological or sociological explanation is not sufficient. Instead a
doctrinal issue is raised. In this case the issue is what we
might term "the two wives."

Elder Yates's first wife reportedly ran off with another man
to Maryland. Yates, accompanied by a contemporary who is
also a young elder and protégé of Elder Roten of the Senter
Association, pursued and discovered Yates's wife together
with the other man, after which Yates sued for divorce in
North Carolina on grounds of adultery. He was instructed by
Evans to proceed in this way since, according to Evans, only
in a case where adultery is the grounds for divorce can an
elder legitimately be divorced and remarry and continue to
serve as an elder.

Yates did marry a second time after his divorce. Yates's second wife, who works in a textile factory, is a member of the leading church in the Senter Association where her father is a deacon and where Elder Roten was pastor for many years.

On the basis of Yates's divorce and remarriage, Elder Reed and others claim that Yates has "two wives" and therefore continues illegitimately to be an elder. Reed and his supporters cite Titus 1. 6 in support of their contention, while Evans asserts that a more contextual reading of the whole Bible permits an exception in the case of an elder whose wife is guilty of adultery. Evans challenges Reed's interpretation of the passage in Titus because, he says, of "two words: save and except." Evans argues that these exceptions make adultery a just cause for divorce and a second marriage following such a divorce acceptable. Evans is careful to insist that Yates got a divorce on that ground, and he even went to the courthouse to check that this was the ground.

Reed is known as a "duty" preacher, namely, a preacher who stresses duties to the church on the part of its members, while Evans is widely viewed as a doctrinal preacher. Reed emphasizes that if one is called by God, one must live by the scriptural imperatives. He cites the falling away of members with the elder out of order. He emphasizes that the local church must retain its purity, must choose elders and deacons carefully, not yield to the temptation of aging elders and deacons to ordain someone just to carry on; and deacons should "call out" elders who preach wrong doctrine, while presbytery should not ordain men known to be weak in either doctrine or behavior. Reed's own strongest sermons turn around this issue of maintaining morality and ethics, an example of which is the two wives question stated in Titus.

Elders Reed and Yates were once co-pastors of Peach Bottom Church, which is only seven miles from Reed's home in Virginia, while it is some twenty-five miles from Yates's residence in North Carolina. Conflicts between them and their allies in the church at Peach Bottom apparently prompted Reed to resign. At least two important male members of Peach Bottom followed Reed to Cross Roads Church, where he already held a position as co-pastor. (Anticipating our description below, we note that the Peach Bottom Church was the site of the first day's session of the 1983 Mountain District Association meeting.) Reed pastors three churches, two in Virginia, as noted, and one in North Carolina, Elk Creek. This church was once pastored by Elder Evans, who resigned over differences with the laity over their wish for stained-glass memorial windows, a kind of churchly aesthetics Evans did not believe warranted by Primitive Baptist readings of scriptures, which stress simplicity. Reed refuses to invite Yates to preach in any of the churches he pastors and discourages, as we have noted, the churches he leads, especially Elk Creek Church in North Carolina, from "turning out" for Peach Bottom, which Yates leads. Yates, in turn, does not invite Reed to preach in his four churches.

Reed believes Evans may be losing "his gift," in part for his backing of Yates on the two wives issue, in part because of problems in Evans's distant past and, no doubt, in part because of Evans's decision to intervene in the affair at Low Valley. Because Reed believes Evans and Yates are tainted by the two wives issue, a topic that inclines him to risk losing his normally mild demeanor, the polity question about Low Valley and the controversy over the marital status of elders combine to build his opposition to Yates and Evans.

Two Factions, Four Leaders: Evans and Nichols, Yates and Reed

Nichols, then, mirrors in his life and character the communal solidity of Baywood. His house, his cabin, his land, and his church are extensions of his craftsmanship and his systematic building through his life. In the same steady way he has kept the minutes (and note, later, that when he resigns as clerk it is because his hand is not steady anymore; minutes are defined as a handcraft). As a responsible official, the epiphany he remembers is not an occasion when he was blessed in preaching or a vision, but an administrative act: he

recounts with special verve how he was somehow inspired to
vote to appoint at once not only Reed but also Elmer Sparks.
Nichols's calling is not to preach but to enable those who
could to preach.

Reed, then, was the protégé of Nichols. Perhaps their work
with heavy road machinery was a point of commonality; all
of these men are handworkers, but these two worked with
machines. Perhaps it is their slow, deliberate manner. Perhaps it is their proximity, a half hour from each other on the
Virginia side of the river. In any case, it is Nichols who spoke
for Reed to become an elder, and Nichols who has acted as
clerk of the association and a leading layman in the Cross
Roads Church, even as Reed has made his way into pastorates
in Cross Roads Church as well as others in the association,
and now assistant moderator. While Reed had a supernatural
experience, a calling from God that got him from his sickbed
and obligated him to preach lest he fall ill again, Nichols
claims no such experience and no such calling (and his
health, except for a chronic allergy, has apparently stood
steady throughout a life of hard work). Yet the result of this
experience has induced in Reed, like Nichols, a strong sense
of duty; if he does not fulfill it he will fall ill. So Reed is a "duty
preacher." In his sermons, which are not the rhetorical mar-
vels of Evans, he stresses the duties of the "bishop": elders,
clerks, and deacons. Among these duties is that of having only
a single spouse, and it is the duty of this spouse to behave
properly and contribute appropriately. Here, too, Nichols and
Reed are alike, for each has a wife who is a steady helpmate
in church affairs. In fact, the wife of Nichols could be observed
instructing the wife of Reed in proper administration of these
wifely duties.

Evans's life is recounted as one of personal visions, struggle,
and translation into transcendental experiences and understandings sometimes distilled into sermons, in which he at
times enjoys the experience of being blessed. As a stone
mason, Evans is like John Bunyan, the tinker, the independent artisan who by his charisma rather than any social orga-

nizational status gains power in the religious community. Evans's images are of the pilgrim, the stranger, the sojourner, and he gives brilliant descriptions of occasions when he felt alienated from even the religious community, standing aloof, a detached observer of rituals that, he says, meant nothing to him. Such images of alienation are balanced against those of ecstatic engagement, in his translation, his baptism, and being blessed in his sermons. From his lonely sojourn, he is brought back to the fold. He says, "Quoting the Georgia preacher, 'I've quit a thousand times; but never really succeeded in quitting.'"

If Reed is the protégé of Nichols, so is Yates of Evans; in Yates, Evans has a tiger by the tail. A John Henry or Paul Bunyan, Yates is strength and energy—the former point man in Vietnam who now works two jobs, sixteen-hours-per-day hard labor, while preaching four or five times on a weekend, relaxing by bow hunting bucks. Yates represents the vitality that Evans once manifested himself but now sees as sadly on the wane. Evans defends the legality of Yates's two wives against the legalism of Reed, and Yates in his own bullish strength has, in 1982, vindicated Evans's trust by becoming moderator of the neighboring association; still, he is an object of controversy, denied preaching at any churches associated with Reed and the Cross Roads group.

Charismatic and communalistic modes of translating the transcendental into the real are, then, personified in the paired figures of the Virginia and the North Carolina factions. Both modes are beset with paradox and dilemma. Charisma is not quite acceptable within Calvinism, which denies spiritual power to the person. Yet the gift is manifested on occasion. Evans can show it, as does Yates; yet again it is lost, so the life of the charismatic preacher is up and down. Nor is the communal, institutional axis acceptable either. A symbol of this is the attempt of Reed's wife to inject instrumental music into the wedding of their daughter at the Cross Roads Church. The best she could do was to play the wedding march on a record player situated on the edge of the church, in the foyer beside the restrooms. Doctrine limits ritual, and the Cross Roads move toward incorporating the mainline Protestant Southern culture, with its greater bureaucratization of religious and social life, can go only so far.

Lacking, in this Calvinistic setting, any firm authorization, both the charismatic and the communal modes of institutionalizing the transcendental are, then, subject to continuous debate and conflict. Alliances shift, boundaries are fuzzy, and issues such as the two wives cause rancor and disturbance.

Top: Old style pews. *Bottom:* New style pews, at Cross Roads.

Top: Remodeled stand, at Cross Roads. *Bottom:* Elder Walter Evans at home.

Top: Elder Walter Evans showing family graves at Salem Church. *Right:* Elder Walter Evans at his earliest stone construction. *Bottom:* Raymond Nichols beside the ramp for the handicapped he helped build at Cross Roads Church.

CHAPTER SIX

The Wind Bloweth Where It Listeth

Schisms and Complexities

The prior history of mentorship between younger and older elders, scriptural disputes about "two wives," divisions among elders and laity, and a dense pattern of reciprocity and exclusion among churches and their leaders were some of the key features behind tensions in the Mountain District Association. We have highlighted major divisions and personalities, but we need to indicate some of the further complexities. We focus on Cross Roads Church. At this church, Elder Reed is pastor—but there is an additional elder, Elder Elmer Sparks, who, we recall, was put forward by Raymond Nichols at the same time that he put forward Reed for ordination.

In addition to his duties at Cross Roads Church, Elder Sparks also co-pastors an independent Primitive Baptist church in North Carolina near his home, a very small church (approximately ten members), Woodruff. There Sparks has a co-pastor, Elder Lyle. Lyle has another church of which he is the sole pastor, in the Low Valley Association, which must be distinguished from Low Valley Church. Both church and association have the same name, though the church by this name is no longer a member of this association, which we explain below. In addition to his work as pastor of one church in the Low Valley Association and as co-pastor with Sparks of the independent church at Woodruff, Lyle, who is an instructor in automotive mechanics at a technical institute, is the respected clerk of the Low Valley Association and well read in local church history. (His informative comments will be recalled at various points in our narrative.)

Elders Sparks and Lyle as co-pastors enjoy fellowship with each other; they preach together, and Sparks has preached in churches of the Low Valley Association as well as Low Valley Church; and, of course, he has preached at Elder Lyle's other church. They are very much in fellowship. Elder Sparks has had many attachments over the years to various churches and associations and claims that he wants to be in fellowship with all the churches, and professes not to understand why there has to be so much fuss and exclusion.

But the problems of fellowship and exclusion are actualities. For example, Elder Lyle is a member of an association, Low Valley, which is not recognized by either the Senter Association, which is near Lyle's residence and church, or the Mountain District Association. Elder Lyle's grandfather was a renowned leader of the Senter Association prior to the reign of Elder Roten. This particular history is similar to the Cahooney brothers, whose father was a leading elder in the Low Valley Church and association for many years.

Elder Lyle is alleged to have split off from the Senter Association over the issue of "radio preachers." This conflict occurred in the late fifties and sixties; the issue was whether a church or an association should invite an elder to preach who had appeared as a preacher over the radio. The conflict over "modern inventions" continues. Out of this controversy, which was by no means confined to the Senter Association, but reached into many associations and churches in Virginia, North Carolina, West Virginia, and Kentucky, Elder Lyle left the Senter Association, taking his church into the Low Valley Association. Both Elder Roten and Evans, leaders of the Senter and Mountain District associations, approved of radio preaching.

These alignments place Elder Sparks in the following position vis-à-vis the Mountain District and Senter associations:

Sparks as Lyle's co-pastor is in fellowship with a man who is not in fellowship with the Mountain District or the Senter associations. As Reed's co-pastor at Cross Roads Church in the Mountain District Association, Sparks is very much in fellowship with at least that church, and, through it, with the Mountain District Association. Yates and Evans take a very dim view of the fact that Reed and Nichols, and their church, Cross Roads, continue to be in fellowship with Lyle through Spark's position as co-pastor with Lyle at Woodruff. To make matters worse, the church at Cross Roads regularly invites another elder to preach, also a pastor of an independent church, and it is well known that this elder invites Elder Lyle to preach in his church. Of course, Yates, Evans, and their allies refuse to invite Lyle, Sparks, or any other elder known to have been in fellowship with them. These relations and denials of relation limit the churches where these elders can preach and, presumably, have built up a history of resentment.

It is notable that in both Low Valley, the independent church in Virginia, and Woodruff, the independent church in North Carolina, it is the issue of fellowship between *independent* Primitive Baptist churches and those churches and elders joined together in *associations* that causes conflict. These tensions, which usually are in a dormant state, are immediately available for new life when a major controversy occurs. The Low Valley Church's internal division, with the intervention by Evans, Yates, and their fellow elders in that affair, was just such a controversy. Nichols and Reed and their followers were already predisposed to be critical in relation to Evans and Yates, differing in temperament, polity, and marital ethics. Autonomous churches outside the boundaries of the Mountain District and Senter associations engender conflict within the associations, through uneven and contradictory patterns of reciprocity.

Sometimes conflicts over divergent patterns of fellowship spur new associations. When the authors paid a visit to Low Valley Church in southwestern Virginia in October 1983 (after the Mountain District associational meetings in September of that year, which we narrate below), they found two other visitors present for the Saturday night and Sunday morning services. These Primitive Baptist visitors were from a church in North Carolina that had withdrawn from fellowship in the Senter Association. Part of the reason for this church's action in breaking fellowship with the Senter Association was disagreement with the official actions of that association when it authorized Elder Yates, as moderator, to lead a delegation from the Senter to the Low Valley Church to labor with the brothers and sisters there in their conflict. We have referred to this as the first delegation to Low Valley. The visitors, a man and his wife, had come to the Low Valley Church and the Cahooney brothers seeking ties of fellowship. The Cahooney brothers already pastor two churches in this part of Virginia. Should a third church join them in fellowship, there exists the possibility that a new association of these churches could emerge.

The cycle of splitting and combining continues, a cycle that becomes the prevailing pattern when we recall that the Low Valley Church itself split from its former association. We note again that the Low Valley Church and the association from which it split have the same names, a fact that reminds us of the important history of this church, founded in 1775, in the Primitive Baptist world of this region. (See Appendix G for chart of relations sketched in this chapter.)

The issues that precipitated that split are recurrent as well as germane to the present case.

Some years previous to the present case, the Low Valley Association passed a rule forbidding any of its member churches to invite any elder from a church not in fellowship with the Low Valley Association to preach. This rule, if observed by the Low Valley Church, would prevent it from inviting a distinguished elder from Maryland, the pastor of a historic Primitive Baptist church and author of a widely read spiritual autobiography, who happened to be a close friend of the Cahooney brothers and their own distinguished father. Such a rule placed a limit on the choices of member churches and their elders as to whom they could invite while remaining in peace and fellowship with the association and, thus, also reduced the network of reciprocity that is so vital to an elder if he aspires to gain recognition beyond the boundaries of his own church, association, and region. The rule exercised prior restraint on the circulation of elders and hence reduced the number and extent of preaching appointments elders in the Low Valley Association could accept. The church at Low Valley and the Cahooneys were not likely to observe such a limitation on their affiliations and movements. But another issue intruded upon the disenchantment at Low Valley over the preaching rule.

A sister of the Cahooney brothers and a member at Low Valley Church was divorced, then remarried. For these actions, she, daughter of old Elder Cahooney and sister of the three Cahooney brothers, was excluded by the Low Valley Church from its fellowship. This action upset many of the other members in the churches of the Low Valley Association. Conceivably, on this issue the Cahooney brothers and Elder Reed would be in agreement.

Out of these two familiar conflicts—one over a polity issue that would restrict the circulation of elders, the other over divorce, remarriage, and the proper scriptural teaching on these issues—Low Valley Church split off from the Low Valley Association (or the Low Valley Church was dropped by the Low Valley Association). So Low Valley became independent, the status it had when the present conflict occurred. By the early winter of 1983, however, Low Valley Church seemed, as we noted, on its way to becoming the center church in a new configuration of churches formerly aligned with the Senter and Low Valley associations. If so, the new association will be divided, like the Mountain District Association, between churches in Virginia and North Carolina. Whether geographical division will become symbolic of theological and ecclesiastical divisions in the future is an open question. But if precedent is prophecy, a new cycle of conflict is likely.

Whether in that case splitting will result in multiplication or subtraction, we cannot say.

The Fall of an Elder?

Old Elder Roten, long moderator of the neighboring Senter Association until his replacement in 1982 by young Yates, told of a dream he had in his youth while in conflict with a revered moderator we shall call Reynolds. Roten dreamt of peering at a beautiful pool of calm and clear water, when suddenly a black snake came out of the bank. Drawing his gun, he shot it, and it turned into Elder Reynolds who, he says, "crippled away," followed by many baby snakes.

Soon after, at the association meeting, Elder Roten was "blessed" in preaching against the position of Reynolds, and he defeated Reynolds, breaking his authority. Reynolds had been like a father to Roten, who had revered him, and before the meeting when asked what side he would take, Roten had replied, "I will side with the old Elder." His conscience had forced him though to go instead with the scripture, and on his deathbed, Reynolds had forgiven him and said he was right. Shortly after the meeting, Roten told his dream to a fellow Primitive Baptist, who replied, "You certainly did shoot Reynolds."

Elder Roten recounted this experience to us in the context of discussing the forthcoming Mountain District Association meeting and the Low Valley affair. He probably had in mind the parallel between Reynolds being shot down by himself and the impending possibility of his close friend Evans being shot down over the Low Valley issue at the association meeting a month hence. Certainly this possibility was in the minds of many as the meeting approached. Evans was widely acknowledged to have been given the "gift," an acknowledgment which, as noted, extended widely. In many ways, he is a "genius," possessing a remarkable memory, poetic power, acuity of analysis, and eloquence. And he had once been physically vigorous, working at hard labor all day while preaching and traveling constantly.

Yet now he is almost seventy-four years old, afflicted with emphysema, which has diminished his once powerful tenor voice. Though wonderfully kind and engaging, he had always been more preacher than pastor, and his health now restricts organizational activity as his labor had done previously. One of his three churches has shrunk to an attendance of less than a dozen, and his allies appear neither strong nor numerous.

As the day approached for the association meeting, the prospects for the fall of Elder Evans were strong: if it did not happen this year, then soon he would be replaced as moderator, like his close friend Roten of the Senter Association the year before. As we rode around with him revisiting the old places of his life—the cabin where he was born; the house where he first offered public prayer; the church where he obeyed a vision in first preaching the Primitive Baptist doctrine of sovereign grace; the stone buildings he had erected—he was alternately cheered by memories and gloomy about what would come, at least in this world.

Would gifted men like Evans give way to prudent and pragmatic men like Nichols? Would the rule of strong clerks prevail over the remote and elevated elders? Would the Virginia faction win out over the lone rule of Evans and the North Carolina faction?

The way we formulate these questions gives a sharp edge to the rhetoric of conflict, from the point of view of the narrators. But what of the point of view of the chief protagonists? Are they adequately represented by this dramatic mode?

It was true without doubt that the controversy, in its several aspects, was present in their conversations, if not in their preoccupations. But as observers we need to remind ourselves that Evans and Nichols, Yates and Reed did not see themselves acting within the compact and highly visible limits of a theater (though the meetinghouse where the association held its meeting in its stark simplicity can be termed Old Baptists' ritual theater). Rather, as we know from their life histories and from the collective histories of the Primitive Baptist associations, these men and women were acting within a long history of "divides." The memories and feelings from these earlier divisions were a part of the present scene. As we suggest later in our commentary on the case history, these Old Baptists are who they are; their actions disclose their habits of association and division. So what appeared to us as singular events and high drama, "high" even in the understated speech and gesture of Appalachians, was for them a fresh installment in a familiar history. This traditional character of the conflict made it no less a conflict, but the dramatic formulations of our questions may distort the character of their common life, which is not theatrical but rather, as we have said, understated. Whatever the intensity of their feelings, Old Baptists speak with "a flat out" style. Even when they are relating their experience of grace, the rhetoric is subdued, their manner dignified. Only when under the inspiration of the "living word of God" do elders reach a pitch of climactic speech, never in the politics of associational life.

As their speech about divine grace in their lives is reticent and sparse, so is their speech and activity in the world of practical affairs indirect. It is doubtful that much political planning occurred prior to the association meeting, particularly on Evans's part. We imagine that reticence about the political dimensions of their ritual life resides in their consciousness of the equivocal status of politics or any other human affairs, owing to the doctrines of election and predestination. Lacking any certainty that they are elected, in the cosmic sense of that luminous term within the ambience of Calvinism, Old Baptists are not likely to conduct political campaigns with the vigorous certainty explicit advocacy demands. In the account that follows the reader will note that no nominations and no speeches are made on behalf of particular candidates for the election of the moderator and clerk. The election itself is secret, like the inscrutable decrees of God who elects and predestinates. Divine grace cannot be earned by works, spiritual or political. Old Baptists' style of political conduct matches their tact and indirect demeanor in things spiritual.

We invite the reader to compare the ethos of Primitive Baptist Calvinists with scenes that occur on the floors of national conventions of the evangelical Protestant denominations. The assertive advocacy of leaders convinced of their status as saved children of God contrasts sharply with Mountain District Primitive Baptists. For Southern Baptist fundamentalists there is no doubt of destination and no reticence in their rhetoric. Like the Old Baptist, they display a striking fit between their manner of politics and their religion.

Despite the reticence and however subtle the tactics of indirection, there is drama in the election scene we relate below. Reed, a mild-mannered person, is strongly convinced that Evans is in error on the "two wives" question. Nichols, the sturdy clerk, is convinced that Evans intervened improperly in the affairs of the Low Valley Church. Evans confesses to the assembled brothers and sisters that the Old Baptist church is the only home he has. For Evans the metaphor of "home" is no mere commonplace, as the struggles he recounts in his autobiography make evident. The death-threatening agony for this "pilgrim in a barren land" has been to find a home in a church where he can preach without rejection the hard doctrine of predestination. This struggle is reenacted in the election scene of the first session of the Mountain Association annual meeting, particularly in Evans's entrance, with its echoes in the dream that was prelude to that other fateful entrance he made, to a meeting where he preached the sermon that drove him from the Union Baptists and into the Primitive Baptist church, by way of the icy waters of the Little River.

The Meeting of the Mountain District Association

We set the scene for the momentous opening of the one hundred eighty-fifth annual session of the Mountain District Primitive Baptist Association with a description of the ending scene of the one hundred eighty-fourth meeting of the association, held in Sparta, North Carolina, beginning on Friday before the first Sunday in September 1982.

Elder Evans, the moderator, speaks:

> Next association go to Peach Bottom, same time, Friday before the first Sunday in September. The Lord tarries and time goes on. Some of us that have gathered here today, and have been gathering through this meeting may be sleeping and gone on . . . And all . . . like Brother [Reed] said, if he will pardon me, and others have said, Brother Roten mentioned it, and been brought to our attention, I would to God that our people would pray to the Lord of the harvest our little churches, all of us pray to the Lord of the harvest . . . Now we are going to close . . . Going to baptize Brother Lloyd Absher, church at Antioch, this evening . . . I want to mention before we start singing (all our elders that are here come up front) that those who say that handshaking is not scriptural . . . just one minute [reads Galatians 2. 9] "and they gave to me and Barnabas the right hands of fellowship. . . ."

But before the singing could begin, the clerk of the association, Raymond Nichols, spoke up firmly to the assembled group in the high school auditorium:

> I've got some extra minutes [of the 1981 meeting] . . . just what we had left. Now . . . in reading the letters to our churches, we are losing ground every year . . . and looking at this crowd, I know that's people here who needs to join the church . . . come with us. We are getting old [had difficulty continuing to speak] . . . so, I'd like to see people do their duty. Come on! . . . We are all old, or the majority, I might say, is old . . . Today [pauses and had further difficulty in speaking] is the sixtieth association year I have attended association. In 1922, my mother joined this association, and I have never missed one since . . . I would like to see it go on . . . [cannot finish].

Elder Evans says again, "now we are gonna close, Number 175, 'Amazing Grace.' Church doors open. Let's all the elders line up here in front." Thus the 1982 meeting closed with the long line of members slowly going along the line of elders shaking hands as they sing of a grace that is, for Old Baptists, particularly amazing.

In the precise directions for finding each of the churches in the Mountain District Association, always reprinted in each year's minutes, we find this entry for Peach Bottom Church: "Independence, Virginia. Located one mile north of Independence at intersection of Route 21 and 654."

Cars and trucks of members crossed the bridge spanning Peach Bottom Creek, which eventually flows into the New River, and turned into the grassy front yard of the church. They parked and got out into a misty slow drizzle. Leaving hampers of food in their vehicles, members did not pause, but entered directly through a small foyer and the center aisle of the meetinghouse. They left behind clouds lowering over the mountainsides just beyond a pasture at the back of the church house where several cows grazed. It was 10 a.m., Friday morning, September 2, 1983.

Soon the singing began with Clerk Nichols of the Cross Roads Church leading, as he and other deacons and clerks from sister churches sat in the front pew. Nichols sat next to Elder Reed, his pastor from Cross Roads, and to his left sat a cousin, also named Nichols, an executive with a furniture manufacturing company in Galax, Virginia. Cousin Nichols sang with great enthusiasm and volume. Several other members, including women members, seated themselves around the church in no particular order except that the women sat to the left of the stand.

On the table in front of the stand were carved the words "In remembrance of me." As the closing words of Elder Evans and Clerk Nichols at the associational meeting the previous year make altogether clear, the annual gathering is a collective historical act that brings to fresh life the latent memories of the group and the individuals who compose it. The meetings mark the turn in the history of fellowship and division; they also mark presences in these gatherings. It is an association in the polity of the Old Baptists, and it is an association of anniversaries and memories as well. Each meeting is an evidence of endurance, loss, and hope.

As we entered the church with our tape recorder and notebooks, we recognized about half of the so-far-assembled members. This was our second associational meeting with the Mountain District Primitive Baptists. We noticed as we set up our machine that Elder Yates, who is the regular pastor of Peach Bottom Church, was sitting in the very back pew on the men's side of his own church. His position was notable since the customary place for a pastor and elder is in the front row, where Clerk Nichols, Elder Reed, and Nichols's cousin were sitting singing. Our readers will recall that Elder Yates, while pastoring Peach Bottom, is a member and moderator of the Senter Association. Peach Bottom Church, however, is a member of the Mountain District Association. We discovered later that both of us were immediately struck with this observation: Elder Reed, in the front row, and Elder Yates, in the back pew, had about as much distance between them as the small church would allow. Elder Walter Evans, the moderator of the association, had not yet arrived.

A visiting elder from Swainsboro, Georgia, George McNure, who had preached at Elder Evans's Little River Church in North Carolina the previous June, walked in out of the weather and moved with ease up the aisle, having a good overview of the church from his tall frame. Elder McNure is a special friend of Elder Evans. He was a large, square, deep-voiced man, in dark suit and cowboy boots. Elder McNure had been a member of the second delegation, headed by Elders Evans and Yates, to the divided church at Low Valley.

McNure sat down in the second row corner of the men members' bench, accompanied by a thinner, compact, and bespectacled elder, M.E. Temples, from Vidalia, Georgia. Elder Temples was making his first visit to the Mountain District Association.

Following McNure and Temples came the faithful young man from Cross Roads, a disabled victim of a muscular disease that caused his limbs to splay and his mouth to remain open in an exaggerated grin. After he had struggled to seat himself in the front row, his mother smoothed his hair and took her seat one row behind him. By this time the gathering congregation had sung several long hymns from the old style (notes without words) hymnal, Goble's *Primitive Baptist Hymn Book*. As the singing proceeded well into the hour, nearer eleven o'clock, Evans entered. He was dressed in a dark suit with vest. His face wore a somber expression. As we have related in chapter five, walking up an aisle, slowly as he was doing that day at Peach Bottom Church, was a action fraught with background and import for Evans. During his last year as a Union Baptist he had struggled with the scriptures that, more and more he believed, taught predestination, particularly 2 Thess. 2. 13–14: ". . . God hath from the beginning chosen you to salvation." For two meetings over the space of two months, Evans had suffered, "condemned in my heart for not proclaiming this message." It was a few days later that he had had the dream related above, the dream in which he saw himself entering the door of the church, in which "the congregation had gathered. As I walked up the aisle. . . ." Later in fact he had reenacted his dream: "As I walked up the aisle, I looked directly at the pulpit to see if my dream was true." And everything was exactly as it had been in the dream. He preached the doctrine of predestination and soon left the Union Baptists for a home with the Primitive Baptists. Now he was entering another church; would his walk down the aisle end with an experience similar to both his dream and his experience of earlier years, when he was "carried above every trouble, every fear in this world"? Was he walking up this aisle this day as he had that day, with his legs working with the weight of lead, his soul in fear of death?

The scene, so ordinary, so typical on its surface, becomes both highly individualized, yet, at the same time, for Old Baptists, archetypal. For sedimented within this entrance is a life that Evans describes as "my travels" and a person who believes passionately, out of doctrine and experience, that he is a pilgrim and a stranger.

In the sermon that soon followed his entrance, Elder Evans confessed, as we have noted, "the Old Baptist Church is the only home I've got." That confession condenses his spiritual autobiography into a single sentence, evokes scriptural archetypes, and translates the doctrine he believes into the image of pilgrim and traveler. As we will show in our re-presentation of that sermon, "translation" was a persistent topic in his meditations, on this day of election of a moderator and for many weeks before and after.

As the moderator moved toward the front of the church, he caught sight of the two elders from Georgia, his friends from far off, cocked his head humorously, and trained his one good eye on them. McNure broke into a broad grin. After embracing McNure and shaking hands vigorously with Temples, Evans took his seat with the home elders and deacons on the bench across from McNure and Temples, giving a quick handshake to Elder Reed and Clerk Nichols as he did so. He joined in the singing.

The singing continued in a minor key, the sound matching weather and mood:

> Tell me no more of this world's vain store.
> The time for such pleasures with me now is o'er.

Then followed another hymn:

> I am a stranger here below,
> and what I am 'tis hard to know. . . .

And finally, the Isaac Watts hymn, "Hark From the Tomb a Doleful Sound. . . ."

With messengers from all nine association member churches seated, along with representatives of corresponding churches and associations, Elder Evans, the moderator, took the stand, declaring that this was the one hundred and eighty-fifth meeting of the Mountain District Association. "Someone said, it makes no difference whether or not it exists," said Evans. "It makes all the difference in the world for me." He called for the singing of the introductory hymn, number 131, itself a doleful sound:

> Hungry, and faint, and poor.
> Behold us, Lord, again
> Assembled at thy mercy's door.
> Thy bounty to obtain.
> Thy word invites us nigh,
> Or we must starve indeed;
> For we no money have to buy,
> No righteousness to plead.

Evans then professed that he was "deeply moved" and began to preach "the introductory discourse," which is not always preached by the moderator. We assume this year Evans decided to preach the opening sermon himself rather than invite a visiting elder, which sometimes is done.

He stated that his "primary subject is translation," and he introduced some of the themes that he had mentioned in the sermon and conversations noted earlier. This subject of translation had been on his mind for several months, he said, perhaps because he saw his own life coming to an end.

Then he slipped into another mode, personal reflection. He said he was not trying to disturb the peace, but that he could not hold still on things close to him. "If I cease to be a member of the Old Baptist church, there is nowhere else for me to go." He said he had a strange feeling about this association, that his life was marked by periods . . . he trailed off. At other times, he had mentioned to us that twenty-one years had passed between his joining the Union Baptists and the Primitive Baptists. Now that twenty-one years were passed since that second joining, he implied that a third transformation was due.

Then he shifts from the theme of translation, not finishing his argument as he had in previous sermons. He remarked on the Primitive Baptist doctrine, how it contrasted with that set forward by Jacobus Arminius (1560–1609). He exclaimed, "I thank God for the promise! A hope for eternal life!"

He concluded, reiterating that "this 185th annual session does mean something to me!" Then he dismissed everyone for dinner on the wet grounds outside, asking them to return at the sound of "singing in the house."

Dinner on the grounds was an unusually joyless time, as people hurriedly ate amidst drizzle. Mrs. Nichols, the clerk's wife, later noted to one of us that attendance was way down, giving her view that it was because of uncertainty about what the association would do about Evans and Low Valley.

Sermons on Translation and Translations in the Life of an Elder

The grand division between the world of history and the world of scripture is a preoccupation of Primitive Baptists. Like the divide between the predestinating acts of God before the foundations of the world and the world that was founded by divine creation, the division between scripture and history is set deep in the outlook and sensibilities of these Baptists. Where such cosmic divisions are sharply etched, there typically follows a keen interest in connection, crossing, and translation. Old Baptists are no exception. Like Bunyan's Christian who must make a final crossing to Mount Zion, Primitive Baptists on their pilgrimages are looking for crossings. In their doctrine, calling must precede crossings just as the acts of divine election preceded the creation of the world. Calling of God must be intimately associated with scripture.

Elders read from the King James Version of the Bible for morning meditations and texts for sermons. The reading from this version and this version alone is mandated by the Articles of Faith of the Mountain District Association. Between 1972 and 1979 the second Article of Faith was amended to add: ". . . as translated in 1611 into the King James Version of the Holy Bible. . . ." There is more than a tinge of paradox, if not contradiction, here. Making a specific historical translation normative for faith and practice does confer on a historical event authority not normally accorded. The challenge of multiple translations of the Bible, many of which, so Primitive Baptists judged, stressed or strongly implied conditionalism (or Arminian denials of sovereign grace for salvation), was met by making the long-favored King James Version canonical in doctrine as well as in practice. No doubt the increasing numbers of "radio preachers" and "TV preachers" using a variety of translations appropriate to their evangelical doctrine were part of the reason.

We note this fact to highlight the ambiguity in this official doctrine that derives more from "history" than "scripture," yet which is thoroughly motivated by doctrinal reasons. But this is only one version of the ambiguity; others attend the use of the metaphor of translation. Primitive Baptists are well aware that the Bible is a collective work translated from ancient languages. This causes them no basic difficulty, since the letter as such is not sacred. It is the world represented by scripture, the Word of God, the cosmic plot, that is sacred. It is true that elders pay close attention to the grammar of scriptures; they are particularly attuned to the use of the past tense and the definite article, since both of these grammatical signs are indications that the decisive events in cosmic history have already occurred and that only a particular group is elected by divine choice. Even the word "all" refers, in their reading, to the elect or the damned. Any grammatical hint of universalism is corrected according to a grammatical reading under the governance of doctrine of election and predestination.

The Bible is first a translation of the fundamental order of things into the written Word of God. It is then translated into varied languages. Primitive Baptists also note a third translation, from the written Word to the spoken Word of God, particularly applicable when an elder is "blessed" in his preaching. So the language of the Bible is already a translation before it is written in a language, i.e., scripture, and scripture, under the inspiration of God's blessing, may become translated by the mind and voice of the elder into the spoken Word of God. The crossings and transfers constitute the vital economy of the divine and human exchange, though for these Calvinists the exchange is decidedly asymmetrical, with the divine initiative always preceding human response; the gift-giver always predominates, including motivating the gift-receiver for a proper response.

The ways this divine-human exchange works are not subject to any human calculus. A favorite scriptural text in the preaching of Elder Evans is "the wind bloweth where it listeth." Experience is shot through with unevenly spaced irruptions usually of a quiet rather than an ecstatic character. The person may be a member of the laity attending a series of services when "nothing happened" ("I didn't get nothing out the service"), or an elder attempting to preach, not being blessed, and "getting on out of the way so some one else can try." In addition to the unpredictable quality of religious experience, which is not assured by any regularity based on the routine of the rituals of worship or of private meditation, the focus and the means for grace, namely, the scriptures, are themselves places of mysteries, passages so full of meaning, connection, cross-reference, types and shadows and allusive echoes, that elders confess as they close sermons on a cluster of texts tied together by a theme like "translation," or "pilgrimage," or "regeneration": "I cannot get the half of it! It's too deep for me!" They invoke the mysteries of the text, its unnumbered connections and meanings.

The singular most hoped-for translation is that special liberty elders sometimes get when they are especially blessed. Elder Evans reckons he has had special liberty perhaps a dozen times in his life, and Elder Roten makes a similar observation. In the dream Elder Evans recounts in his autobiography, we recall, he finds himself preaching, finally, the doctrine of election to Union Baptists who do not hold such hard doctrine. Of the dream he says:

Time came for preaching and I arose to my feet and announced the text that I had run from twice before. I was carried completely above everything that pertains to this world.

In the dream he falls dead. Then he wakes, "speechless and couldn't even move my fingers." He recovers, disturbed by his dream. He says he promised the Lord he would not rebel again, he would go next time and preach "and tell the people that the family of God were chosen in Christ from the beginning, even before the foundation of the world." He continues, "with all this fear before me, and yet trying to keep my vow to God, I started my journey walking [to the meetinghouse of his Union Baptist church]. My dream was constantly before my face all the way."

The dream was translated in experience. As Evans approached the church, he thought he must die in defense of the gospel:

I walked up to the open door. I almost knew what I would see. My dream was so plain, and so impressive, I opened the door and stepped inside, and as I walked up the aisle, I looked directly at the pulpit to see if my dream was true, there set the men in the stand. Exactly where I saw them in my dream . . . I cannot find words to express the burden of my heart in the hour . . . One of the brothers invited me to the stand, and I was fearful to move. But I did, and took my seat about the center of the stand, just about direct behind the book board. As I viewed the scene my mind was rushing back to my dream, and then what I was facing at present. Everything pointed directly to death . . . I thought if I could but feel what I felt in my dreams, it wouldn't be so bad to die after all. I rose to my feet and addressed the congregation, and said I've rebelled against God the last two times I've been here. I promised God if he would only let me live to come back once more, that I would rebel no more. I said, I have carried the weight of a scripture three months, I will now read the text, which is as follows: "We are bound to give thanks always to you brethren, beloved of the Lord, because God hath from the beginning chosen you to salvation through sanctification of the spirit, and belief of the truth." [2 Thess. 2. 13–14] I began to enter into the choice of God, the salvation of poor lost ruined and helpless sinners, my mind was so exercised greatly on the subject, or was exercised greatly on the subject at hand. My whole body was trembling under the weight of God's eternal spirit. My voice was then loud and clear, I delivered this message with all the power of my being. I still thought this was my last message. I was carried above every trouble, every fear in this world. Just as I closed the two white she bears came before me [as in his earlier dream].

We have made reference to Elder Evans's autobiography where a version of these interrelated dreams and experiences is recounted. But the quotation we have just used did not come from the text of the autobiography, which was written several years prior to 1981, but from an interview we had with him on July 22, 1983, about six weeks before the association meeting where he preached his sermon on translation. A comparison between the transcript of the interview and the text of the autobiography shows their amazing similarity, though perhaps our amazement registers the distance we share from an oral culture.

The sermon he gave, which, as we have noted, spelled his break with the Union Baptists and his public acceptance of the doctrine of sovereign grace, was itself constituted by several translations. His dream was translated into actual experience. His struggles to preach on the text were translated by his dream and his sermon. There is also the experience of this elder as he preached this doctrine: "I was carried above every trouble, every fear in this world." Given Old Baptist elders' inclination to interpret their experiences as types and shadows of biblical events, the experience of being carried above the world would suggest another meaning of translation, those found in the biblical writings. Indeed, the clue of the white she bears leads to one of the classical places in scripture of a translation from this world to the next, a text Evans used in a sermon at Antioch Church the day following our interview.

The text is 2 Kings 2. The chapter recounts the translation of Elijah into heaven in a chariot of fire (verse 11) leaving Elisha, who later in the chapter is mocked by a band of children. "And there came forth two she bears out of the wood, and tare forty and two children of them" (verse 24). When Elder Evans first dreamed of the she bears, before he ate his breakfast the morning after the dream, he found this passage in scripture.

In his sermon opening the associational meeting, Evans used the text Colossians 1. 12–13: ". . . Father who hath delivered us from the power of darkness, and hath translated us into the kingdom of his dear Son." Against the dream and the sermon that fulfilled it as he publicly declared his belief in particular election and his farewell to the Union Baptists, this text for the association sermon gains several textual contexts as well as autobiographical echoes. In the associational sermon he also quoted the text from 2 Kings 2. 11, cited earlier.

The links and cross-references, in textual citation and in the preaching experience of Evans, did not stop with the interview (and the autobiography preceding it) and the associational sermon. The connections are even more intimate. The day following the interview we quote above, Elder Evans preached a sermon at Antioch Church (July 24, 1983) on the subject of translation. He was also to preach a sermon the following December at the Peach Bottom Church, the same church that hosted the opening of the early September associational meeting, and this sermon was to be on the subject of translation. Like his associational sermon, the sermon six weeks before at Antioch also focused on the text of Colossians 1. 12–13. In this sermon he suggested that being a new creation in Christ, for the elect, is also translation: "The work of God's grace in the hearts and souls of his people is described as not only being born again, but it's called a translation."

In the Antioch sermon, Elder Evans arranges his discourse in a manner typical of Primitive Baptists. In so doing he employs the major interpretive strategy of these Calvinists, the typological method of scriptural use, or, in the language of these elders, "types and shadows," a phrase that turns up in one of their favorite hymns as well as in their discussions with each other about preaching.

The sermon under review arranges a sequence of biblical figures, each an instance as well as a type of men of God who have experienced translation. While Elder Evans does not say so directly, the listener is left with the strong impression that in a modest way he lines himself within this sequence, and this impression amounts to a probability when we recall his narration of his experience in his written autobiography, in his interviews with us where his language so closely resembles that of his autobiography, and, finally, in the allusions he makes in these sermons from June to December 1983 to "my travels." This term, amounting to a term of art, refers to an individual's pilgrimage in this life, beginning with the first strong impression that "this world is not our home." "Travels" also fits the movements of elders among the various churches where they preach, keeping appointments across a wide expanse of counties and states in the course of a year. So the specifically religious image of the traveling pilgrim matches the actual movements in the life of elders and to a large extent also the laity as they travel from one church to another, from one associational meeting to another. The experience of translation that elders sometimes have when they are powerfully blessed adds depth and personal resonance to that term. And finally, the term is important to any community that employs as its master canon a collection of sacred texts held to be ultimately translated from God to men, from men to other men, including the men of the King James Version of the Bible. The metaphor of translation acknowledges the gap, so abysmal for Calvinists, between the created and the Creator, which makes every crossing inherently equivocal, and which makes each successful translation, as in preaching and becoming sweetly blessed, precious for both preacher and his listeners. So translation is a theological, interpretative, personal, and collective point of reference, each of which implicates and resonates with the other uses of this favored term.

In his sermon at Antioch Elder Evans speaks about Enoch (Genesis 5. 23):

"All the days of Enoch was three hundred and sixty five years," and verse 24 said, "And Enoch walked with God; and he was not; for God took him." That's about all he said about that. He was not found, he was not, he was translated Paul said . . . My mind was going plumb to Hebrews [in the New Testament], look like, before I got to it. But I want to go now to the 11th chapter of Hebrews, at verse 5, and shed a little more light on what I'm talking about. And yet it brings in another word that's completely missed here [in the Genesis passage], in the text, and that's the word "faith." By faith Enoch was translated that he should not see death. [Hebrews 11. 5]

This movement from one testament to the other, in both directions, is characteristic of typological interpretation, a way of reading that ignores any constraints imposed by temporal sequence or historical context. Elder Evans begins with Enoch, and interprets that text by a text from Paul. Evans says in the sermon he believes Paul wrote the Epistle to the Hebrews though others differ from him. He then moves to an account of Elijah, but before he makes that key move he delays with a personal recollection in which his use of the term "called" is intended to echo the repeated use of the term "translation" in the earlier part of the sermon.

. . . when I begin to look back through the years, and I was called here in 1952, first part of it, thirty-one years ago. Old church stood out here a little further. The old walls would weave when the wind would blow so hard. I've been coming year after year, I've seen our people come, I've seen them go. And I can see me going, you see . . . But God took Enoch, translated him from this world to the world beyond . . . And Paul said he translated him. And I want to emphasize one point, and before his translation, he had this testimony that he pleased God. How on earth can a man have a testimony, can I get this to you somehow?, when he didn't feel something inside, let me say it that way.

The faith or testimony of which Elder Evans speaks here would not be possible without the motivating grace of God. The recurrent point Evans makes throughout each of the several sermons he preaches on translation, from June to December 1983, is that the human is the passive side of the translation, and God the active side. Faith or testimony is a gift, not a human achievement. This, incidentally, is why the translation of the Bible from one language to another causes these Calvinists no trouble, since the human translators are passive under the guidance of active Spirit of God, directing the written Word by his Living Word.

The center of the sermon at Antioch, as at the associational sermon at Peach Bottom just a few weeks later, is the scriptural account of the translation of Elijah in 2 Kings 2. By beginning with Enoch, as interpreted by Paul in Hebrews, Evans prepared for his reading of the Elijah translation, the "greatest such event, other than the day the Lord of glory died." By moving from Enoch to Elijah, each a foreshadowing of Jesus's resurrection, Evans opens the way for these translations to become emblems for events and dreams in the lives of persons living in history and the flesh. These powerful images are grasped as tokens of hope, idioms for understanding divine calling here in time.

> In the second Kings, second chapter, you'll find one of the greatest, most mysterious days other than the day the Lord of glory died, when there was a great earthquake and shook this old earth, and it quaked and trembled, and one said reeled him like a drunken man, and the sun went out, as the old colored preacher said, in the middle of the day, refused to shine, everything got dark and black as sackcloth. But other than that, perhaps, the day of translation of the great servant of God that the ravens fed, one time and drank water from the brook and the ravens, God sent the ravens to bring him bread and flesh in the morning, and bread and flesh in the evening, but he drunk water from the brook. And by and by that dried up. . . .

Now Elder Evans moves to make an important connection, a connection with unstated references to his own experience and view of the world.

> And Elijah as a man subject to like pleasuring as we are, and he prayed as I've told you, that it might not rain. A man like

this, in this world. Now. But there was a time come when he was to leave this world, and in that very day that he left, and this is the thing that we got into the other day in our discussion, and it's like old Charles Alexander said one time, I can't hardly talk about this, cause it gets so close to some things that's, I've been so close to some things in my little time in this world, right on this mountain up here as you've heard me tell, but I'm embarrassed to speak of it this morning lest I be just completely overcome with emotion, cause I've been so close to this thing.

The merging of the Elijah account with veiled references to his own experience on Sheep Pen Ridge, a ridge that can be seen from the front door of the Antioch Church where this sermon on translation is being preached, will be alluded to again in the association sermon. Evans's own words about this experience, in imagery and tone, bear strong resemblance to both the dream and the experience of preaching the doctrine of predestination to the Union Baptists, his farewell sermon from that body, and the sermon that opened the way for his translation, by testimony and baptism, into the Primitive Baptist church. This passage also has a reference to the Reverend Charles Alexander, a Baptist elder from Liverpool, England, who visited in "this country" some years previously and whose friendship Evans prizes greatly. The passage quoted at length before this passage, containing the phrase "and this is the thing that we got into the other day in our discussion," refers to discussions with the two of us and Daniel Patterson just the day before on the subject of translation in which the Elijah texts played an important role, texts Evans quotes from memory with amazing accuracy.

After multiple textual references to the term and to the experience of translation, interspersed with oblique and explicit personal references, Elder Evans arrives at the summary teaching he finds in these texts, undoubtedly reconfirmed by the personal experiences we have cited.

I'm dealing, Brothers and Sisters, with the power that's active, and subjects that's acted upon, or shortly to be acted upon . . . As they went on (Elijah and Elisha), and as they went on talking, there appeared—and here it is—there appeared a chariot of fire, and horses of fire parted them both asunder and Elijah went up by a whirlwind into heaven, and that's where Enoch was taken . . . Enoch and Elijah and the Lord Jesus Christ is there bodily. All right. Here's a power that's active, which is God, and a subject Elijah that's acted upon . . . But here is a power that's active, in translation, here's a subject that's acted upon in translating. Being taken from this place to another, from this world to the world unknown to us, and that's where he went, into heaven. That's where Jesus came from, you know, and went to. That's where the Lord's people will eventually be carried to. We are not going to sprout wings and fly, that's why I don't much like to hear that song sung, "I'll fly away old glory, I'll fly away."

But the sermon did not end there. Elder Evans kept finding new ways in the texts to speak about translation, or rather new ways to emphasize the dominant activity of God and the passive status of humans. The simple phrase in this passage—"Being taken from this place to another, from this world to the world unknown to us"—is the resounding voice of Primitive Baptist hope, a hope that is given some warrant in the particular experiences of translation Elder Evans recounted in person and alluded to over and over in this sequence of sermons and interviews. Facing an election as the association opened its annual meeting in the Peach Bottom Church (where Elder Evans had preached the communion sermon two weeks previously), this elder was the passive subject of the activity of voting; his only means for interceding was his introductory discourse on "translation."

The Meeting Resumes

The sound of singing in the house rescues the members from the damp out-of-doors and from strained lunchtime conversation. Back in the church, around one o'clock, Evans begins the agenda of the meeting. He asks his friend McNure from Georgia to open the meeting with prayer. The first item is the receiving and reading aloud the letters from each member church in the association, each church having elected its delegation to the association a month before in the conference following the Saturday afternoon or evening preaching service. This is conducted by Clerk Nichols and his son the assistant clerk. The two stocky figures stand at either side of the small table, below the stand, taking turns reading the letters from each of the member churches in strong, stolid voices. There is a move to receive the letters and seat the messengers from the member churches. Then there is a call for petitionary letters from other churches who desire admission to the Mountain District Association. There are none. Evans then announces the next item, the election of the officers. A moderator, assistant moderator, a clerk, and an assistant clerk are to be elected. Evans then states: ". . . we choose them annually by a majority of the messengers present, so, whatever your desires and ideas at this point, why let's present them."

Nichols asks leave to speak, and makes a firm statement. He has been clerk seventeen years (his voice breaks as he recalls those times), but now he must step down. His hand is crippled, and he cannot write. He suggests that Roy Truitt, the jewelry store owner in Galax, who only a month ago was ordained deacon at Cross Roads, be elected. Nichols's exact words are these:

> Seventeen years ago today you elected me as clerk. And I appreciate the confidence you all have in me, and seventeen years is a long time, and I've got to where I'm not capable of doing the work. What I mean, I can't write . . . Now it's been a pleasure working with you all, and there's been a lot of heartache, there's been a lot of hard work . . . And we've got a lot of young men that can take the job. We've got two, especially, in our church, brother Roy Lee Truitt, and his son Tony, and in about every church there's somebody . . . So, I'll just ask you all to relieve me of my duties.

Now Nichols's son speaks, saying he can continue as assistant clerk but cannot take over as clerk (as normally might be done) because of travel commitments in his job with a large national textile corporation.

Now a third man, cousin to Nichols, one associated by kin and place with Cross Roads Church, stands and moves that the election for clerk and assistant clerk, as well as moderator and assistant moderator, all be decided by private ballot, with every messenger, representing the churches of the association, writing on a slip of paper whomever he prefers for each job. This procedure has not been used for a number of years, comments Evans, but since it was used before, he says he finds it all right.

Nevertheless, the motion to have a private ballot is almost certainly moved by the unrest associated with Evans's intervention in the Low Valley Church business. Evans accepts the suggestion, saying that the election has indeed been so conducted in past times. (The contrast is with recent times, when the officers have simply been nominated, then elected by affirmation.)[1]

The ballot vote is held. A certain tension while the ballots are counted, by the two visiting elders from Georgia, appointed by Evans, is signaled by the opening of windows by men at the four corners of the church.

The results: Evans is returned as moderator, Reed as assistant moderator, Nichols's son as assistant clerk, and the only new officer is Roy Lee Truitt for clerk, replacing Nichols.

Evans then remarks that he, Evans, appreciates their confidence, while Reed (his heretofore unannounced opponent, from the Virginia faction) would have made a better moderator, and "I'll certainly make some errors, I'm certain to, I'll just promise to do the best I can, the year, and that's as far as I'm expecting to go."[2] He recognizes Reed: "Brother [Joseph]." Reed: "I appreciate the confidence of people and like Brother Evans said I know I'll make some mistakes. I ask you to pray for us, and to help us, that's what we need." Evans asks the new man, Truitt: "Brother Roy, come on up here." Truitt, echoing the humility of the others, replies: "I feel like you've made a very poor choice to be doing this, I'll just do the best I can."

There follow some remarks by the other officers and a little anecdote by Nichols about his replacement Truitt (that he's busy, which is why he'll do a good job), who has now taken his seat. There is a call for visitors from sister associations and sister churches to be seated. Nichols moves that the moderator make the appointments to committees. Evans does, with some hesitation and difficulty in remembering names. Appointments are made to the following committees: preaching, finance, arrangements, and distribution of minutes. He gives most positions to persons from his own churches from North Carolina, although he does put Nichols on the arrangements committee, joking that "If Raymond ain't gonna clerk, get him right there." Now he announces the time and place of the next day's preaching, by Temples, from Georgia. Elder Reed gives the closing prayer.

So Evans is returned as moderator for another year. During the remainder of the weekend, the following events or remarks bear on the conflict.

Friday evening, the retired Clerk Nichols (pivot of the losing faction) does not come to services, nor do any of the Virginia faction save for Assistant Moderator Reed.

Appointments to preaching omit Assistant Moderator Reed, while placing at the penultimate position on the last day the "two wives" offender and archenemy of Reed, Yates. Yates preaches on sin. Reed walks out.

The final sermon is delivered by Elder Jess Higgins, pastor of the Galax Church, generally considered a close ally of the Cross Roads Church. Higgins grew up on a ridge across the road from Cross Roads Church; his father, a vigorous man in his late eighties, still lives in Baywood; and Higgins is a frequent and popular preacher at Cross Roads. A robust, friendly man, he bridges the Virginia and North Carolina line in that he often shares baptizing duties with Elder Evans. His sermon appeared to us (and was so received by others) to mediate the schisms and tensions. It is on the subject "Hands," including allusion to the hand of fellowship. This sermon leads to the final remarks of Evans.

Evans says this may be his last time to be present, and he

emphasizes that central in the faith is not only the hand but the hand of fellowship, citing scripture to back this assertion, as he had at the association's previous final closing. He calls for the hand of fellowship before they close, with everyone shaking hands with everyone else. The last word, however, comes from Nichols the clerk, who shouts to everyone, "Pick up your copies of last year's minutes!"

CHAPTER SEVEN

Pilgrims and Paradoxes

Nichols's shout ended the one hundred eighty-fifth meeting of the Mountain District Primitive Baptist Association, and there our narrative ends as well. We turn now to the task of identifying themes and implications of general significance.

Ritual

Among the many elements described in the case, we begin with ritual, those repeated and sacralized forms that creep only to the edges of this narrative, but which tacitly inform and frame it. As we have noted in the introductory section of this volume, many circumstances within which this case is embedded cannot be related within the genre of narrative. The cyclical pattern of ritual provides the matrix in which the actions we recount occur. If social dramas highlight occurrences, ritual is recurrence. In the case of the Primitive Baptist it is the recurrence of ritual that must be appreciated, and its particular status understood, if this case is to be fully situated.

Stern Calvinists of separatist Puritan tradition, the Primitive Baptists are in many respects anti-ritualistic, particularly if ritual is seen from their rigorous scriptural guard against any hint of magical or sacramental practices. They oppose any fusion of church and state, ritual and community, or ritual and family, as taught by Durkheimian theory and historically embodied by Christian groups from medieval Catholicism to Falwell's neo-Christendom movement. Primitive Baptist churches do not recognize Memorial Day, Fourth of July, town or county commemorations, or Father's Day and Mother's Day. To wed ritual to community, family, or state is to lose the transcendence of the sacred. Hence, in neither theory nor practice do Primitive Baptists support any semblance of American civil religion. In this they depart from their Genevan ancestors as well as the New England Puritans who moved from elect invisible saints to visible Americans with a manifest destiny.[1]

The Primitive Baptist sets the Spirit over and against both ritual and community. Mistrusting form, since a condition of all created things is decay and deception, they affirm meaning as given by the Spirit, and as revealed by the scriptures, interpreted through the gift of liberty granted now and again to elders in their sermons and to lay persons in their meditative solitudes. The Spirit moves like the wind, touching and electing whom it ordains.

Ever alert to the danger and temptation of "modern inventions," Primitive Baptists permit no musical instruments, no robes, no stained-glass windows, no pictures or crucifixes or flags in the churches. "What is a cross?" thunders Elder Yates, "but a timber on which criminals were hanged; what matters is not the cross but Christ." Rejecting idolatry of form, they reject also any destruction of form for transcendence; unlike their Pentecostal neighbors, they give no credence to speaking in tongues or "the shout," where words lack clear meaning, even if, as among Pentecostals, the spiritual message is heard and interpreted by spiritual adepts.

Against ritual routines, they affirm the Word, as spoken, as written, as lived, always as expressions of the Holy Spirit. A person cannot prepare routinely to join the church; he or she must receive and report a spiritual "impression," for which he or she may wait a lifetime, only then to come forward, like Nichols after thirty years, to present themselves for membership. An elder must be called, liberated to preach, and finally ordained by a presbytery: then again, he can lose the gift for both manifest and unknown reasons. An elder cannot prepare a sermon in advance. He must mount the stand without notes hoping to be blessed by the Spirit to preach and, as we have seen, if he is not blessed, he will say, "I am not being blessed today, and I am going to get on out of the way and let someone else try."

Seeking the guidance of the Spirit, the Primitive Baptist prays and meditates in the hollows and low places, occasionally to be lifted to the mountaintop. Such a quest is accompanied by the private intense study of scripture and theology.

Yet despite their suspicion of ritual and their reliance on solitary quests for meaning framed by history and theology, the Primitive Baptists have constructed public ritual patterns. This ritualization turns around such familiar overlapping oppositions as the sacred and profane, public and private, male and female, and it entails an acute sense of history and doctrine, and of possible conflict between them.

The degree of ritualization of the administrative and political process is striking. Each month, following the Saturday service, a church is declared "in conference," and the pastor moderates a brief business meeting. The meeting follows rules of decorum printed in the minutes. Noteworthy is the constancy of this format, which, as we have noted, has remained essentially the same for three centuries, maintaining old English Baptist procedure. It appears that most matters are worked through from start to finish in this context, rather than reflections of prior deliberations. Business is thus conducted in the context of sacral space and time—right there in the church within the context of the service—and publicly. Business is ritualized. With this background, one can understand Nichols's objection to Evans's holding the meeting concerning the Cahooneys "in the house of a sister," rather than "in the church." Said Nichols: "What is started in a church should be finished in a church."

Women as Type

"In the house of a sister" was the other side of Nichols's objection. Business meetings are dominated by men, although the sisters are present. Not only may women not preach, they should not speak at business meetings, which are led by the pastor and the deacons.

Business, then, is not only sacral and public, it is masculine. "What do the women do?" one of us asked Elder Lyle in an interview, at which point his wife, a highly intelligent mathematics teacher, stuck her head around the kitchen door and said, laughing, "They cook!" The major job of women is indeed to prepare the meals for dinners on the grounds of communion and foot washing services. Although the cooking can spill into sacral spheres, as when the deacon's wife prepares the bread and wine for communion, the women are, practically speaking, consigned to the profane and private.

Into this opposition, Evans has injected a reversal. "You sisters who listen in silent reverence," he preached, "are a 'type.'" "You," he said, turning to the men's pew, "are not a type." By this, he explained, he meant that women are symbolically the bride of Christ, hence they are the symbol of the church itself.[2]

Discussing Evans's argument with him, we proposed the kind of interpretation suggested by Rodney Needham,[3] that here was an opposition between explicit, instrumental power (that of the men, who publicly dominate church ritual and business) and mystical power (here associated with the women) that resides not in what one does or controls but in what one is, what one symbolizes and manifests. Evans neither accepted nor rejected the interpretation but instead shifted the ground to scripture, justifying his own argument by exegesis of the Song of Solomon. Here is an excerpt from that conversation:

> Peacock: Ok, let me see if I got part of it. If the church has a female symbolism in that it is married to Christ, then women in the church can symbolize that femaleness in a way that men cannot. Is that it?
>
> Evans: Yeah, that's what it is, Solomon 2. 2–3 (he quotes from the Song of Solomon).
>
> Patterson: I was wondering whether there's any parallel in the experience of the woman, as she feels moved by the spirit to enter the church, does she fight it less than men do?
>
> Evans: . . . well I doubt it. When it comes to that part of the experimental phase of it . . . I think it affects both the man and woman, or boy and girl, about the same . . . It don't affect all the sisters the same, nor the male members either . . . Experiences are different.

We continue pressing to discover what the symbolic equation might mean behaviorally, but Evans refuses to accept a direct relation between the symbolic and the experiential. Finally he refers us back to the Song of Solomon, which he quotes at length from memory, and he cites a number of scriptural references to the relation between women and the church.

Elder Evans in these responses to our probes is true to the Calvinist refusal to accord any concord between the experiential and the symbolic or transcendent on a regular or substantial basis. "Signs" become such in a highly contingent fashion; there are no preordained sacral objects, not even sacred types, which assure a connection between the experiential and the sacred. (We note again that Evans's term was "experimental," a term in use by English speaking persons since the sixteenth century and a commonplace for Old Baptist referring to direct experience of things.)

Elder Evans, then, prefers to emphasize the scriptural basis for his symbolic equation of church and woman, whereas we emphasize the implications for practice. Such an equation bestows on women meanings and powers outside the formal administrative and ritual routine of the church. This symbolization could then explain how Evans and his colleagues could accept the "sister's house" as a suitably liminal place in which to bring together the excluded members of Low Valley and re-constitute them as a new church. For women at a mystical level are the church.

Nichols, less mystical and more bureaucratic, simply re-jected this betwixt and between category represented by the sister's house: business should be public, formal, and sacral. What starts in the church should be finished in the church.

The difference between Evans's and Nichols's attitude about the role of women may reflect personal experience. Evans's wife, who has never joined the Primitive Baptist church, plays no role even in its profane sphere of cooking and hospitality, while Nichols's wife is active in these re-spects. Nichols's wife also informally influences affairs of the church, while Evans grumbles about "women who run the church through the telephone . . . women trying to run things now." Nichols the administrator permits women to slide into the sacral pragmatically, while Evans the preacher restricts their role to the symbolic—a difference in ritualiza-tion rooted in the private lives of the two men as well as in many segments of the culture at large.

Whatever their differences, Nichols and Evans share the general Primitive Baptist dichotomization of male and female in the church. Women are silent, men speak. Women cook the food, men repair the building. Women sit on the left hand of the preacher, men on the right. The dichotomization pene-trates even into the music, in that, unlike in most Western singing, including that of mainline Protestantism, where the soprano carries the melody, among Primitive Baptists it is the men who sing the melody, while women harmonize. In short, relations among men and women within the church are highly ritualized, part of a dichotomy that is rigidly defined and defended, buttressed by scriptural and symbolic text and cosmology and elaborated in a social order.

The distinction between male and female roles in the church does not, however, imply a difference in eligibility for election to salvation; a woman is as eligible as a man, so far as anyone can know; distinctions of gender cannot forecast chances of election any more than can other earthly distinctions, such as race or religious affiliation. Nor would the other kinds of ritualized patterns to which we have referred be regarded as having significance in the transcendental and eternal. The format of meetings and minutes may be adhered to with constancy bolstered by a long heritage, but this is merely history; we recall the ambivalence with which history is viewed. Church procedure, social arrangements within the church, even the order of services are regarded, no matter how highly ritualized they seem to the observer, as merely human arrangements. Yet, again, they are part of the visible church, the most nearly perfect manifestation of God's plan by humans in an imperfect world.

In short, ritualization has an important but ambiguous place in the religious life of the Primitive Baptist.

Now let us return to the outcome of the association meeting. What did the vote mean? Evans was reelected moderator and Nichols resigned as clerk. Evans then cemented his position through the two structural means at his disposal: appointments to committees and appointments to preach, in both of which positions he placed his own men, largely excluding those of the other faction.

Charisma and Bureaucracy?

Charisma beat bureaucracy, North Carolina beat Virginia, Evans beat Reed? Such a bare bones assessment of logistics fails to capture the ritual context of these actions.

Evans's conduct during the association meeting was not that of the political strategist so much as the man of sorrows, acquainted with grief. He was absorbed in reflections on his own life, his coming death, and the history and fellowship of the association as it is bound with these. His mournful remarks and somber countenance were in evidence throughout.

One could of course interpret his spiritual posture as itself a political weapon. What guilt would be laid on him who would dare, at this point in Evans's life, to crucify him?

Such a cynical psychological interpretation distorts the ritual frame within which Primitive Baptist business is conducted. The spiritual and the tactical are not so sharply differentiated as pragmatism would assume in its separation of ways and means from spiritual symbols. Accepting that the two spheres fuse, that politics are ritualized, we interpret the case in the following vein.

At one level, political maneuvering of a deliberate and rational type is indeed taking place, by both Evans and Nichols and by their factions. Awareness of that is revealed in comments and actions, though it is often tacit. At another level, accustomed forms are followed; the conflict is worked through as part of a sacral fellowship and a sacral rite. And at a deep level, Evans's reelection is a drama embodying a profound set of isomorphic symbolizations. These symbols include Evans's life pilgrimage—"my travels," as he calls it, his gift and his coming death; the biblical archetypes of death ranging from Elijah's translation to Christ's crucifixion; and the collective history of the Primitive Baptist association, its struggle and decline. Resonances among such symbols are made surprisingly explicit by Evans's mournful utterances and demeanor that set a heavy mood at the final meeting.

Behind all of this is the question of ritual within the reformist sect, of which this group is a type. Growing out of a purifying movement, such a sect must be skeptical of communal ritualism. Sternly individualistic, members seek meaning not in the public rite so much as in private experience, yet those experiences and understandings discovered in them are "translated" by the gifted charismatic spokesman like Evans into public statements. For such Protestants, forms and fellowship are deeply felt, perhaps more intensely than in the case of those who take communal ritual for granted. Ritual, for these pilgrims, is constructed, negotiated. Ritual is not liturgically prescribed, but a creative struggle to wrest meaning from disorder and dispersion, but always with awareness of history— the looming destruction of such forms, together with all that is mortal.

Suspensions

Like some members in the Mountain District Association who are suspended between Evans and Nichols, we are situated—not between charisma and bureaucracy, but between Weber and Durkheim. Durkheim instructs us about public ritual and collective solidarity—in Primitive Baptist terms, about the meanings of fellowship. Weber instructs us about the private spiritual conditions induced by theological doctrines that sever all natural and social ties and promote a rich inner life of self-examination and meditation—in Primitive Baptist-Calvinist terms, the problematics of "effectual calling."

Our case reminds us of the dialectical and mutually supporting relations between the public and the private, the community and the individual, though never without the incorrigible unease induced by Calvinist doctrine. This doctrine, and the practices of public and private spirituality it authorizes, places an indelible suspicion over every alleged concord between consciousness and the external world: intention and action, feeling and expression, meaning and sign. The doctrine of predestination builds into the fabric of the Primitive Baptist view of the world the permanent possibility of recall for every human election, and all forms of human associations. Such a doctrine places the meaning of fellowship, so richly experienced among Primitive Baptists as a mode of personal and interpersonal transcendence, in question.

Lest we commit the fallacy of simple location in our focus on the conflict embodied in Evans and Yates, on the one side, and Reed and Nichols on the other, we turn again to major themes in the lives and thought of Primitive Baptists. We address the problematics of fellowship and sociality in the world of Primitive Baptists with their recurrent controversies in doctrine and polity, and we consider the issue of leadership and authority. We consider first the individual, especially with regard to the place of charisma within a Calvinistic framework, then we consider the group and the issue of fellowship given the interdictions of Calvinism.

Charisma

As Calvinists, the Primitive Baptists elevate God and deni-
grate the human. Accordingly they are suspicious of imputing
charisma to persons.[4] "We believe in divine healing, but not
divine healers," they say, in criticism of charismatic Christians who verge on worship of overpowering personalities who
have such gifts as healing. They avoid special titles and clothing for preachers, as well as ornate pulpits or other signs of
imputing special powers to individual ministers.

Is charisma, then, absent? We have seen that a certain charisma is possible, enlivening the austere skeleton of a strict
Calvinism. Preachers can hope (though not strive) to be
blessed. The preacher must take the stand, hoping to be
blessed though knowing he may draw a blank and then have
to sit down. But those who are blessed report a momentous
experience. Elder Evans describes one. He took the stand,
having no idea what he would say, and, once beginning, was
unconscious of saying anything; nor could he remember anything later; but, he reports, a "brother" had timed his sermon
as lasting more than an hour, and many were greatly moved.
He recounts the vivid and compelling circumstances of the
experience, describing the precise format of the church, the
location of each listener, and the exact scriptural reference
of his text. But he cannot recall a word of his sermon. Elder
Roten, in his eighties, counts seventeen such occasions in his
lifetime of preaching. (The meticulous recording and counting of occasions on which one preaches is, by the way, typical
for the Primitive Baptists; one elder's log records thousands
of such "appointments," blessed or not.) Balancing the experience of being blessed, every elder recounts the experience
of going blank, of taking the stand and having one's mind go
dark. One elder suggests that this is the difference between
preaching and acting; an actor has a script so that he can always say his lines, but a preacher depends solely on being inspired by God, hence the proof of that inspiration is as much

his drawing a blank on some occasions as his being blessed on others.

A certain charismatic power is, then, acknowledged, provided that it is God-given; but as God giveth, so he taketh away. We have noted the speculation of Elder Reed that one preacher lost his ability to preach owing to misconduct. But most leave such speculation aside and accept the inscrutability of God.

The charismatic occasion can be repeated, as when a preacher is blessed many times. Such gifts then translate into an enduring reputation and personality. But does this charisma come to be, in Weber's sense, a type of authority? The Primitive Baptists block such a translation; this they do by minimizing organization itself. There is no ecclesiastical hierarchy, no bishop, and the pastor is unpaid and given few requisites of office. Yet because of their very lack of bureaucratic organization, the Primitive Baptist association can pivot around the charismatic inspiration of certain figures, as is the case with Elder Evans. The charismatic qualities of such leaders are seen as of the spirit, not of the person, however. While this distinction may blur in practice, as when admirers of a gifted preacher slip into an attitude of admiring the man himself, Primitive Baptists carefully draw this distinction when reflecting on the meaning of being blessed in preaching. And the distinction has sociological implications in that the Primitive Baptists do not permit themselves the unquestioning, irrational worship of a charismatic leader that Weber observed in cults and movements. So the Primitive Baptists do recognize more charisma than a strictly rationalistic typology of Calvinism might predict, yet they limit the authority of charisma in practice as well as in theory.

If not in the person, is charisma immanent in the group? Is there, among Primitive Baptists, what Weber terms a "charismatic community"? The church cannot be consistently blessed if for no other reason than, as Primitive Baptists insist, a church contains those who will be damned as well as those who will be saved; it is not a society of saints. But as the blessing of God can descend on an individual, for a moment, so it can descend momentarily on the group. Especially is this felt, as we shall shortly elaborate, during the hand of fellowship at the close of the service. The poignancy of this fellowship is charismatic, in contrast to a coldly bureaucratic type of sacralized sociality. But like the individual, so the group is only a momentary vessel of spiritual gifts. The poignancy of the blessed moment of fellowship does not translate into any claim of charismatic authority by those momentarily blessed. Those who enjoy this fellowship may be prominent in the church. But their fellowship, however sweet, is temporary. When they next meet some will be absent, perhaps— who knows—predestinated to hell rather than, as they hope, a "home in heaven." They cannot claim, nor would they try to claim, that they are a community of the elect.

The doctrine, then, firmly limits the translation of charismatic attitudes into charismatic authority, whether of person or group. But what of the doctrine itself?

Their doctrine, the Primitive Baptists say, is a "hard doctrine," for it separates the elect from the damned, with no recourse and no reasons except those known to the omniscient and inscrutable God. But to this doctrine itself is imputed a kind of charisma. This Calvinistic theology is not merely, as Weber observed, magnificent in its logic, it is also beautiful in its aesthetic, or rather in an aesthetic of the sublime. It is elegant in its very hardness, impressive in its tragic solemnity, moving in its requirement of total belief and humility despite all human impulse to believe and feel otherwise. And it is expressed in the compelling rhetoric of the King James Bible. Preaching that is truly intellectual as well as eloquent is admired, and the intellectual excitement that surrounds theological debate renders these mountain towns more like Geneva than Barchester. In the doctrine and the word, then, we find a kind of charismatic authority through aesthetic articulations. Yet this doctrine limits its own charisma. If at one level its very rationalism is charismatic, at another this rationalism dampens the spirit, questions the excitement, and channels enthusiasm back into sober reflection. But this process is richer and more complex, when we see it in the conversations and introspections, the sermons and tracts, than one would guess from a simple extrapolation from the doctrine.

Fellowship

Preachers charismatic in their eloquence, doctrine magnificent in its logic and paradox—these inspire many and often. But especially among the laity, preaching and doctrine sometimes pale in contrast to fellowship. We recall that Green Ward, a deacon in the Peach Bottom Church, remarked once as we walked with him in his pastures: "I sat through a whole association meeting [lasting three days with nearly a dozen sermons] and did not get anything out of it until the end when we had the hand of fellowship."

The hand of fellowship is the affecting ceremony that concludes every service. As we have described, a line is formed by the members and any guests invited to join. As the members move in a semicircle toward the receiving line of elders standing just below the stand or pulpit, they sing the closing hymn, shake everyone's hand, and, frequently, embrace each other as they move along at a slow pace in time with the hymn. During these movements of gesture and song, the Primitive Baptists shed tears of joy and sorrow, joy in the immediate experience of peace and fellowship with their fellow members, sorrow at the memories of departed loved ones. The closing of every service elicits such sorrows, reminders of the uncertainty of their ultimate destiny.

The term fellowship also refers to the condition of the collective membership of the church. The first order of business at the monthly "conference" of every Primitive Baptist church is an inquiry into the state of the church. The moderator, usually the pastor, asks the assembled members: "Is the church at peace and fellowship?" If the reply is negative from a single member, no further business may be transacted until the impediment to peace is removed. Should the service the next day (the conferences are held, we recall, after service on Saturdays prior to services on Sunday) be the annual communion service, the church cannot proceed with its communion until peace and fellowship are restored. Fellowship, then, is both a ritual experience and a condition of polity upon which the ritual is permitted to proceed.

By extension we have been using the term "fellowship," following Primitive Baptist practice, to refer to relations between churches and associations, and to indicate the condition of recognition or rejection that obtains between various churches and their elders. The description of the complicated pattern of acceptance and rejection that radiates from the co-pastorate of Elders Lyle and Sparks at Woodruff is an illustration of the meaning of this use of the term.

The taint of nonrecognition is not limited to individual churches and to particular elders: nonrecognition is systemic and can be transmitted to anyone who keeps fellowship with a church or to an elder who is not recognized by a church or an association. Such acts of recognition and rejection, purity and contamination, are transacted between churches with each other (their elders included) and between associations with each other (their elders included). Such practices of inclusion and exclusion limit the ability of elders to preach, or exercise their gift, as well as the ability of the laity to visit freely in many churches as is the normal rule for active members.

It would be a profound error, one perhaps encouraged by the standpoint of outside observers, to understand the attendance at church by the laity and the invitation to take the stand by elders to each other as routine acts of minor importance. What is happening in these apparently routine acts, again perhaps unduly obscured by inclination on the part of analysts to assume importance only when high drama occurs, is a social process of election. One church recognizes another, opening the way for members and elders to elect to attend and preach there. The same occurs at the associational level. We have explained why the ecclesiastical action of excluding a member from a local church carries such extraordinary resonance, theologically and spiritually. The converse is true when a new member is voted into the church and baptized into the fellowship. These same doctrinal and polity structures are at work when churches and elders exclude and include one another. An act of inclusion or exclusion by a church or association is not a single self-limiting instance. On the contrary, each act of election by one church or association of another implicates networks whose boundaries are never closed, though such actions may redistribute parts of the network. So every act of accepting or rejecting fellowship is at once an action of conviviality and separation. Such acts express sentiments of affiliation and disaffiliation in affective, doctrinal, and political modes. They declare an identity for members and churches that is constituted by acts of fellowship: recognition and rejection.

It is not difficult to appreciate how the divorce of a member (particularly of an elder), the act of excluding an individual from the fellowship of a local church, and the vote of a church or an association to sever relations with a church or another association are sacred acts predicated upon the sacrality of fellowship, itself constituted by, as well as constituting, the identities of Primitive Baptists. As polity and as experience, election is doctrine translated by such actions and in such experiences. With these multiple relations among polity, experience, and doctrine, it is easier to understand some of the implications for individuals and for churches of the theological doctrine of *particular* election. The meaning of election, at least in this world, is understood through the translations of fellowship as inclusion and as exclusion. But since Primitive Baptists can claim no certainty about their own prior divine election before the beginning of the world, they know that every human election and exclusion suffers the probability of "dread presumption," to use John Calvin's words about knowledge of predestination.

> Let it, therefore, be our first principle that to desire any other
> knowledge of predestination than that which is expounded by
> the word of God, is no less infatuated than to walk where there
> is no path, or to seek light in darkness. Let us not be ashamed
> to be ignorant in a matter in which ignorance is learning. Rather
> let us willingly abstain from the search after knowledge, to
> which it is both foolish as well as perilous, and even fatal to as-
> pire. If an unrestrained imagination urges us, our proper course
> is to oppose it with these words, "It is not good to eat much
> honey; so for men to search their own glory is not glory." (Prov-
> erbs xxv. 27.) There is good reason to dread a presumption
> which can only plunge us headlong into ruin.[5]

If human impotence and presumption make acts of fellowship constitutionally equivocal, such acts of recognition and
rejection make controversy and conflict inevitable. A theology that makes acts of polity constitutive of normative human
identity yet teaches at the same time that such acts are apt
to be tainted with error and presumption nourishes movable
feasts of conflict and controversy. Understood with this perspective the conclusion is hard to resist that the case we have
sketched here is not unique or eccentric but exemplary of
normal relations among Primitive Baptist churches and associations, elders, clerks, and deacons.

So routine acts of fellowship and exclusion carry, if most
frequently in a minor key, moments and patterns of transcendence. Handshaking, hugging, and weeping are actions
and emblems of fellowship. The meanings of these acts vary
according to individual members but they share in these public expressions of solidarity, hope for election, and memory
of members who have "passed on." Rooted in the affective
sentiments of these gestures, ordered by freshly preached images of biblical figures and scenes, and revivified by the hymns
accompanying the closing ritual, the Primitive Baptist experiences the translation of doctrine into emotion. Such mutual
translation between feeling and doctrine win for the church
strong affection. Such acts as accepting a new member, declaring an old member excluded, and meeting in conference
and associational gatherings lend authority to the doctrine

and the experience of worship. The repeated elaboration of doctrinal subtleties practiced by many elders and by some members of the laity receives experiential confirmations through the gestures of ritual and acts of polity. The doctrine of particular election and the theological suspicion of all things finite exert a steady pressure on all ritual actions as well as particular doctrinal formulations. Under such constant questioning ritual acts can never be considered as routine and habitual.

The acts of conviviality render hard doctrine digestible, while doctrines of election and the visible church are translated into experiences and practices.

The experience of the practices of fellowship, thus informed, allows sensuous gestures to become "spiritual emotions," which are distinguished in Primitive Baptist spiritual directions from "fleshly emotions." In the play of such spiritual affections doctrine and polity cease their status as written Articles of Faith and a Constitution of Laws. Their externality is temporarily transfigured as fellowship—handshaking, hugging, and weeping—fragile and brief actions that compose a public world within which to enact an identity.

In the divisions in the Low Valley Church, perhaps members of the Mountain District Association saw, as if in a mirror, not only parts of their past, but an image of normal affairs in the world of many Primitive Baptists. Evans and Nichols, Yates and Reed perhaps saw the same situation. They read it differently and acted accordingly. In their differing positions they were very much Primitive Baptists.

The divisions in the Low Valley Church, while initially on the margins of the Mountain District Association, pulled its churches and leaders into a conflict of their own. We have seen how the conflict worked in several ways, from personal style and geographic loyalties to difference in judgment about the practical import of doctrine as guidance for associational politics. The debate over doctrine, recounted in our opening anecdote in chapter one, between old Elder Cahooney and Elder Evans in the living room—and the bedroom—of Clerk

Nichols's home, occurred long before the affair at Low Valley, yet the practice that little story tells is a part of the story of the case we have told. The habit of talking scripture and arguing doctrine rehearses, if not predicts, differences that manifest themselves in the conflict between Nichols and Evans over the leadership of the young Cahooney elders, all with important ramifications for the life of their cherished Mountain District Association.

If we have succeeded in placing the factions in the Mountain District Association within the context of Primitive Baptist ritual supported by doctrine, polity, and the experience of transcendence that comes through fellowship, we can return to our main protagonists without fear of abstracting them from the world in which the events of our narrative occurred. If, as we have previously stated, to settle for the concluding summary—"Charisma beat bureaucracy, North Carolina beat Virginia, Evans beat Reed"—is extremely reductive, we can, however, pursue this dictum to the benefit of this case.

Did Evans win over Reed because he is a gifted preacher whose eloquence worked to his political benefit from a long history of deference and admiration on the part of many? These factors no doubt played key roles, but to leave the analysis in such a formulation is to defer too much to Weber's heroic understanding of charisma and exclude Durkheim's stress on the ineluctable role of collectivity. We must further analyze charisma.

If we leave out any elaboration of bureaucracy, it is because there is rather little of that social form in Primitive Baptist proceedings, and what there is does not partake of the impersonal mechanisms usually associated with the term. It is true that Primitive Baptist organizational forms and rules of conduct, so much admired by Elder Reed and Clerk Nichols, are understood by persons of Reed's and Nichols's dispositions to be carriers and expressions of fundamentally serious meanings for Primitive Baptists. Again, with our predispositions for the heroic and the dramatic, we tend to neglect expressions of charisma that take the form of love of order: business con-

ducted according to approved rules of decorum (which are reprinted each year in the Mountain District Association minutes); and behavior, in sexual relations, for example, that
conforms to theological ethics according to the way Primitive
Baptists read scriptures. These forms, cherished by Nichols
the clerk, are charismatic for those of similar dispositions.[6]
Such routines, like the routines of attending services and enjoying fellowship, are for Primitive Baptists modes of transcendence, forms for disclosing and claiming their identity.
This is particularly true for Primitive Baptists since they cannot conceive, according to their understanding of theological
doctrine, how any human form of perfectionism is possible
under the conditions of existence spelled out in Calvinistic
doctrine, not to mention again the normal occurrence of splitting and reunion among Primitive Baptists. With these ac-
knowledgments we turn to Evans: Why was he reelected?

Gifts
We have used the term "gifted" with respect to Evans. We
mean by this his impressive powers of speech, breadth and
availability of scriptural knowledge, his interpretive and argu-
mentative skills. Besides encompassing these features, we had
two other reasons for using this term. First, we used it to
avoid overuse of the term charisma, and endowment, or gift,
is assuredly one of its prime meanings. Secondly, we used the
term gifted to build into our description of Evans a way of ac-
counting for the consequences, at least in part, of his long
career of preaching and travel within the Primitive Baptist
world from Maryland to Texas.

Gifted suggests gift-giving, implying a reciprocity of giving
and receiving. Primitive Baptists would say that Evans's gift
comes from those special times he has been particularly
"blessed" by the Holy Spirit "to feed the flock," namely, as
an elder being "liberated from the flesh" and used as an organ
for the divine word. Primitive Baptists distinguish between
the living, the written, and the spoken Word of God, and
preaching under the sovereignty of the Holy Spirit is under-

stood to be the spoken Word of God. In such experiences the elder who is so blessed, we noted, loses all sense of time and may well find himself chanting his sermon. The congregation will know that he is blessed by the extent and depth of their own spiritual affection.

If theologically Evans and his auditors are the recipients of such gifts, anthropologically he is the giver of his words and the congregation is the receiver of his sermon. To be moved by an elder elicits gratitude from Primitive Baptists, since such movings of spirit, "the spiritual emotions," may be signs of "effectual calling," pearls priceless in value to the uncertain soul of a Calvinist. Such appreciative responses are especially apt in the cases of churches Evans has visited and revisited over the years, not to speak of the members of his own three churches. The elders of churches he has visited and elders with whom he has traveled, like old Roten, are the admiring recipients of his gifts, and conversely.

Within this large group of elders there are younger men, like Yates of the Senter Association and McNure of Georgia, who defer to Evans as a mentor, just as the younger Evans once deferred to old Elder Kilby who baptized him in the icy waters of November when he left the Union Baptist to become a Primitive. One of the highest honors that can come to an elder, besides being elected moderator, is to be asked to preach a person's funeral. We have noted that Evans ventured into a winter storm to meet such a request of an old sister at Low Valley Church. Evans has preached hundreds of sermons at funerals. Primitive Baptist elders do not "conduct" or "hold funerals," they "preach funerals." The gratitude of many families is thus generated. All these appointments across a career work to intensify colleagueship with some elders and to distance relations with others. The friendship between old Elder Cahooney and Elder Evans, so evident in the story Clerk Nichols told, could be repeated many times for both men. Colleagueship and mutual indebtedness for preaching appointments work among elders within the same pattern of reciprocity and exclusion we have sketched in earlier sections of this study.

Evans's religious virtuosity as a preacher, practiced within a long and varied career, redounds to Evans's political standing and supplies him with expendable political capital. A part of the power that comes from this exchange of gifts is that it is never articulated in political or economic terms, or as personal achievement. The normative language is always scriptural and doctrinal: "The Lord sure did bless him today." We have noted in our description of Evans at the fateful association meeting, that when he was not ostensibly aloof, by being correct according to the rules of decorum, he expressed himself in a vocabulary used since the sixteenth century in Puritan spiritual autobiography: pilgrimage, stranger in a strange land, translation, etc.

However, given the networks of fellowship and exclusion within which elders in the Primitive Baptist church must work, theological charisma cannot be separated from the political economy of the distribution of gifts, particularly the gifts of a virtuoso preacher. As indicated, the rhetoric through which this political economy is articulated is scriptural and spiritual, of holy book and personal pilgrimage. Evans appears in this case as a major character who has a long career of participation in the economy of Primitive Baptist preaching appointments and from these exchanges derives his political power, which, of course is never secure, always subject to critical pressures from the same sources—the scripture, the polity, and the doctrines of the Primitive Baptist fellowship which support him in his achieved status. So Evans's charisma is jointly constituted by the exchanges between natural talent and major experiences of "sweet liberty" in preaching; and by grateful responses on many occasions by his auditors and admirers.

Charisma as gift exchange cannot be understood on individualist or heroic premises alone. The meaning of bureaucracy, within the Primitive Baptist world, cannot be understood as routine or mechanical forms of organizations and rules. The extraordinary is a property of the charismatic preacher, but the ties, born of giving and receiving spiritual gifts, affect the ordinary and make the ordinary essential to the appreciation, indeed the efficacy, of the extraordinary.

Both rhetorical charisma and skill in the administration of churches are essential, not just to the instrumental functioning of the church, but to the experience of fellowship. In the world of Primitive Baptists both charisma and bureaucracy are subject to the erosions, interdictions, and equivocalities of the doctrine of predestination, that form of ignorance that is learning, according to Calvin.

Why was Evans reelected moderator of the Mountain District Association? He was elected by charisma and by bureaucracy, which, in the case of the Primitive Baptists, is difficult to distinguish from fellowship.

Routinization of Charisma and the Charisma of Routine

We note certain aspects of the outcome of the case. First, although Evans was elected there was no exultation or celebration; the outcome, like the proceedings, was low-key. Second, the outcome did not appear, and was not taken, to move the Primitive Baptist community into some new phase of being; it did not signal an evolutionary step or a new level of transcendence, or anything of that sort, but instead retained, for a while, the accustomed arrangement. Third, although the election obviously had political aspects, the language used in the church meeting was generally rather apolitical—blunting the sharp edges of the conflict by framing it in terms of ritual and doctrine.

In these senses, this case was a non-case; the dramatic potential was not permitted to explode and evolve, and the actors subordinated themselves to the higher principles and affections of fellowship on which their order is built. Such an emphasis accords with the distinctive view of Calvinism. God is transcendent, man cannot transcend his own flawed condition except in the next life through God's plan. Therefore, any present arrangement is flawed, yet it is all that humans can have for manifesting what of God's will can be imperfectly expressed. This conflict between Evans and Nichols was not, then, so much a drama as a ritual. Whatever charisma Evans may have mustered was routinized not only by the bureaucratic organization of the association but also by the conviction that any such organization is intrinsically deficient. Yet in the rituals of fellowship hymns they sing, Primitive Baptists experience signs of the presence of an inscrutable God, the only contact permitted on this side of the chasm between the world of nature and history and the sacred cosmos represented in the holy books of scripture. They are pilgrims who wait in hope for a home in heaven.

This case is not unique or new to the experience of the Old Baptists. To them, steeped in a history and in a reality seen as existing "since the foundation of the world," this small case is neither climatic nor anticlimactic. It is simply part of what there is. That reality, whether rural, or Appalachian, or traditional, is Calvinist; for them, this case is only an instant in God's eternity and His plan.

Paradoxes

Here in our conclusion we have reviewed a set of Primitive Baptist paradoxes and tensions; these are not episodic, but continuing, not born of a particular case of conflict but built into the structure of individual and common life. In large part, these paradoxes stem from Calvinistic doctrine; but they are played out as a process of struggle as humans endeavor to live these doctrines in the world.

The fundamental premise, to repeat for a final time, is that God is transcendent and the world is temporal and fallen. Therefore, all that is in the world is suspect and ineligible for sacred authority. Such worldly entities include the person, things, the community, nature, and history. Yet, as humans living in the world, the Primitive Baptists do invest these entities with sentiment and meaning. They are by no means detached ascetics.

Normatively, history has no authority, and is, as we see, sharply distinct from scripture, which does. Yet history is cherished and is employed as part of study of doctrine. Their own church history is retold with pride.

Normatively, humans have no authority, hence, as we see, Primitive Baptists are deeply suspicious of claims to charisma. Yet preachers can be blessed, and a certain power is imputed to them and received from their preaching.

Normatively, communities and institutions are without sacrality, hence, as we see, the church has no special status in terms of ultimate destinies. Yet fellowship is cherished, and there is a doctrine of the visible or organic church, an ark of repose amid the uncertainties of the world.

Normatively, ritual and aesthetic forms are meaningless, and the ritual and aesthetic values of the Primitive Baptists are, to put it mildly, minimalist. Yet they do love the rituals, music, and other forms, and they call their doctrine beautiful.

Normatively, if all is predestined, then no "work" is of value, and no religious experience has significance. Yet Primitive Baptists work at jobs long hours and years and exercise great care for their homes and gardens. Amid a world of snare and delusion, Primitive Baptists seek signs of hope and evidences of election.

Such paradoxes inculcate a distinctive ethos and distinctive patterns of experience. Primitive Baptists oscillate between hope and conviction on one hand, and irony, skepticism, and doubt, on the other, about themselves and each other. They displace meaning toward God and the scripture or doctrine, resisting organic embracing of forms experienced as symbols embodying religious power. Rather than on participational symbols, their emphasis is on allegory: a more intellectualized and critically suspended trope for expressing relations between belief and experience.

Their favorite allegory is the sojourner, the pilgrim and

traveler in this world which is not home, for the pilgrim is only here en route to a final destiny. Yet this allegory is balanced by the image of the visible church: the church as garden and ark. The "Old Baptist Church" is a lovely garden of flowers amid the briars and rocks of the world. And this image, eloquently invoked, is weekly refreshed in experience by the rituals of fellowship. Yet again the experienced meaning is never consummate for it is diminished by a doctrine that declares that the church, though visible, is only a "type," a foretaste and shadow of heaven. Even those who have been part of the fellowship of the church for a lifetime remain uncertain whether heaven will be their home, for this destination was set before they or the world began.

For Primitive Baptists of the Blue Ridge, then, the institutionalization and the living out, in human terms, of Calvinism, is a continuous struggle, beset by paradox and doubt yet also sustained by endurance fed by hope. The paradoxes are always present, though they become more resonant through such localized conflicts as that between the association and the local churches, or issues such as the two wives question.

A certain assurance comes in the argument that paradox itself is a sign of the good Calvinist. Primitive Baptists can feel a unity in their propensity toward divisiveness, for they know that division reflects a shared conviction that the human community is frail in the sight of God.

Their despair can be hopeful because these pilgrims say that the first sign of grace is the growing conviction that this world is not home, an experience that makes a spiritually ignorant sinner a spiritually discerning mourner. Tears of sadness mixed with tears of hope are evidences of grace, if one be not deceived.

CHAPTER EIGHT

Theory and Ethnography

Calvinism and the World

The reader will have noticed a certain movement in our presentation: we introduce the concept and genre of case study, then we say how it is mixed and carries an unsteady identity. We employ such standard anthropological concepts as social drama, ritual, and charisma, then in every instance show how these terms undergo particular translations with respect to Primitive Baptist belief, sentiment, and practice. We use the term bureaucracy, then hasten to shape its meanings to accord with Primitive Baptist understandings. We write of protagonists, actions, drama, crisis, then radically qualify these terms by using such terms as "minor key" and muted. When we write of the characters in our case, we warn the reader away from imagining them in exclusively Weberian terms as heroic individuals in lonely struggles by situating them with as much rootage as we can muster from our data and observations. Thus we invoke for balance Durkheim, Weber's dialectical counterplayer, in our situation between these two characters in our own histories.

We have been made sharply aware of some of the problematics of translation by our conversations with Primitive Baptists and by our attendance at their services. We find ourselves in a constant movement within the ambiguities of translation as we have briefly indicated. We are not, of course, the first ethnographers to hit upon that metaphor for ethnographic work, whether ethnography refers to fieldwork or a genre and practice of writing.[1] *In our case*—and we leave the double meaning of that phrase to stand—Primitive Baptist doctrine and practice have moved us to reimagine, or reconceive, many of the standard terms in the anthropological repertory, for example, "charisma," and "ritual," and "case study." We have been taught by these Calvinists new aspects of, and new translations for, these terms. Such translation is entailed as we confront, again, Weberian theory.

In Weber's analysis, Calvinism is set against the world, and none of the traditional social or religious means of mediating between the world and the transcendent are of use. This viewpoint can be illustrated at many levels.

Of all the concepts contributed by Max Weber, "charisma" and the "Protestant Ethic" perhaps have widest currency. Yet these two prominent concepts are not, in Weber's theorizing, systematically interrelated. In neither of Weber's major works—neither *Wirtschaft und Gesellschaft*, nor *Aufsätze zur Religionssoziologie*—are these concepts joined, although they are developed at length separately. It is true that Weber saw Calvinism as heir to Judaism, and the concept of charisma was salient in his analysis of the Judaic prophets. Yet Weber's account of Calvinism, as the core of the Protestant Ethic, says almost nothing about charismatic leadership. Not Luther, but Lutheranism, not Calvin, but Calvinism, are elucidated. Those figures who are discussed, such as John Bunyan and Benjamin Franklin, are cited primarily as authors of texts rather than as charismatic leaders of movements, which, in comparison to the prophets or the great reformers, they were not. Conversely, in Weber's major exposition of charisma, he omits discussion of Calvinists.[2]

Why this avoidance of charisma in discussion of Calvinism? Weber, we recall, is elucidating ideal types. The major emphasis of Weber's ideal typical depiction of Calvinism, at the base of the typological construct termed the Protestant Ethic, is that of rationalization. Based on God's plan, which was designed before the foundation of the world, existence should be rationalized at the levels of both thought and action. Thought, including doctrine, should be systematized logically, while action, including business and other practical endeavors, should be systematized functionally. (These are the major implications in this context of Weber's multiple uses of the term rationalization or *rationalität*.) In terms of such an ideal (and an ideal type) of rationalization, human qualities, such as charisma, have little significance. In fact, given the doctrinal position of Calvinism, the imputation of charismatic power to a person is blasphemous. All authority belongs to God and his plan.

Calvinist doctrine, as typologized by Weber, not only denies authority of the charismatic type to individuals, but also to all other entities of the world: the emotions, ritual, aesthetic forms, and, of special importance for Weber as a sociological theorist, the community. While Weber has much to say about community as well as about Calvinism, he has little to say about the relationships between them. In comparison to his relatively rich explication of the psychology of Calvinism, he did not explore deeply the sociology of Calvinism, particularly its rituals and polity.

Owing to Weber's ideal typical treatment of Calvinism, based primarily on doctrinal texts, then, Weber leaves those afflicted with the Protestant Ethic without social means to live their beliefs in the world. Their solution is primarily individualist and economic: to work methodically for the glory of God, thereby providing themselves some degree of psychological assurance that they are of the Elect.

What does our ethnographic portrait of the Primitive Baptists contribute to this typological portrait? Normatively, as we have seen, the Primitive Baptists fit the type; their doctrine and the interdictions it imposes on life in the world are cogently predicted by Weberian theory. Behaviorally, as we have seen, the relationship between doctrine and life is richer and more complex than predicted by theory. The Primitive Baptists live in a world of bodies, buildings, wine, bread, pews, and books. They show a human need for precious objects and human community, and they impute a certain charisma to their leaders. They cherish history, even though denying it doctrinal authority. They doubt but they also hope, they suspect but they also act.

Ethnographically, then, we are reminded of ways humans mediate between the transcendent and the world; and between the cultural logics of doctrine, the sociological requirements of community, and the existential imperatives embodied in nature and time.

But the ethnography demonstrates not simply that sociological and existential exigencies mediate cultural logics. It is not that the Primitive Baptists simply forsake their doctrine and embrace the communal or the charismatic. To the contrary, the doctrine forces them to regard their worldly creations in a paradoxical way. Skeptical of charisma and community, they have an acute sense of their fragility. The "sweet seasons" of fellowship during the shaking of hands and embracing and weeping are, for the moment, to be relished with a special poignancy for that reason but not to be trusted as an eternally firm foundation. Likewise, the man who is raised up and blessed surely will fall and lose his gift, and no elder with a gift fails to recount when he has lost it—all the more reason to cherish it when he has it, as a gift from God. If the human and institutional significances are, among these Primitive Baptists, greater than predicted through a Weberian typology based on doctrine, likewise they are more vexed and dubious than predicted through a Durkheimian sociologism— which would be no surprise to them.

Yet the Primitive Baptists do reach a kind of resolution, and it differs from that discerned by Weber. Their solution is not capitalistic striving to demonstrate their status as elect. They do work hard under harsh conditions, and some do well, but success is no indication of salvation. Rather, their solution is in a shared understanding of the very ambiguity and paradoxicality of their lives as doctrinally framed. Together, they ac-

cept and explore their divisiveness and their loneliness as so-
journers in a fallen world.

Case, Ethnography, and Social Drama

We have attempted to interpret meanings the Primitive Baptists find in their lives, and those we find, particularly the
events at Low Valley that led to the 1983 Association Meeting
of the Mountain District. In this effort we have been especially
concerned with Calvinism as a framework of meaning. This
motif reflects the centrality of Calvinism in the worldview of
the Primitive Baptists, and it also establishes a relationship
between them and broader cultural historical frames: Calvinism, Protestantism, American culture, Western civilization,
on the one hand, and theoretical interpretations of these religions and cultures, especially the Weberian, on the other. The
Primitive Baptists have much to teach those of us who are situated within these confluences. They can enrich our understanding of more abstract questions by showing us how they
work them out in particularities of their situation, individual
lives, and ritual procedures. In doing so, they teach.

Yet another universe of discourse is addressed by our study
as we have noted in the preface and in chapter two. This is
the discipline of ethnography, the focus of the Series in Ethnographic Inquiry in which this work is published. We have
already traced some of the major developments in this discipline: the move from holistic to more focused description, re-
finement of methods to include close reading of native representations, and attention to the role of the ethnographer in
construction of ethnography. Reflecting these trends, we have
developed them in several directions.

Along with others, our purpose is to deepen a sense of the
relationship between representations and political process,
and we have shown how in the Primitive Baptist case both are
framed by theological premises. We acknowledge our work as
ethnographers in the composition of this ethnography, and

we argue further that just as natives and ethnographers are not entirely distinct neither are natives and guiding theorists. The Primitive Baptists and their theological guides are as formidable as our theoretical guides, and they both converge in certain interpretations that reflect common cultural historical heritage and direction. Max Weber's having blood kin and ethnographic experience within the subculture that his theories partially illuminate is only one reminder of this relationship between theory and the case as well as theorists, ethnographers, and the case.

With such considerations in mind, we return to our case, now to view it not so much in its own dynamics as from the standpoint of what it, and our efforts at interpreting it, can teach us about ethnography.

Earlier we have cited social anthropological approaches to case study. The most notable of these is Victor Turner's "social drama." Here, in a Durkheimian way, social process unfolds in a rather mechanistic pattern, determining the symbolic and cultural content of the ritual. As we have noted, Turner, as a superb ethnographer, was deeply aware of the significance of such symbolic and cultural content. In his analysis of the historical drama that led to the death of Thomas Becket, for example, he sought to analyze what he termed the "root paradigm. . . ."[3] And the third term in the title of the volume in which this essay appeared was "Metaphors." As Turner expanded his interests beyond ritual per se to cults, pilgrimage, and modern theater, he enriched his views of symbols. But the most constant paradigm through Turner's work, and the one to which he returned after forays into literature, hermeneutics, and psychology, was this paradigm of social drama, conceived as a four-phase process that unfolded according to a social dynamic: conflict leading to resolution. Cultural and symbolic phenomena were typically interpreted as products of this social process. In fact, in a revealing argument with Geertz, Turner subordinates the cultural to the social by relegating issues of meaning to the third phase of the social process—the reflexive, when the group ponders its conflicts. Turner goes further to suggest that modern drama and the search for meanings generally are derived from the reflexive phase in the social process.[4] In sum, the most resonant and recurring message of Turner's theory of social drama is that the drama is social: social process determines the cultural meanings.

Geertz, for his part, tends to emphasize cultural meanings as determinants of social and historical events. In his writing of the Javanese funeral as a kind of social drama, he stressed the interplay between social processes and cultural meanings. But his approach, while inserting an important balance, was, in accord with its times, mechanically functionalist, and the cultural and social forces elucidated are too abstract to explain adequately the particular acts and emotional expressions of the participants, for example, the hysterical behavior of the mother.[5] In later accounts of dramatic and historical events, such as the Balinese cockfight, or the mass suicide of Balinese nobility in the late nineteenth century, Geertz laid more emphasis on the overriding cultural themes, such as hierarchy or centrism, of which the events are iconic expressions.[6] While Geertz's analyses escape the social determinism of Turner's, he encounters a difficulty: how to explain particulars of events by necessarily abstract cultural premises. Thus, his own cultural emphasis deters his movement toward the general prescription he sets forth for ethnography: addressing large issues by small cases. This is not an issue peculiar to Geertz, of course, and is addressed not only by him, as in his critique of structuralism, but at a general level by such theorists as Sahlins and Giddens, who would somehow unite culture and process.[7]

Nor is our own case analysis perfectly articulated with the theories and issues posed by a more general social and cultural analysis. The dominant themes in the lives and thought of the Primitive Baptists—their Calvinistic theology, especially—certainly hover around the edges of the case and frame it. Without the Calvinism, there could have occurred a somewhat similar case socially defined. Schism is not peculiar to the Primitive Baptists, and Evans, Nichols, and the Cahooneys would perhaps divide and multiply regardless of their Calvinism. But, if so, they would need idioms in which to debate and larger doctrinal frames to make connections between case and cosmos. Could there be an Elder Evans or a Raymond Nichols in an Arminian context? Based on our own studies of the Arminian groups within American Protestantism, we would say there could not. At the same time, Calvinist theology is not a heavy hand in the action in explicit ways; the debate is not one of theology per se. The association meeting is not explicitly about creeds or confessions. Yet both Evans and Nichols, and the others, devoutly and stoutly strive to adhere to the doctrine. We argue that this very adherence affords them at once a unity at one level and division at another. Sharing a Calvinist mistrust in any claim that a human arrangement expresses God's will, they express their faith by such skepticism. This skepticism, which corrodes authority and spurs division, is at another level a shared value. For them skepticism is communal. But this argument is rather formalistic. We cannot conclude that this case alone definitively demonstrates the place of theology in structuring a social drama.

The case is, though, a drama, particularly in the root meaning of the term as doings and deeds. It has, to use a phrase suggested by an anthropologist whose own work is sternly structuralist rather than dramatistic, "affecting depictions."[8] As a drama, in both ritual and social action, it calls into play the forces and tensions which such literary theorists as Kenneth Burke have analyzed: victimage, victims, and plots of sacrifice.[9] Yet if this type of theory is invoked by the use of the term drama, modifications are necessary. This understanding of drama, with its analogues in archaic mythopoetic patterns, is not in our case merely aesthetic in either a tragic or comic mode. The theology of the Primitive Baptists, which we have persisted in calling Calvinist in spite of their own disclaimers, while based on the victimage of Christ, has a reduced or self-limiting dramatic intensity for the best possible reason in their terms: namely, the dramatic events of Christ's life were, of course, already predestined before the foundation of the world. What we have called the a priori character of this Primitive Baptist-Calvinist doctrine exerts a prosaic effect on the narrative of Christ's life as recounted in the New Testament. The doctrine of predestination limits the dramatic representation of the events of redemption. So the systematic doctrine of Calvinism overlays dramatic representation of the narrative of salvation, placing an anxious question mark over its outcome for every human career. The subdued character of Primitive Baptist ritual and customs may indicate the displacement of final meanings from the mimetic actions of ritual and church life to the mysterious priority of divine election. Allegorical resonances may be at play in this qualified drama, but no imitation of the life and death and resurrection of Christ is discernible, either in the worship rituals or in counsels for living daily in the world.

Comparison with other non-Calvinist groups, such as the Arminian ones, does suggest that the demeanor, procedures, and the way Primitive Baptists enact their dramas—and suppress their climatic potential—translate Calvinism in practice, even when they do not make explicit at every turn the relevant points of doctrine. This difference has led us frequently to qualify heavily the usual assumptions and images inscribed in the term dramatic.

Whatever the theoretical or theological allusions that the Primitive Baptists may evoke in us or in themselves, our firmest sense of them is, in the end, as characters, neither as a Jamesian or a Weberian type. Their reality ethnographically for us is as Evans, Nichols, Yates, and Reed. But these characters are driven, they would insist, by a grand design—for them, foreordained before the foundation of the world; for us, if not that, at least nurtured in rich media of social forces, theological debate, shared affections, and dramatic exigencies that together constitute a Primitive Baptist way of living life and making history.

1983 Minutes of the Mountain District Primitive Baptist Association

Minutes of the One Hundred and Eighty-Fifth Annual Session of the Mountain District Primitive Baptist Association held with Peach Bottom Church, Independence, Virginia

Beginning on Friday before the first Sunday in September, 1983

The next session will convene with Galax Church, Galax, Virginia, located at the intersection of Painter and McArthur Streets, beginning on Friday before the first Sunday in September, 1984, at 10:30 a.m.

Officers

Elder Walter Evans . . . . Moderator
Elder [Joseph Reed] . . . . Asst. Moderator
Roy L. Truitt . . . . Clerk
Leslie T. Nichols . . . . Asst. Clerk

Proceedings of the Mountain District Primitive Baptist Association

The association met with Peach Bottom Church for its one hundred eighty-fifth annual session.

After singing by the congregation and prayer by Elder Manning Temples from Original Upper Canoochee Association, the introductory sermon was preached by Elder Walter Evans, text: Colossians 1:12,13, "Translation."

After intermission of one hour during which lunch was served, the messengers assembled in the meeting house to attend to the business of the association. We were called to order with prayer by Elder George McNure from Original Upper Canoochee Association.

1. Called for, received, and read letters from the churches.
2. Called for petitionary letters from other churches for the same faith and order desiring admission to the association. None came.
3. Organized by move, second, and approval to elect Elder Walter Evans, moderator; Elder [Joseph Reed], assistant moderator; Roy L. Truitt, clerk; and Leslie T. Nichols, assistant clerk.
4. Called for visitors from sister associations and sister churches. The following came forward and were welcomed to our midst.

ORIGINAL BEAR CREEK ASSOCIATION of North Carolina: Elder Guy Parks and wife, and Elder Roy E. Speir.

UPPER CANOOCHEE ASSOCIATION of Georgia: Elder George McNure and Elder Manning Temples.

SENTER ASSOCIATION of North Carolina: Elders G. D. Roten, Steven P. Douglas, Billy Yates and wife, Brethren Norman Brown and wife, Willard Hartzog and wife, Sisters Lillian Richardson, Zell Walker, and Dorothy Brown.

NEW LIBERTY ASSOCIATION of West Virginia: Brother Finley Ratliff and wife.

MOUNT CARMEL CHURCH: Bel Air, Maryland: Brother James Dixon and wife and Brother Guthrie Caudell and wife.

CRAB CREEK CHURCH: Ennice, North Carolina: Brother Roy Carr and wife, Brother Reuben Easter and wife, and Sister Mabel Caudill.

CHESTNUT GROVE CHURCH; Lamsburg, Virginia: Elder Lester Faulkner and wife and Elder Bruce Thomas and wife.

NORTH VIEW CHURCH: Danbury, North Carolina: Elder Milton Gunter.

LANDMARK PRIMITIVE BAPTIST CHURCH: Pennsylvania: Brother Elzie Reynolds and wife.

PULASKI PRIMITIVE BAPTIST CHURCH: Pulaski, Virginia: Elder Jay Harris and wife, and Sister June H. Goins.

COMMUNITY PRIMITIVE BAPTIST CHURCH; Stuart, Virginia: Sister Virginia Hylton and husband.

CINCINNATI PRIMITIVE BAPTIST CHURCH: Cincinnati, Ohio: Licentiate Bob Brubaker and wife, and Sister Mae Head.

PINE GROVE CHURCH; Hillsville, Virginia: Elder Ray Rotenizer and wife, Elder Ronald G. Bowman, and Brother Leonard Myers.

CHILHOWIE PRIMITIVE BAPTIST CHURCH; Chilhowie, Virginia: Elder Leonard W. Davis, Elder Howard M. Davis, Jr., Brother Howard M. Davis, Sr., and wife, Brother Glenn Blevins, Sisters Margaret Hayden and Jessie L. Adams.

INDIAN CREEK PRIMITIVE BAPTIST CHURCH; Greenville, West Virginia: Elders Norvel P. Mann and wife, Paul Williams, Licentiate Thomas B. Mann, Brother Junior Lyle and wife, Brother Ferd Slusher and wife, Brother Estel Henley and wife, and Sister Wyatt Marshall.

5. Received minutes from the following associations: Mt. Zion, Senter, Original Bear Creek, Original Mates Creek, Union, Little Yadkin River, Ebenezer, and Sand Lick District.

6. By move, second, and approval, the moderator will make all temporary committee appointments for this session.

   (A) Preaching Committee: Brethren John Nichols, Jack Nichols, and Arol Choate, and the messengers from Peach Bottom Church: Brethren Paris Hackler, Green Ward, Arvel Newberry, and Thomas Farmer, Alternate.

   (B) Finance Committee: Brethren Arthur Gambill, David Fields, and Cary Edwards.

   (C) Committee to distribute corresponding minutes: Brethren H. Bayne Caudill and Everette Cox.

   (D) Committee on arrangements: Brethren F. G. Dillard, Carl Williams, Raymond Nichols, R. L. Gambill, and Johnny Truitt. By motion, second, and approval, the moderator and clerk to serve on this committee: Elders Walter Evans, [Joseph Reed]; Brethren Roy Truitt, and Leslie Nichols.

7. By motion second, and approval, the association adjourned until Saturday morning at 10:00 a.m. Closed with prayer by Elder [Joseph Reed] from Mountain District Association.

Saturday, September 3, 1983

After singing by the congregation, the association was opened with prayer by Elder Ronald Bowman from Pine Grove Church.

1. Called roll of messengers and marked off those that were absent.
2. Called for visitors, those that came forward were added to Friday's list.
3. Called for committee on arrangements to report. They recommend the following:

   (A) To have 800 copies of these minutes printed and distributed as usual.

   (B) Next session of the association to convene with Galax Primitive Baptist Church located in Galax, Virginia, at the intersection of Painter and McArthur Streets.

   (C) To have a memoriam of our deceased members printed in the minutes. Also, obituaries and pictures that are requested by the churches.

   (D) The members of the Building Committee: Brethren Garfield Dillard, Raymond Nichols, John Nichols, Green Ward, C. S. McBride, Arol Choate, Everett Cox, Arthur Gambill, Franklin Wood, and Thomas Farmer are to poll their individual churches to find how much money and materials they would be willing to give toward the building and report at the next association.

   By motion, second, and approval, the recommendations of the committee on arrangements were adopted.

4. Committee on finance gave the following report and were discharged when their duties were completed.

Received from the churches $567.00
For printing of minutes 425.00
Gave to moderator. 65.00
Gave to assistant moderator 25.00
Gave to Peach Bottom Church for expense of school 50.00
Balance in treasury from last year. 351.51
Balance in treasury to carry over for next year 353.51
Received from brethren, sisters, and friends which was distributed to visiting elders. $555.00

5. Committee to distribute corresponding minutes made their report and were discharged.
6. Committee on preaching made their report and were discharged when their duties were completed.

Friday Afternoon:
  Elder Manning Temples, text: 1 Peter 2:5
  Elder Ray Rotenizer dismissed with prayer

Friday Night:
  Elder Walter Evans opened with prayer
  Elder George McNure, text: 1 John 4:10
  Elder Manning Temples. text: Psalms 121
  Elder [Joseph Reed] closed with prayer

Saturday Morning:
  Elder Ronald Bowman opened with prayer
  Elder George McNure, text: Proverbs 16:25
  Elder Manning Temples, text: Song of Solomon 3:9,10

Saturday Afternoon:
  Elder Lester Faulkner opened with prayer
  Elder Norvel Mann, 2 Corinthians 11:28,29
  Licentiate Bob Brubaker, text: Ruth 2:15
  Elder Guy Parks, text: Matthew 7:7
  Elder H. B. Thomas dismissed with prayer

Saturday Night:
  Elder Leslie Faulkner opened with prayer
  Elder James McLamb, text: "Kingdom of Heaven on Earth"
  Elder Samuel Whittington, text: Genesis 2:21–24
  Elder H. B. Thomas dismissed with prayer

Sunday Morning:
Elder Franklin Oresta introduced with prayer
Elder H. B. Thomas, text: 2 Thessalonians
Elder Billy Yates, text: James 1:15
Elder Jess Higgins, text: Zechariah 13:6
Elder Walter Evans dismissed with prayer

7. By motion, second, and approval, the clerk was appointed as treasurer and to superintend the printing of these minutes.
8. Resolved that we return thanks first to God, then to brethren, sisters, and friends for their hospitality and kindness during this association.
9. By motion, second, and approval, the association voted to give thanks first to God and second to Brother Raymond Nichols for his seventeen years of faithful service as clerk of the Mountain District Association.
10. These minutes were read and approved.
11. By motion, second, and approval, the association ajourned to the time and place of the next meeting. Closed with prayer by [Elder Joseph Reed].

Elder Walter Evans, Moderator
Elder [Joseph Reed], Assistant Moderator
Roy L. Truitt, Clerk
Leslie T. Nichols, Assistant Clerk

Thus closed the one hundred and eight-fifth session of the Mountain District Association in peace and fellowship. Each minister who filled the stand was wonderfully blessed to preach the gospel in its purity and love to a large congregation.

Roy L. Truitt, Clerk.

Visiting Elders
Elder Roy E. Speir: 1506 Huntingdon Rd., Kannapolis, NC 28081
Phone: (704) 938–3424
Elder Ray Rotenizer: Rt. 4, Box 53, Hillsville, VA 24343
Phone: (703) 728–2577
Elder H. Bruce Thomas: 508 South Main St., Galax, VA 24343
Phone: (703) 236–3696
Elder Billy Yates: Rt. 1, Sparta, NC 28675
Phone: (919) 372–5311
Elder Jay Harris: P. O. Box 288, Pulaski, VA 24301
Phone: (703) 980–3891
Elder George McNure: P. O. Box 762, Swainsboro, GA 30401
Phone: (912) 237–5487
Elder Manning Temples: P. O. Box 103, Vidalia, GA 30474
Phone: (912) 537–2180
Elder Paul Williams: 230 Burnett Street, Richlands, VA 24641
Phone: (703) 964–4938

Elder Howard M. Davis, Jr.: Rt. 1, Box 177, Glade Spring, VA 24340
Phone: (703) 429–5757
Elder Leonard W. Davis: 329 Piney Avenue, Piney Flats, TN 37686
Phone: (615) 538–7645
Elder Milton Gunter: Rt. 2, Box 193 AA, Stoneville, NC 27048
Phone: (919) 871–2680
Elder Steven P. Douglas: Rt. 1, Box 466, Crumpler, NC 28617
Phone: (919) 982–2958
Elder Dewey Roten: Rt. 2, Box 65, Fleetwood, NC 28626
Phone: (919) 877–4834
Elder Norvel P. Mann: Rt. 1, Box 39, Lindside, WV 24951
Phone: (304) 832–6341
Elder Guy Parks: Rt. 2, Box 213, Albemarle, NC 28001
Phone: (704) 982–9371
Elder Lester Faulkner: Rt. 9, Box 212, Mt. Airy, NC 27030
Phone: (919) 789–3405
Elder Ronald G. Bowman: Rt. 1, Box 214-H, Austinville, VA 24312
Phone: (703) 728–7089
Elder Samuel Whittington: Rt. 2, Box 263 C, Millers Creek, NC 28651
Phone: (919) 667–4935
Licentiate Thomas B. Mann: Rt. 1, Box 39, Lindside, WV 24951
Phone: (304) 832–6341
Licentiate Bob Brubaker: 1410 Springfield Park #63D, Cincinnati, OH 45215
Phone: (513) 821–2592
Elder Franklin Oresta: Rt. 1, Box 14, Bluefield, WV 24701
Phone: (304) 325–7207
Elder Jess B. Higgins: Rt. 6, Box 45, Galax, VA 24333
Phone: (703) 236–5574
Elder James McLamb: Rt. 4, Box 108, Shallotte, NC 28459
Phone: (919) 287–3746

Home Ministers
Elder Walter Evans: Rt. 1, Box 348, Sparta, NC 28675
Phone: (919) 372–5559
Elder Elmer Sparks: Sparta, NC 28675
Phone: (919) 372–8136

Communion Times

Antioch	June, 4th Saturday
Little River	June, 3rd Saturday
Union	July, 1st Saturday
Peach Bottom	July, 2nd Saturday
Saddle Creek	July, 4th Saturday
Rock Creek	August, 1st Saturday
Galax	August, 2nd Sunday

Elk Creek .... August, 2nd Saturday
Cross Roads .... August, 3rd Saturday
(And the Sunday following in all the churches.)

Memoriam

It is with sadness and grief that we pause in the solemn tribute to our dear members who have passed away since our last association. Even though our hearts are grieved now, we rejoice in the glorious hope that there is an eternal city not made with hands beyond this life, where we will ever be with the Lord, where there will be no sadness and farewells.

Peach Bottom: Margie E. Owens, James K. Cassell, Abe Anders, Dewey Wingate, Clarence Ward,
Galax: Laura Ethel Harmon, Virginia Ruth Pope, Alice Hampton Paisley,
Elk Creek: Owen Clinton Busin
Cross Roads: Cora Boyer
Little River: Lon Mac Reeves

Margie E. Owens
Margie E. Owens was born on April 15, 1890, in Allegheny County, North Carolina, and passed from this life on April 23, 1983, in Twin County Community Hospital, Galax, Virginia. She was the widow of William B. Owens and the daughter of Bart and Ester Andrews Stedham.

Margie, was a very saintly person, possessing many virtues. She was a member for many years of Peach Bottom Primitive Baptist Church.

Her funeral service was conducted on April 25, 1983, at Reins-Sturdivant Chapel, Independence, Virginia, by Elder Robert Norman, Elder Olin Shupe, and Elder Jess B. Higgins, with interment in the Independence Cemetery.

Survivors are as follows; three sons, Thomas F. Owens and Bart Owens of Independence, Virginia, and Dan L. Owens of Ocala, Florida; also seven grandchildren and six great-grandchildren.

Abe Anders
Brother Abe Anders was born on January 12, 1905, and departed this life on August 6, 1983, making his stay on earth seventy-eight years and almost seven months.

Abe was a faithful member of Peach Bottom Primitive Baptist Church and served as deacon for many years. He loved the church with all of his heart, always desiring the best for the church. It certainly was a privilege to know Brother Abe Anders. He and his wife, Ossie, had many friends as evidenced by the great congregation at his funeral service.

Survivors are as follows: His wife, Ossie Murray Anders; one son: Bob Anders, one daughter: Mrs. Pauline Edwards; one brother: John Anders; and three sisters: Mrs. Ethel Carrico, Mrs. Alberta Edwards, and Mrs. Reba Jennings.

His funeral service was held on August 8, 1983, at Peach Bottom Primitive Baptist Church by C. H. McKnight and Elder Jess B. Higgins. His body was laid to rest in Pleasant Grove Cemetery, near Independence, Virginia, to await the glorious resurrection day.

[The obituaries of the following members of the Mountain District Primitive Baptist Association have been omitted here: Cora Boyer, Owen Clinton Busic, James K. Cassell, Laura Ethel Harmon, Lon Mac Reeves, Alice Hampton Paisley, Virginia Ruth Pope, Clarence Ward, Dewey Wingate.]

Rules of Decorum

1. The Association shall be opened and closed by prayer.
2. A Moderator and Clerk shall be chosen by the suffrage of the members present.
3. Only one person shall speak at a time, who shall arise from his seat and address the moderator when he is about to make his speech.
4. The person thus speaking shall not be interrupted in his speech by any except the Moderator till he is done speaking.
5. He shall strictly adhere to the subject, and in no wise reflect on the person who spoke before, so as to make remarks on his slips, failings, or imperfections; but shall fairly state the matter as nearly as he can so as to convey his light or ideas.
6. No person shall abruptly break off or absent himself from the Association without liberty obtained from it.
7. No person shall rise and speak more than three times on one subject without liberty obtained from the Association.
8. No member of the Association shall have liberty of laughing during the sitting of the same, nor whispering in the time of public speech.
9. No member of the Association shall address another in any appellation but the title of Brother.
10. The Moderator shall not interrupt any member in his speech or prohibit him from speaking till he gives his light on the subject, except he break the rules of this Decorum.
11. The names of the several members of the Association shall be enrolled by the Clerk and called over as often as the Association requires.
12. The Moderator shall be entitled to the same privilege of speech as any other member, provided the chair be filled, and he shall not vote unless the Association be equally divided.
13. That any member who shall willfully and knowingly break these rules shall be reproved by the Association as they think proper.

Constitution

1. The Association shall be composed of members chosen by the different churches in our union, and duly sent to represent them in the Association who shall be members whom they judge best qualified

for that purpose, and producing letters from their respective churches, certifying their appointment, shall be entitled to a seat.

2. In the letters from the different churches there shall be expressed their number in full fellowship, those baptized, received by letter, dismissed, excommunicated and dead since the last Association.

3. The members thus chosen and convened shall have no power to lord it over God's heritage, nor shall they have any ecclesiastical power over the churches, nor shall they infringe on any of the internal rights of any church into the union.

4. The Association, when convened, shall be governed by a proper Decorum.

5. The Association shall have a Moderator and Clerk who shall be chosen by the suffrage of the members present. In the absence of the Moderator and Assistant Moderator, the Clerk shall stand as Moderator until a new Moderator can be elected.

6. Any church may be admitted into this union, who shall petition by letter and messengers, and upon examination, if found orthodox and orderly, shall be received by the Association, and manifested by the Moderator giving the messengers the right hand of fellowship.

7. Every church in the union shall be entitled to representation in the Association.

8. Every query presented by any member of the Association shall be once read, and before it be debated the Moderator shall put it to vote, and, if there be a majority for its being debated, it shall be taken into consideration and be deliberated; but, if there by a majority against it, it shall be withdrawn.

9. Every motion made and seconded shall come under the consideration of the Association, except it be withdrawn by the member who made it.

10. The Association shall endeavor to furnish the churches with the minutes of the Association, the best method for effecting that purpose shall be at the discretion of the future associations.

11. We think it absolutely necessary that we should have an Associational fund for defraying the expenses of the same, for the raising and supporting of which we think it the duty of each church in the union to contribute voluntarily such sums as they think proper, and send by the hands of their messengers to the Association, and the money thus contributed by the churches and received by the Association shall be deposited in the hands of a treasurer by the Association who shall be accountable to the Association for all money by him received and paid out according to the direction of the Association.

12. There shall be an Association Book kept, wherein the proceedings of every Association shall be regularly recorded by a secretary appointed by the Association, who may receive a compensation yearly for his trouble.

13. The minutes of the Association shall be read and corrected, if need be, and signed by the Moderator and Clerk before the Association arises.
14. Amendments to this plan or form of government may be made at any time by a majority of the union, when they deem it necessary.
15. The Association shall have power (1) To provide for the general union of the churches; (2) To endeavor to preserve inviolably a chain of communion among the churches: (3) To give the churches all necessary advice in matters of difficulty; (4) To inquire into the cause why churches fail to represent themselves at any time in the Association; (5) To appropriate the means contributed by the churches for an Associational Fund to any purpose they may think proper; (6) To withdraw from any church in the union which shall violate the rules of this decorum or deviate from the orthodox principles of our religion; (7) To admit any of the distant brethren in the ministry who may be present, to assist in the transaction of business during their setting; (8) To adjourn themselves to any future time and place they may think most convenient to the churches in the union.

Articles of Faith

1. We believe in only true and living God, and that there are three persons in the Godhead, the Father, the Son, and the Holy Ghost.
2. We believe that the scriptures of the Old and New Testament, as translated in 1611 into the King James Version of the Holy Bible, is the written word of God and the only rule of faith and practice.
3. We believe in the doctrine of eternal and particular election.
4. We believe in the doctrine of original sin.
5. We believe in man's impotency to recover himself from the fallen state he is in by nature of his own free will and ability.
6. We believe that sinners are justified in the sight of God only by the imputed righteousness of Jesus Christ.
7. We believe that God's elect are called, converted, regenerated and sanctified by the Holy Spirit.
8. We believe the saints are preserved in Jesus Christ and called and shall never fall finally away.
9. We believe that baptism and the Lord's Supper are ordinances of Jesus Christ, and that true believers are the only subjects of these ordinances, and that the true mode of baptism is by immersion.
10. We believe in the resurrection of the dead, both of the just and the unjust, and a general judgment and the punishment of the wicked will be everlasting and the joys of the righteous will be eternal.
11. We believe that no minister has the right to administer the ordinances only such as are regularly called and come under the imposition of hands by the presbytery, and in fellowship with a church of our faith and order.

Mailing Addresses for Minutes
Cary E. Edwards, Rt. 4, Sparta, NC 28675 40
H. Bayne Caudill, Rt. 4, Box 95, Sparta, NC 28675 40
Roy L. Truitt, 102 Gentry St., Galax, VA 24333 75
Green Ward, Rt. #3, Independence, VA 24348 40
Blake Roberts, 117 Branch St., Galax, VA 24333 70
Paige Wagoner, Sparta, NC 28675............................... 75
Rose Jenkins, Independence, VA 24348.......................... 30
Arthur Gambill, Sparta, NC 28675 60
C. S. McBride, Independence, VA 24348.......................... 30
Blanche Wyatt, Rt. 1, Piney Creek, NC 28663 10

Distribution of Minutes to Sister Associations
Sandlick District: Robert Jackson, Rowe, VA 24646................ 20
The Christian Baptist Library, P. O. Box 68, Atwood, TN 38220....... 5
Senters Earl W. Severt, 4798 N. Cherry St.,
    Winston-Salem, NC 27105 20
Mount Zion: Tommy Joe Pack, 402 Cedar Ave., Hinton, WV 25951 ... 20
Union: Tommy Adams, Box 48, Eolia, KY 40826................... 10
Mates Creek: Stearl Hatfield, McCarr, KY 42544 20
Ebenezer: Aubrey E. Utz, Madison, VA 22727 10
Ketocton: L. E. Farley, Rt. 3, Box 168, Williamsport, MD 21795...... 10
Little Yadkin River: Curtis Harbour, Rt. 2, Dobson, NC 27017 20
W. J. Berry, Rt. 2, Elon College, NC 27244...................... 5
American Baptist Historical Society: 1106 South Goodman St.,
    Rochester, NY 14620 3
Original Little River: c/o Elder Worth Stephenson,
    Rt. 1, Box 385-A, Wendell, NC 27591 10
A. B. Hall, Rt. 3, Box 112, Arab, AL 35016...................... 5
Original Bear Creek: Kenneth R. Austin, Rt. 2, Box 808,
    Monroe, NC 28110 25
Daniel W. Patterson, The University of North, Carolina at Chapel Hill,
    228 Greenlaw Hall 066A, Chapel Hill, NC 27514................ 5

Church Directory
Union Church, Whitehead, North Carolina. Located four miles southwest
    of Sparta, NC on Route #18. White, frame building on south side of
    #18.
Galax Church, Galax, Virginia. Located at the intersection of Painter and
    McArthur Streets.
Saddle Creek Church, Independence, Virginia. Located four miles west of
    Independence on Route #58. White, frame building on south side of
    #58.
Cross Roads Church, Baywood, Virginia. Located seven miles west of
    Galax, Virginia. Turn off Route #58 (five miles west of Galax) onto

Route #639 for .3 mile. Turn right on Route #626, and church is just beyond Baywood Elementary School.

Little River Church, Sparta, North Carolina. Located on Memorial Park Drive, one block east of Route #21.

Rock Creek Church, Independence, Virginia. Located two miles east of Independence. Turn off Route #58 onto Route #274 for one mile. Turn left onto Route #685 for one mile and church is on the right.

Peach Bottom Church, Independence, Virginia. Located one mile north of Independence at intersection of Route #21 and 654.

Antioch Church, Stratford, North Carolina. Located six miles southwest of Sparta, NC. Turn off Route #221 onto Route 1167 (Antioch Church Road), go two miles, turn left on Route 1163. Just .4 mile to brick church on left of road.

Elk Creek Church, Sparta, North Carolina. Located five miles west of Sparta. From Route #21 at Twin Oaks, North Carolina, take 221 south, turn right on Route #93, just two miles to church on right of road.

Statistical Table 1983

Churches and Pastors	Clerks	Messengers	Received by Baptism	Received by Letter	Received by Relation	Rest to Fellowship	Dismissed by Letter	Excluded	Deceased	Ordained Elders	Licentiates	Sunday of Meeting	Month of Communion	Total No. in Fellowship	Contributions
Galax Elder Jess Higgins	Blake Roberts Galax, VA	John Nichols, David Fields, Marvin Smythers, & Clifford Roberts	1						3			2	August	40	$70.00
Little River Elder Walter Evans	Paige Wagoner Sparta, NC	Elder Walter Evans, Garfield Dillard, Jack Nichols, & Paige Wagoner								1		3	June	55	$117.00
Saddle Creek Elder Elmer Sparks	Rose W. Jenkins Independence, VA	Rose Jenkins										4	July	11	$20.00
Elk Creek Elder [Joseph Reed]	Authur Gambill Sparta, NC	Authur Gambill, J. R. Gambill, Dean Halsey, & Blanche Halsey							1			2	August	36	$50.00
Rock Creek Elder Bruce Thomas	C. S. McBride Independence, VA	Elder [Joseph Reed], C. S. McBride, & Paul Hash								1		1	August	7	$45.00
Union Elder Walter Evans	H. Bayne Caudill Sparta, NC	H. Bayne Caudill & Everett Cox										1	July	56	$35.00
Cross Roads Elder [Joseph Reed]	Roy L. Truitt Galax, VA	Raymond Nichols, Roy Truitt, Leslie Nichols, & Johnny Truitt	6					2	1	1		1 & 3	August	44	$125.00
Antioch Elder Walter Evans	Cary E. Edwards Sparta, NC	Cary E. Edwards, Arol Choate, Carl Williams, & Troy Irvin	7			1						4	June	34	$85.00
Peach Bottom Elder Billy Yates	Green Ward Independence, VA	Paris Hackler, Green Ward, Arvel Newberry, & Thomas Farmer					1		5			2	July	31	$50.00

Excerpts from the London Meeting of 1689

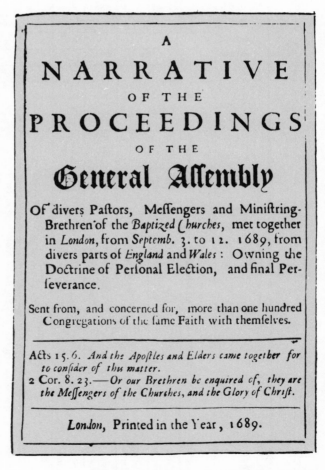

A

NARRATIVE

OF THE

PROCEEDINGS

OF THE

General Assembly

Of divers Pastors, Messengers and Ministring-
Brethren of the *Baptized Churches*, met together
in *London*, from *Septemb.* 3. to 12. 1689, from
divers parts of *England* and *Wales* : Owning the
Doctrine of Personal Election, and final Perseverance.

Sent from, and concerned for, more than one hundred
Congregations of the same Faith with themselves.

Acts 15. 6. *And the Apostles and Elders came together for
to consider of this matter.*
2 Cor. 8. 23.——*Or our Brethren be enquired of, they are
the Messengers of the Churches, and the Glory of Christ.*

London, Printed in the Year, 1689.

Narrative of the London Meeting of 1689.

A General Epistle to the Churches

And now, Brethren, in the first place, with no little Joy we declare unto you how good and gracious the Lord hath been to us, in uniting our Hearts together in the Spirit of Love, and sweet Concord, in our Debates, Consultations, and Resolves, which are sent unto you, there being scarcely one Brother who dissented from the Assembly in the Sentiments of his Mind, in any one thing we have proposed to your serious Considerations, either in respect of the cause of our Witherings, nor what we have fixt on as a means of Recovery to a better state, if the Lord will.

And therefore, in the second place, be it known unto you that we all see great cause to rejoice and bless God, that after so dismal an Hour of Sorrow and Persecution, in which the Enemy doubtless designed to break our Church to pieces, not only us, but to make the whole *Sion* of God desolate, even so as she might become as a plowed Field, the Lord was pleased to give such Strength and Power in the time of need to bear up your Souls in your Testimony for Jesus Christ, that your Spirits did not faint under your Burdens in the time of your Adversity; so that we hope we may say in the Words of the Church of old, *Though all this is come upon us, yet we have not forgotten thee, neither have we dealt falsly in thy Covenant. Our Heart is not turned back, neither have our Steps declined from thy way. Though thou hast fore broken us in the place of Dragons, and covered us with the shadow of Death*, Psal. 44.17,18,19. Yet nevertheless we fear Christ may say, *I have somewhat against you, because you have left your first Love*, as he once charged the Church of *Ephesus*, and may possibly most Churches in *England*; it is therefore good *to consider from whence we are fallen, and repent, and do our first works*, Rev. 2.5.

We are persuaded one chief cause of our decay is for want of holy Zeal for God, and the House of our God; few amongst us living up (we fear) to what they profess of God, nor answering the terms of that sacred Covenant they have made with him; the Power of Godliness being greatly decayed, and but little more than the Form thereof remaining amongst us. The Thoughts of which are enough to melt our Spirits, and break our Hearts to pieces, considering those most amazing Providences of the ever blessed God under which we have been, and more especially now are exercised, and the many signal and most endearing Obligations he is pleased to lay us under. The Spirit of this World we clearly discern is got too too much into the Hearts of most Christians and Members of our Churches, all seeking their own, and none, or very few, the things of Jesus Christ; if therefore in this there be no Reformation, the whole Interest of the blessed Lord Jesus will still sink in our Hands, and our Churches left to languish, whilst the Hands of poor Ministers become as weak as Water, and Sorrow and Grief seize upon their Spirits.

Thirdly, We cannot but bewail that great Evil, and neglect of Duty in many Churches concerning the Ministry.

1. In that some though they have Brethren competently qualified for the Office of Pastors and Deacons, yet omit that sacred Ordinance of Ordination, whereby they are rendered uncapable of preaching and administring the Ordinances of the Gospel, so regularly, and with that Authority which otherwise they might do. Those who have failed herein, we desire would in the fear of God lay it to Heart, and reform.

2. In neglecting to make that Gospel-Provision for their Maintenance, according to their Abilities, by which means many of them are so incumbred with Worldly Affairs, that they are not able to perform the Duties of their holy Calling, in preaching the Gospel, and watching over their respective Flocks.

Fourthly, We find cause to mourn that the Lord's Day is no more religiously and carefully observed, both in a constant attendance on the Word of God in that Church to whom Members do belong, and when the publick Worship is over, by a waiting on the Lord in Family-Duties, and private Devotion.

But because we have sent unto you the whole Result of this great Assembly particularly, we shall forbear to enlarge further upon these Causes of our Witherings and Decays.

One Thing you will find we have had before us, and come to a Resolve about, which we are perswaded will prove an exceeding great Blessing and Advantage to the Interest of Jesus Christ in our Hands; and if the Lord enlarge all our Hearts, give a revival to the sinking Spirits of the Mourners in *Sion*, and to languishing Churches too, which is, that of a general or Publick Stock, or Fund of Mony to be raised forthwith. First, By a Free-Will Offering to the Lord: And, secondly, by a Subscription, every one declaring what he is willing to give, Weekly, Monthly, or Quarterly, to it.

And now, Brethren, we must say, the Lord is about to try you in another way than ever you have been tried to this Day, because, till now, no such Thing was settled amongst us, and so not propounded to you. It will be known now, whether you do love Jesus Christ, and his Blessed Interest, Gospel, and Church, or no; *i.e.* Whether you love him more than these, or more than Son or Daughter. O that you would at this time shew your Zeal for God, and let all Men see the World is not so in your Hearts, but that Jesus Christ hath much room there: 'Tis to be given towards God's Holy Temple, to build up his Spiritual House which hath a long time lain as waste. Remember how willingly the Lord's People offered upon this Account formerly; 'tis some great as well as good Thing the Lord, and we his poor and unworthy Servants and Ministers, do expect from you. God has wrought a great Work for us, O let us make some suitable return of Duty to him, and act like a People called, loved, and saved by him. Shall so much be spent needlessly on your own ceiled Houses, on costly Attire and Dresses, and delicious Diet, when God's House lies almost waste! We are therefore become humble Supplicants for our dear Master, and could entreat you on our bended Knees, with Tears in our Eyes, to pity *Sion*, if it might but move your Hearts to Christian Bounty and Zeal for Her and the Lord of Hosts. We fear God did let in the Enemy upon us to consume us and waste our Substance, because to this Day we have with-held it from him, when his Cause, Gospel, and Churches called for more than ever yet you parted with, and that a Blast has been upon our Trades and Estates for our remissness in this Matter. May we not say, *Ye looked for much, and lo it came to little; and when ye brought it home, the Lord did blow upon it*? Why, because, saith God, *mine House that is waste, and ye run every one to his own House*, Hag. 1.9. But if now we reform our Doings, and shew our zeal for Christ and his Gospel, and love to him, and act as becomes a willing People professing his Name, you will see you will be no losers by it: *For I will*, saith the Lord, *open the Windows of Heaven, and pour out a Blessing that there shall not be room enough to receive it*, Mal. 3.10. If the Worth of Souls, the Honour of God, the Good of the Church, the glorious Promulgation of the Gospel in the Nation, the Credit of your Profession, your own Peace, and that weight of Eternal Glory be upon your Spirits, we doubt not but you will give evidence of it at this Time; and so shall you *build the old waste Places, and raise up the Foundations of many Generations; and be the Repairers of the Breaches, and Restorers of Paths to dwell in*, Isa. 58.12.

We to these great and good Ends, have thought upon and appointed a Solemn Day to Fast and Mourn before the Lord, and to humble our selves, and seek his Face, that a Blessing may attend all that we have done, and you with us may yet further do for his Holy Name sake.

A General Fast appointed in all the Congregations on the 10th *of* October *next*, 1689. *with the Causes and Reasons thereof.*
The main and principal Evils to be bewailed and mourn'd over before the Lord on that Day, are as followeth.

First; Those many grievous Backslidings, Sins, and Provocations, not only of the whole Nation, but also of the Lord's own People, as considered in our publick and private Stations; particularly that great decay of first Love, Faith, and Zeal for the Ways and Worship of God; which hath been apparent, not only in our Churches, but also in private Families.

Secondly; That this Declension and Backsliding hath been, we fear, for a long series of time, and many fore Judgements God has brought upon the Nation; and a strange Death of late come upon the Lord's faithful Witnesses, besides divers painful Labourers in Christ's Vineyard called Home, and but few raised up in their stead; little success in the Ministry; storms of Persecution having been raised upon us, a new War commenc'd by the Beast, (through the Divine Permission of God, and Hand of his Justice) to a total overcoming to appearance the Witnesses of Christ in these Isles; besides his more immediate Strokes by Plague and Fire, *etc*. God blasting all Essays used for deliverance, so that we were almost without hope, therefore our Sins that provoked the Righteous and Just God to bring all these Evils upon us, we ought to bewail and mourn for before him. But withal not to forget his Infinite Goodness, who when he saw that our Power was gone, and that there was none shut up or left, that he should thus appear for our Help and Deliverance, in a way unexpected and unthought of by us.

Thirdly; The Things we should therefore in the next place pray and cry to the Lord for, is, that he would give us true, broken, and penitent Hearts for all our Iniquities, and the Sins of his People, and wash and cleanse away those great Pollutions with which we have been defiled; and also pour forth more of his Spirit upon us, and open the Mysteries of his Word, that we may understand whereabouts we are, in respect of the latter Time, and what he is a doing, and know our Work, and that a Blessing may attend all the Churches of his Saints in these Nations, and that greater Light may break forth, and the Glory of the Lord rise upon us, and that the Word may not any more be as a miscarrying Womb and dry Breasts, but that in every place Multitudes may be turned to the Lord, and that Love and sweet Concord may be found among all the Lord's People in these Nations, that the great Work begun therein so unexpectedly, may go on and be perfected, to the praise of his own Glory.

Likewise to put up earnest Cries and Supplications to the Lord for the lineal Seed of *Abraham*, the poor Jews, that they may be called, and both Jews and Gentiles made one Sheepfold, under that one Shepherd Jesus Christ.

These are some of those Things we have thought good to lay before you, and which we hope we shall be helped with you to spread before the Lord on that Day, with whatsoever else you or we may be help'd to consider of: hoping you will not forget your Pastors and Ministers in your Prayers, and what we have been enabled to come to a Resolve about, so that all may be succeeded with a glorious Blessing from the Almighty, that the present Churches, and those Saints who shall come after us, may have cause to praise his Holy Name: Which is the unfeigned Prayer and Desire of us, who subscribe our selves your Servants for Jesus sake.

Hanserd Knollys,
William Kiffin,
Andrew Gifford,
Robert Steed,
Thomas Vaux,
William Collins,
John Tomkins,
Toby Wil_es,
George Barrett_,
Benjamin Ketch,
Daniel Fi___,
John Carter,

Samuel Battall,
Isaac Lame,
Christopher Price,
Robert Keate,
Richard Tidmarsh,
James Webb,
John Harris,
Thomas Winnell,
James Hitt,
Hercules Collins,
Richard Sutton,
Robert Knight,

Leonard Harrison,
Edward Price,
William Phips,
William Facey,
John Ball,
William Hankins,
Samuel Ewer,
Paul Fruin.

In the Name and behalf of the whole Assembly.

[*Memorand.* 'Tis agreed to by us, that the next General Assembly be held at *London*, on that Day which is called *Whitson-Monday*, 1690.]

The NARRATIVE *of the Proceedings of the Elders and Messengers of the Baptized Congregations, in their* General Assembly, *met in* London on Septemb. 3, *to* 12, 1689.

Whereas we the Pastors and Elders of the several Churches, in and about *London*, did meet together, and seriously take into our consideration the particular States *of the Baptized Churches* among our selves; and after a long Persecution, finding the Churches generally under great Decays in the Power of Godliness, and Defects of Gifts for the Ministry; Also, fearing that the same Decays and Defects might be among the Churches of the same Faith and Profession throughout *England* and *Wales*, many of their Ministers being deceased, many having ended their Days in Prison, many scattered by Persecution to other Parts, far distant from the Churches to which they did belong. From a due sense of these Things did by their Letter, dated *July* 28. 1689, write to all the aforesaid Churches throughout *England* and *Wales*, to send their Messengers to a General Meeting at *London*, the 3d of the 7th month, 1689. And being met together, the first Day was spent in humbling our selves before the Lord, and to seek of him a right way to direct into the best Means and Method to repair our Breaches, and to recover our selves into our former Order, Beauty, and Glory. In prosecution thereof, upon the 4th day of the same Month, We, the Elders, ministring Brethren and Messengers of the Churches in and about *London*, and Elders, Ministring-Brethren & Messengers of the several Churches from several parts of *England* and *Wales* hereafter mentioned, being again come together, after first solemn seeking the Lord by Prayer, did conclude upon these following Preliminaries, and lay them down as the Foundation of this our Assembly, and Rules for our Proceedings; Wherein all the Messengers of the Churches aforesaid, in City and Country (as well for the Satisfaction of every particular Church, as also to prevent all Mistakes, Misapprehensions and Inconveniencies that might arise in time to come concerning this General Assembly) do solemnly, unanimously, profess and declare;

1. That we disclaim all manner of *Superiority, Superintendency* over the Churches; and that we have no *Authority* or *Power*, to prescribe or impose any thing upon the Faith or Practice of any of the Churches of Christ. Our whole Intendment, is to be helpers together of one another, by way of Counsel and Advice, in the right understanding of that perfect Rule which our Lord Jesus, the only Bishop of our Souls, hath already prescribed, and given to his Churches in his Word, and therefore do severally and jointly agree,

2. That in those things wherein one Church differs from another Church in their Principles or Practices, in point of Communion, that we cannot, shall not, impose upon any particular Church therein,

but leave every Church to their own liberty, to walk together as they have received from the Lord.

3. That if any particular Offence doth arise betwixt one Church and another, or betwixt one particular Person and another, no Offence shall be admitted to be debated among us, till the Rule Christ hath given (in that Matter) be first Answered, and the Consent of both Parties had, or sufficiently endeavoured.

4. That whatever is determined by us in any Case, shall not be binding to any one Church, till the Consent of that Church be first had, and they conclude the same among themselves.

5. That all things we offer by way of Counsel and Advice, be proved out of the Word of God, and the Scriptures annexed.

6. That the Breviats of this Meeting be transcribed, and sent to every particular Church with a Letter.

7. That the Messengers that come to this Meeting, be recommended by a Letter from the Church, and that none be admitted to speak in this Assembly, unless by general Consent.

The Letters from several Churches being read, the Meeting was dismissed till next day, and concluded in Prayer.

Septemb. 5, 1689.

After solemn seeking the Lord, all the Elders, Ministring-Brethren, and Messengers aforesaid, considered, debated, and concluded. That a publick Fund, or Stock was necessary: And came to a Resolve in these three Questions; 1. How to Raise it. 2. To what Uses it should be disposed. 3. How to Secure it.

Quest. 1. *How or by what Means this Publick Fund, or Stock, should be raised?* Resolved,

1. That it should be raised by a *Free-Will Offering*. That every Person should communicate (for the Uses hereafter mentioned) according to his Ability, and as the Lord shall make him willing, and enlarge his Heart; and that the Churches severally among themselves do order the Collection of it with all convenient speed, that the Ends proposed may be put into present practice.

2. That for the constant carrying it on, there be an annual Collection made in the several Churches, of a Half-penny, Penny, 2*d*, 3*d*, 4*d*, 6*d*, *per* week, more or less, as every Person shall be made willing, and that every Congregation do agree among themselves to collect it, either Weekly, Monthly, or Quarterly, according to their own convenience, and that Ministers be desired to shew a good Example herein. *Exod.* 35.4,5. 1 *Chron.* 29.14. *Mal.* 3.10. *Hag.* 1.9. 2 *Cor.* 8.11,12.

3. That every particular Church do appoint their Deacons, or any other faithful Brothers to collect, and to acquaint the Church with the Sum collected, and remit it Quarterly into the Hands of such Persons as are hereafter nominated and appointed to receive it at *Lon-*

don; the first quarterly Paiment to be made the 5*th* of *December* next.

4. That the Persons appointed to receive all the aforesaid Collections, be our Honoured and well-beloved Brethren, whose Names we have sent you in a printed Paper by it self, all living in and about *London*; and when any of these aforesaid Brethren die, then the major part of the Survivors of them, shall nominate and appoint another Brother in his stead, to be confirmed, or refused, at the next General Meeting of this Assembly. And that the said nine Brethren shall disburse it, from time to time, for the uses hereafter mentioned, according to the satisfaction they, or the major part of them, shall have from the Information and Testimony of any two Churches in this Assembly, or from the Testimony of any particular Association of Churches in the Country, or from the Satisfaction they shall have by any other means whatsoever.

Quest. 2. *To what Uses this Fund, or Publick Stock, shall be disposed?* Resolved,

1. To communicate thereof to those Churches that are not able to maintain their own Ministry; and that their Ministers may be encouraged wholly to devote themselves to the great Work of Preaching the Gospel.

2. To send Ministers that are ordained (or at least solemnly called) to preach, both in City and Country, where the Gospel hath, or hath not yet been preached, and to visit the Churches; and these to be chosen out of the Churches in *London*, or in the Country; which Ministers are to be approved of, and sent forth by two Churches at the least, but more if it may be.

3. To assist those Members that shall be found in any of the aforesaid Churches, that are disposed for Study, have an inviting Gift, and are found in Fundamentals, in attaining to the knowledg and understanding of the Languages, Latin, Greek, and Hebrew. These Members to be represented to the Nine Brethren in *London*, by any two of the Churches that belong to this Assembly.

Resolved, The Mony collected, be returned, as is expressed in a printed Paper before mentioned, to one of the Nine Brethren mentioned in the said Paper.

Resolved and concluded, That every quarter of a Year, an Account shall be taken by those Nine Brethren in *London*, nominated in the printed Paper aforesaid, of all the Receipts and Disbursements belonging to this aforesaid Fund, or Stock: With an Account signed by them, or the major part of them, shall be sent and transmitted to one Church in every County, and from that Church to be communicated to all the rest of the Churches aforesaid within the same County, with all convenient speed. The first Account to be made and sent the 5*th* of *January* next.

Resolved, That what Charges soever the said Nine Brethren are at in the Service of this Assembly, shall be discharged out of the aforesaid Stock.

The Questions Proposed from the several Churches, Debated, and Resolved.

Quest. *Whether it be not expedient for Churches that live near together, and consist of small numbers, and are not able to maintain their own Ministry, to join together for the better and more comfortable support of their Ministry, and better Edification one of another?*

Answ. Concluded in the Affirmative.

Q. *Whether it is not the Duty of every Church of Christ to maintain such Ministers as are set apart by them, by allowing them a comfortable Maintenance according to their Ability?*

A. Concluded in the Affirmative, 1 *Cor.* 9.9,10,11,12,13,14. *Gal* 6.6.

Q. *Whether every Church ought not endeavour not only to provide themselves of an able Ministry for the preaching of the Word, but also to set apart to Office, and in a solemn manner ordain such as are duly qualified for the same?*

A. Concluded in the Affirmative. *Act.* 14.23. *Tit.* 1.5.

Q. *Whether it is not the liberty of Baptized Believers to hear any sober and pious Men of the Independent and Presbyterian Persuasion, when they have no opportunity to attend upon the preaching of the Word in their own Assembly, or have no other to preach unto them?*

A. Concluded in the Affirmative, *Act.* 18.24,25,26.

Q. *Whether the continuing of Gifted-Brethren many Years upon trial for Eldership, or any Person for the Office of a Deacon, without ordaining them, altho qualified for the same, be not omission of an Ordinance of God?*

A. Concluded in the Affirmative.

Q. *What is the Duty of Church Members when they are disposed to marry, with respect to their Choice?*

A. To observe the Apostle's Rule, to marry only in the Lord, 1 *Cor.* 7.39.

Q. *Whether, when the Church have agreed upon the keeping of one day weekly, or monthly, (besides the first day of the Week) to worship God, and perform the necessary Services of the Church, they may not charge such Persons with evil that neglect such Meetings, and lay them under Reproof, unless such Members can shew good cause for such their Absence?*

A. Concluded in the Affirmative, *Heb.* 10.25.

Q. *What is to be done with those Persons that will not communicate to the necessary Expenses of the Church whereof they are Members, according to their Ability?*

A. Resolved, That upon clear Proof, the Person so offending, as aforesaid, be duly admonished; and if no Reformation, the Church is to withdraw from them, *Eph.* 5.3. *Mat.* 25.42. 1 *Joh.* 3.17.

Q. *What is to be done with those Persons that withdraw themselves from the Fellowship of that particular Church whereof they are Members, and join themselves to the Communion of the National Church?*

A. To use all due means to reclaim them by Instruction and Admonition;

and if not thereby reclaimed, to reject them. *Mat.* 18.17. *Luk.* 9.63. *Heb.* 10.38. *Jude* 19.

Resolved, That the like method be taken with those that wholly forsake the Fellowship of the Congregation to which they have solemnly given up themselves.

Q. Whether believers were not actually reconciled to God, actually justified and adopted when Christ died?

A. That the Reconciliation, Justification, and Adoption of Believers are infallibly secured by the gracious purpose of God, and merit of Jesus Christ. Yet none can be said to be actually reconciled, justified, or adopted, until they are really implanted into Jesus Christ by Faith; and so by virtue of this their Union with him, have these Fundamental Benefits actually conveyed unto them. And this we conceive is fully evidenced, because the Scripture attributes all these Benefits to Faith, as the instrumental cause of them. *Rom.* 3.25. *Chap.* 5.11. *Chap.* 5.1. *Gal.* 3.26. And gives such Representation of the state of the Elect before Faith as is altogether inconsistent with an actual Right in them, *Eph.* 2.1,2,3,-12.

Q. Whether it be not necessary for the Elders, Ministring-Brethren, and Messengers of the Churches, to take into their serious consideration those Excesses that are found among their Members, Men and Women, with respect to their Apparel?

A. In the Affirmative. That it is a shame for Men to wear long Hair, or long Perewigs, and especially Ministers, 1 *Cor.* 11.14. or strange Apparel, *Zeph.* 1.8. That the Lord reproves the Daughters of *Sion*, for the Bravery, Haughtiness, and Pride of their Attire, walking with stretched-out Necks, wanton Eyes, mincing as they go, *Isa.* 3.16. As if they affected Tallness, as one observes upon their stretched-out Necks, tho some in these Times seem, by their high Dresses, to out do them in that respect. The Apostle *Paul* exhorts, in 1 Tim. 2.9,10. *Women adorn themselves in modest Apparel, with Shamefac'dness and Sobriety: not with Broidered Hair or Gold, or Pearls, or costly Array; but with good Works as becomes Women professing Godliness.* And 1 Pet. 3.3,4,5. *Whose adorning let it not be the outward adorning, of plaiting the Hair, of wearing of Gold, or of putting on of Apparel: but the Ornament of a meek and quiet Spirit, which is in the sight of God of great price. For after this* (fashion) *manner, the holy Women who trusted in God adorned themselves.* And therefore we cannot but bewail it with much Sorrow and Grief of Spirit, That those Brethren and Sisters who have solemnly professed to deny themselves, *Mat.* 16.24. And who are by Profession obliged in Duty not to conform to this World, *Rom.* 12.2. should so much conform to the Fashions of this World, and not reform themselves in those Inclinations that their Natures addicted them to in days of Ignorance, 1 *Pet.* 1.14. From these Considerations we earnestly desire, That Men and Women, whose Souls are committed to our Charge, may be watched over in this matter, and that care be taken, and all just and due means used for a Reformation herein; and that such who are guilty of this crying Sin of Pride, that abounds in the Churches as well as in the

Nation, may be reproved; especially considering what Time and Treasure is foolishly wasted in adorning the Body, which would be better spent in a careful endeavour to adorn the Soul; and the charge laid out upon those Superfluities, to relieve the necessities of the poor Saints, and to promote the Interest of Jesus Christ. And though we deny not but in some cases Ornaments may be allowed, yet whatever Ornaments in Men or Women which are inconsistent with Modesty, Gravity, Sobriety, and a Scandal to Religion, opening the Mouths of the Ungodly, ought to be cast off, being truly no Ornaments to Believers, but rather a Defilement; and that those Ministers and Churches who do not endeavour after a Reformation herein, are justly to be blamed,

Q. *Whether it be not the Duty of all Christians, and Churches of Christ, religiously to observe the Lord's Day, or first Day of the Week, in the Worship and Service of God both in publick and private?*

A. It is concluded in the Affirmative. Because we find that Day was set apart for the solemn Worship of God by our Lord Jesus, and his Holy Apostles, through the infallible Inspiration of the Holy Spirit.

1st. Because it appears that the Son of God, who was manifested in the Flesh, had Authority to make a change of the Solemn Day of Worship, being Lord of the Sabbath. *Mat.* 12.8. *Mark* 2.28. *Luke* 6.5.

2dly. It is manifest that our Blessed Lord and Saviour arose on that Day, as having compleated and confirmed the work of our Redemption. *Mat.* 28.1. *Mark* 16.2. *Luke* 24.1. *Joh.* 20.1. whereby he laid the Foundation of the Observation of that Day.

3dly. Our Lord Jesus did then on that Day most plainly and solemnly appear to his Disciples, teaching and instructing them, blessing them, and giving them their Commission, breathing on them the Holy Ghost. *Luke* 24.13,31,36. *Joh.* 20.19,20,21,22.

Moreover, on the next first day of the Week, he appeared to them again, giving them a further infallible proof of his glorious Resurrection. And then convinced the Apostle *Thomas*, who being absent the first Day before, was now with them, *Joh.* 20.26. Whereby it appears he sanctified and confirmed the religious Observation of that Day by his own Example.

4thly. Our Lord and Saviour remained with his Disciples forty Days after his Resurrection, and spoke to them of the thing pertaining to the Kingdom of God, *Act.* 1.3. And we question not but he then gave command about the Observation of this Day.

5thly. Which appears, in that for a further confirmation thereof, after his Ascension, when his Disciples or Apostles were assembled together, solemnly with one accord, on the Day of *Pentecost*, which (by all computation) was the first Day of the Week; recorded, *Act.* 2.1,2. He then poured out his Holy Spirit in a marvellous and an abundant Measure upon them.

6thly. Accordingly, afterwards, we find this Day was solemnly observed by the Churches, as appears, *Acts* 20.7. where we have the Churches assembling on that day plainly asserted, with the solemn Duties then performed, which were Preaching, and breaking of Bread; and all this recorded as their usual Custom, which could be from no other cause but Divine and Apostolical Institution. And it is most remarkable and worthy the serious Observation of all the Lord's People, that although the Holy Apostles, and others that were Preachers of the Gospel, took their opportunities to preach the Word on the Jewish Sabbath-day, and on other days of the Week as they had convenient Seasons afforded; yet we have no Example of the Churches then assembling together to celebrate all the Ordinances of our Lord Jesus peculiar to them, but on the first Day of the Week. Which manifest practice of theirs is evidently as plain a Demonstration of its being a Day set apart for religious Worship, by the Will and Command of our Lord Jesus, as if it had been exprest in the plainest Words. Forasmuch as they did nothing in those purest Primitive Times in the sacred Worship of God, either as to time or form, but by a Divine Warrant from the Holy Apostles, who were instructed by our Lord Jesus, and were guided in all those Affairs by his faithful and infallible Holy Spirit.

7thly. In like manner the solemn Ordinance of Collection for the necessities of the poor Saints, was commanded by the Lord to be performed on that Day, 1. *Cor.* 16.1,2. by an Apostolical Ordination; which without question, by reason of their observing that Day for their holy assembling and worship, was then required.

8thly, and *lastly*. It is asserted by all the considerate and able Expositors of the Holy Scriptures, that the denomination or Title of the Lord's Day, mentioned *Rev.* 1.10. was attributed to the First Day of the Week, as the usual distinguishing Name given to that solemn Day by the Christians, or Churches, in the Primitive Times; as being a Day to be spent wholly in the Service and Worship of the Lord, and not in our own worldly and secular Affairs, which are lawful to be attended unto on other Days of the Week.

From all which, laid together and considered, we are convinced, that it is our Duty religiously to observe that Holy Day in the Celebration of the Worship of God.

Q. Whether the Graces and Gifts of the Holy Spirit be not sufficient to the making and continuing of an Honourable Ministry in the Churches?

A. Resolved in the Affirmative, *Eph.* 4.8,9. 1 *Cor.* 12.7.

Q. Whether it be not advantagious for our Brethren now in the Ministry, or that may be in the Ministry, to attain to a competent knowledg of the Hebrew, Greek, and Latin Tongues, that they may be the better capable to defend the Truth against Opposers?

A. Resolved in the Affirmative.

Q. Whether an Elder of one Church may administer the Ordinance in other Churches of the same Faith?

A. That an Elder of one Church, may administer the Ordinance of the Lord's Supper to another of the same Faith, being called so to do by the said Church; tho not as Pastor, but as a Minister, necessity being only considered in this Case.

We the Ministers and Messengers of, and concerned for, upwards of one hundred Baptized Congregations in *England* and *Wales* (denying *Arminianism*) being met together in *London* from the 3d of the 7th Month to the 11th of the same, 1689. to consider of some things that might be for the glory of God, and the good of these Congregations; have thought meet (for the satisfaction of all other Christians that differ from us in the point of Baptism) to recommend to their perusal the Confession of our Faith, Printed for, and Sold by, Mr. *John Harris* at the *Harrow* in the *Poultrey*: Which Confession we own, as containing the Doctrine of our Faith and Practice; and do desire that the Members of our Churches respectively do furnish themselves therewith.

Moreover, this Assembly do declare their Approbation of a certain little Book, lately recommended by divers Elders dwelling in and about the City of *London*, Intituled, *The Ministers Maintenance Vindicated*. And it is their Request that the said Treatise be dispersed amongst all our respective Congregations; and it is desired that some Brethren of each Church take care to dispose of the same accordingly.

An Account of the several Baptised Churches in England *and* Wales *(owning the Doctrine of Personal Election and Final Perseverance) that sent either their Ministers, or Messengers, or otherwise communicated their State in our General-Assembly at* London, *on the 3rd, 4th, and so on to the 11th Day of the 7th Month, called* September, 1689.

Barkshire.

1 Reading. . . . .   *William Facy, Pastor.*
                                         Reyamire Griffin, Messenger.
2 Farringdon . . . .   *Richard Steed, Minister.*
                                         William Mills, Minister.
3 Abbington . . . .   *Henry Forty, Pastor.*
                                         John Tomkins.
                                         Philip Hockton.
4 Newberry . . . .
5 Wantage . . . .   *Robert Keate, Minister.*
6 Longworth . . . .   *John Man, Preacher.*
                                         Peter Stephens.

Bedfordshire.

7 Steventon. . . . .   *Stephen Howtherne, Pastor.*
                                         John Carver.
8 Evershall . . . .   *Edward White, Pastor.*

Bristol.

9 Broad-Meade . . . .   *Thomas Vaux, Pastor.*
                                         Robert Bodinam.
10 Fryers . . . .   *Andrew Gifford, Pastor.*

[Remainder of list omitted.]

Number of Primitive Baptist Churches by State

Alabama	146
Arizona	5
Arkansas	54
California	34
Colorado	5
Delaware	3
Florida	79
Georgia	179
Idaho	1
Illinois	34
Indiana	44
Iowa	7
Kansas	3
Kentucky	61
Louisiana	19
Maryland	6
Michigan	7
Mississippi	87
Missouri	41
Nebraska	10
New Mexico	10
North Carolina	70
Ohio	27
Oklahoma	31
Oregon	4
Pennsylvania	6
South Carolina	8
Tennessee	121
Texas	128
Virginia	82
West Virginia	34
Wyoming	1

Total Number of Primitive Baptist Churches in 1983   1,347

Demography of the Mountain District Primitive Baptist Association

	1961	1970	1971	1972	1983	1984	1985	1986
Total Members	531	382	373	382	314	302	246	237
Baptisms	6	14	21	12	14	3	8	3
Letter	5	1	0	10	0	2	3	0
Exclusions	1	0	1	0	3	0	0	2
Dismissals	11	2	3	2	0	2	3	3
Deaths	23	8	7	13	10	14	14	7

Membership of Churches in the Mountain District Association

Year	Smallest Churches		Largest Churches	
1961	Barton's Crossroads	9	Union	75
	Piney Creek	14	Little River	58
	Saddle Creek	16	Cross Roads	54
			Zion	54
1970	Barton's Crossroads	4	Union	69
	Cranberry	5	Little River	68
	Saddle Creek	11	Galax	54
1986	Rock Creek	4	Little River	51
	Union	6	Galax	44
	Saddle Creek	11	Cross Roads	36

Characters and Their Affiliations

North Carolina Group

Elder Walter Evans: Longtime moderator of the Mountain District Association; pastor of three North Carolina churches; joined Primitive Baptist from Union Baptists where he served as elder; widely traveled as a preaching elder from Maryland to Texas; led second delegation to Low Valley; mentor of Elder Yates.

Elder Billy Yates: Moderator of Senter Association; pastor, Peach Bottom Church, Mountain District Association; protégé of Elder Evans.

Virginia Group

Clerk Raymond Nichols: Longtime clerk of the association; longtime clerk of Cross Roads Church, Baywood, Virginia; retired supervisor with Virginia Highway Department; craftsman; mentor of Elders Reed and Sparks.

Mr. Leslie T. Nichols: Assistant Clerk, Mountain District Association; son of Raymond Nichols.

Elder Joseph Reed: Pastor of Cross Roads Church with Elder Sparks; protégé of Raymond Nichols, clerk at Cross Roads; formerly co-pastored Peach Bottom Church with Elder Yates.

Elder Elmer Sparks: Co-pastor at Cross Roads Church with Elder Reed; friend of many in diverse and independent churches and associations; co-pastor at Woodruff with Elder Lyle of the Low Valley Association.

Mr. Roy Lee Truitt: Newly ordained deacon at Cross Roads; elected clerk of the Mountain Association succeeding Raymond Nichols.

Independent of Either Group

Elder Dewey Roten: Longtime leader of the Senter Association, succeeded by Elder Yates as moderator in 1982; longtime friend and preaching companion of Elder Evans; along with Evans, mentor of Elder Yates.

Elder Eddie Lyle: Pastor of a church in the Low Valley Association; clerk of that association; not in fellowship with Low Valley Church; co-pastor with Sparks at Woodruff, an independent church; amateur historian; instructor of automotive mechanics at a technical college.

Elder Cahooney: Longtime pastor of the church at Low Valley; now deceased; father of the current elders of Low Valley Church; longtime friend of Elder Evans; well known as a preaching elder.

Elders Cahooney: The three brothers who pastor Low Valley Church; visitors at Cross Roads Church; their church was visited by delegations from the Senter Association and the Mountain Association.

Patterns of Reciprocity and Exclusion among the Churches

In Fellowship

All churches of the Mountain and Senter associations.

Evans, Nichols, Yates, Reed, et al., through their churches and associations; Yates will not invite Reed to preach; their churches will not "turn out" for each others' communions.

Cross Roads Church (Nichols and Reed, et al.) in fellowship with Low Valley Church (the Elders Cahooney), but none of the other churches in the Mountain are in fellowship with Low Valley and the Cahooneys.

Reed, Nichols, the Cahooneys, Lyle are in fellowship with Sparks, but Yates, Evans, and their churches are unhappy about Sparks's relation with Lyle at Woodruff.

Lyle in fellowship with Sparks, and some of the other independent churches pastored by elders invited to preach at Cross Roads, but Lyle (of the Low Valley Association) not in fellowship with Evans, Yates, Roten and their churches in Mountain and Senter associations.

Mediating

Cross Roads and Low Valley in fellowship through relation of Reed and Cahooneys; Cross Roads and Woodruff in fellowship through relation between Sparks and Lyle.

Out-of-Fellowship

Low Valley Church out of fellowship with both Mountain and Senter associations as well as the Low Valley Association, but in fellowship with Cross Roads Church of the Mountain. Woodruff Church, an independent church, out of fellowship with Senter and Mountain, with possible exception of Cross Roads through Elder Sparks.

Lyle as a member of the Low Valley Association (Low Valley Church is not a member of the association with the same name) is out of fellowship with the Low Valley Church, and both Mountain and Senter associations, but through his fellowship with Elder Sparks, his co-pastor at Woodruff, he is at least indirectly in fellowship with Cross Roads, whose co-pastor is also Sparks.

APPENDIX H

Obituary of Elder Elmer Sparks

Elder Elmer Ray Sparks

Elder Sparks, 74, of Sparta, died on Monday morning, December 30, 1985, at his home.

He was born on June 21, 1911, to Elder John Carlton Sparks and Virginia Edwards Sparks in Sparta, North Carolina, where he lived for most of his life.

He was married to Golar Wagoner on September 7, 1932, in Independence, Virginia. To this union were born six children—three sons, Hoyt (D. F.) Sparks of Antioch, Tennessee, James B. Sparks of Winston Salem, North Carolina, and Wayne C. Sparks of Sparta, North Carolina; three daughters, Eula Ray Cook of Winston Salem, North Carolina, Bonnie Sue Sparks of Rural Hall, North Carolina, and Shelda Jean Upchurch of Sparta, North Carolina. Also surviving are one sister, Mrs. Tressie Edwards; one brother, John Lee Sparks, both of Galax, Virginia; fifteen grandchildren; three step-grandchildren, and five great-grandchildren.

The funeral service was held at 2 p.m. January 1, 1986 at the Cross Roads Primitive Baptist Church at Baywood, Virginia, where he was a member. Elder [Joseph Reed] and Elder Eddie Lyle officiated in the service. The body was laid to rest in the Antioch Primitive Baptist Church Cemetery, Sparta, North Carolina.

He united with the Primitive Baptist Church on Saturday, April 10, 1954, and on Easter Sunday, April 18, 1954 he was baptized. He loved the Primitive Baptist people very much. Wherever he traveled, he strived to bring peace and unity to the Lord's people. He was ordained as an elder at Cross Roads Primitive Baptist Church on February 16, 1974. He became joint pastor of Woodruff Primitive Baptist Church shortly after his ordination. There he remained joint pastor with Elder Eddie Lyle until his death in December. He was pastor of Saddle Creek Primitive Baptist Church (Mountain District Association), Independence, Virginia for several years. He will be missed by his churches and friends. They have lost a faithful and humble leader. In the last year of his ministry, he often went to church when he was unable to go.

On one occasion, he was released from the hospital to go to church, and after the service, he was taken back to the hospital. He was chaplain for the Sparta, North Carolina, Rescue Squad for several years. He served as a reliable member of the squad.

He worked hard farming and doing construction work to raise his family. He was a faithful husband to his wife and a kind and loving father to his children and grandchildren. He was a good neighbor, always ready to help in any way he could in the time of need. He lived an upright and honest life.

I have been Elder Spark's pastor for several years. In those years, I have grown very close to him. I will miss him greatly both in my ministry and as a close friend. He was strong in the faith that "by grace are ye saved, through faith and that not of yourself, it is the gift of God."

He remained a faithful servant of the church until his last day. At Saddle Creek Primitive Baptist Church on Sunday morning, December 29, 1985, Elder Sparks preached his last and one of his most able sermons. The following morning, he passed away in his sleep from a heart attack.

Brother Sparks often said he prayed that, when his time came, God would have mercy on him and take him in his sleep. God did have mercy on him and granted him that prayer.

Independent Protestants: Background Information

The Primitive Baptists of North Carolina and Virginia exemplify the independent Protestant churches found throughout the South and elsewhere. They are independent in that they are not a part of the region's major Protestant denominations (e.g., Southern Baptist, United Methodist), and are usually distinguishable by certain characteristics. The "mainstream" churches are often prominently located in cities and towns; they are parts of a larger hierarchical organization; they employ seminary-educated ministers; and their congregations are relatively affluent. In contrast, the independent churches are more often found in rural areas; they are more egalitarian in organization, with a great deal of congregational autonomy; their preachers often avoid seminaries; and members tend not to be of the affluent elite.[1]

Although they are now distanced from their parent groups, the independent Protestants nonetheless share much of their history with the larger denominational bodies. Most of the independent and mainstream churches in the South are heirs to the British Separatist tradition within Protestantism.[2] A brief historical sketch of the theological roots of independent Protestantism in America may be helpful in situating the Primitive Baptists and other groups.

One of the major influences on independent Protestant churches in America is the Wesleyan tradition. In sharp contrast to his Reformation predecessors Luther and Calvin, John Wesley (1703–1791) gave human perfectibility a central role in his theology. According to Wesley, salvation is granted by divine grace through faith, confirmed and exemplified in the temporal world by good works.[3] Christian perfection, a condition of triumph over temptation and sin, was defined by Wesley as a perfect love of God and one's fellows, qualified by human error and without any guarantee of permanence.[4] Thus, Wesley argued for the sanctification of human life through faith and "taking up the cross daily."[5]

Wesley's Arminianism was obvious. His *Predestination Calmly Considered* (published in 1752) harkened back to Jacobus Arminius's 1608 *Decla-*

ration of Sentiments in its rejection of predestination as unscriptural and antinomian.[6] The preface to the first issue of Wesley's *Arminian Magazine* (January, 1778) declared its support of ". . . the grand Christian doctrine, God willeth all men to be saved and come to a knowledge of the truth."[7]

Wesley's denomination, the Methodists, was among the most successful in early American history. In 1771, there were fewer than 1,000 Methodists in the colonies; a decade later, they numbered 10,000, and by 1790 their ranks had increased to more than 57,000.[8] One of the factors behind this phenomenal growth was the use of the "circuit system," whereby each church was equipped with a group of traveling preachers.[9] This high-mobility ministry enabled the Methodists to establish themselves quickly in the East and expand into the frontier; as Gaustad has written, "when the new homesteader drove his stakes into the ground, the echo was heard somewhere by a Methodist preacher."[10] Another strength of the denomination was Wesley's impatience with divisive and exclusive doctrine: "Methodists do not impose in order to their admission any opinions whatsoever . . . One condition, and only one, is required—a real desire to save the soul."[11]

Wesley's emphasis on human perfectibility, combining with the individualistic ethos of the Jacksonian era, led to the inception of the Holiness movement in the early nineteenth century. The energetic evangelism of Holiness proponents and its personal appeal to individuals aspiring to an earthly life of Christian perfection soon took it well beyond the confines of Methodism; to varying degrees, the Holiness movement became a considerable force in most of the Protestant churches of the United States by the time of the Civil War.[12] For Methodists as a whole, the movement proved to be a mixed blessing. While it attracted many new recruits, the relentless quest for perfection engendered an absolutism among some believers that proved divisive, as witnessed by the 1843 defection of the Wesleyan Methodists from the main body of the church over the slavery issue.[13] After the Civil War, a number of Holiness-influenced churches in the rural Midwest and South began to break away, alienated by the increasing "worldliness" of the church as it grew larger, wealthier, and more "respectable."[14]

Perhaps the best-known offspring of the Holiness movement in the United States are the Pentecostal churches. Pentecostalism is usually traced back to an outbreak of ecstatic behaviors (most notably glossolalia, or "speaking in tongues") in early 1901 at a small Bible college in Topeka, Kansas, run by an independent Holiness preacher and former Methodist, Charles Fox Parham.[15] It grew slowly in the lower Midwest, until a black Holiness preacher converted by Parham, William Joseph Seymour, brought Pentecostalism to Los Angeles in 1906.[16]

Among the early converts at Seymour's Azusa Street Mission was Gaston Barnabas Cashwell, of Dunn, North Carolina. Cashwell received baptism in the Holy Spirit in 1906; returning to his home state, he led the Pentecostal Holiness church of North Carolina.[17] He was later an important figure in the merger of this and other smaller churches to form the Pentecostal Holiness Church,[18] one of the leading Pentecostal groups in the South, with a membership now exceeding 100,000.[19]

Pentecostalism is presently the fastest-growing Christian group in the world. While the tendency toward schism characteristic of perfectionist sects has divided them (there are more than 300 Pentecostal denominations in the United States alone), their numbers are large, estimated at several million domestically and more than 60 million worldwide.[20]

Pentecostal and Holiness churches are a part of the Wesleyan tradition[21] by virtue of their emphasis on earthly perfection. However, whereas Wesley was ambiguous as to whether sanctification was a gradual process or a sudden event,[22] these American churches usually focus on a dramatic experience of grace.[23] For instance, among almost all American Pentecostal groups, glossolalia is stressed as evidence of sanctification through baptism in the Holy Spirit.[24]

The seventeenth-century Baptist pioneers in America were largely Arminian in orientation, with Calvinism becoming prominent in the next century.[25] Because they were stigmatized by their rejection of infant baptism and their denial of the civil government's right to establish a state religion, their early growth was slow.[26] Then, between 1720 and 1780, the number of Baptist churches increased tenfold, from approximately 40 to more than 400.[27] During that same period "In that woeful state of North Carolina," the number of Baptist churches climbed from 1 to 55, outnumbering Anglican churches by a two-to-one margin.[28] The untrained Baptist preachers evoked enthusiasm in their listeners as readily as they provoked scorn and condescension from other denominations. Congregational clergyman Noah Worcester described the appeal of the Baptist ministry in 1794 thusly:

> Many people are so ignorant, as to be charmed with sound rather than sense . . . If a speaker can keep his tongue running, in an unremitting manner . . . and can quote memoriter a large number of texts within the covers of the Bible, it matters not, to many of his hearers, whether he speaks sense or nonsense.[29]

During and after this period of rapid expansion, the tensions mounted between the more "mainstream" Arminian Baptists and the Calvinistic Baptists over issues such as missionization and seminary training for preachers, as well as the basic rift over predestination, culminating in the Black Rock Convention of 1832. These Calvinistic dissenters were the ancestors of today's Primitive Baptists.

Contemporary Primitive Baptists are split along racial and doctrinal lines. The National Primitive Baptist Convention of the United States of America is the umbrella organization of black Primitive Baptist churches. It is important to note that all the churches within the NPBC (which was organized in 1907) are independent; in this and most other respects they are similar to their white counterparts.[30] One exception is the NPBC's support of aid societies and Sunday schools.[31] The Convention claims a membership of 250,000 in more than 600 churches nationwide.[32]

"Factionalism, divisiveness, and politics prevent an accurate report on membership"[33] among white Primitive Baptists, but somewhat more than 70,000 appears to be a fair estimate.[34] Bearing in mind the strict requirements for membership, the number of nonmembers attending Primitive Baptist churches would significantly increase this total.

More than two-thirds of the white Primitive Baptist churches are "Old Regulars" holding to the traditional doctrines of the faith.[35] There are more than 1,300 such churches in the United States, with the highest concentration found in Alabama and Georgia.[36] The "Progressive" element among Primitive Baptists, those congregations approving of instrumental music, Sunday schools, and some other innovations, is made up of approximately 160 churches and some 10,000 members; Georgia and Florida are their strongholds.[37] The smallest group, often called (somewhat pejoratively) "Absoluters" because of their belief in the predestination of all events, number some 7,000 in 390 churches.[38] They are found most frequently in North Carolina and Virginia.[39]

Bibliographic Note: Edwin S. Gaustad's *Historical Atlas of Religion in America*, rev. ed. (Harper and Row, 1976), and Winthrop S. Hudson's *American Protestantism* (University of Chicago Press, 1961), and *Religion in America*, 2d ed. (Charles Scribner's Sons, 1973) are informative and accessible guides to American religious history. For information on specific denominations, doctrines, and theologians, see *The Encyclopedia of Religion*, Mircea Eliade, gen. ed. (Macmillan, 1987), and *Encyclopedia of the American Religious Experience*, ed. Charles H. Lippy and Peter W. Williams (Charles Scribner's Sons, 1988); for those with a particular interest in the American South, Samuel S. Hill's *Encyclopedia of Religion in the South* (Mercer University Press, 1984) is a valuable resource.

Notes

Preface

1. Cf. "Method and Spirit: Studying the Gestures of Religion," introduction to *Diversities of Gifts: Field Studies in Southern Religion*, ed. Ruel W. Tyson, Jr., James L. Peacock, and Daniel W. Patterson (Urbana and Chicago: University of Illinois Press, 1988); also James L. Peacock, *The Anthropological Lens: Harsh Light, Soft Focus* (Cambridge and New York: Cambridge University Press, 1986), 89–91.
2. Henry James, *The Art of the Novel: The Critical Prefaces*, intro. by R. P. Blackmur (New York: Charles Scribner's Sons, 1962), 313.
3. Max Weber, *The Protestant Ethic and the Spirit of Capitalism*, trans. Talcott Parsons, with an introduction by Anthony Giddens (London: Unwin Paperbacks, 1985), 99.
4. Max Weber, "The Protestant Sects and the Spirit of Capitalism," in *From Max Weber*, trans. and ed. with intro. H. H. Gerth and C.Wright Mills (London: Routledge & Kegan Paul, 1952), 304–5.
5. Ibid.
6. See Marianne Weber, *Max Weber: A Biography*, trans. and ed. Harry Zohn (New York: John Wiley and Sons, 1975), 296–300.
7. Weber, *The Protestant Ethic*, 29–31.
8. Ibid., 127.
9. Ibid., 98.
10. Henry James, *The Art of the Novel*, 66.
11. Weber, *The Protestant Ethic*, 29–30.
12. Ibid., 182–83.
13. James, *The Art of the Novel*, 65.

Chapter One

1. These quotations from the Westminster Confession are taken from Max Weber, *The Protestant Ethic and the Spirit of Capitalism*, trans. Talcott Parsons (London: Unwin Paperbacks, 1985), 99–100. The

Westminster Confession is termed by the standard history of the Primitive Baptists "the most able, elaborate, and influential of all Protestant confessions," Cushing Biggs Hassell and Sylvester Hassell, *History of the Church of God, from the Creation to A.D. 1885; including especially the History of the Kehukee Primitive Baptist Association* (Middletown, N.Y.: Gilbert Beebe's Sons, Publishers, 1886), 508.

2. Max Weber, *The Protestant Ethic*, 103.
3. Hassell, *History of the Church of God*, 472.
4. Ibid., 497.
5. Ibid., 499.
6. Ibid., 509.
7. Ibid., 509.
8. Ibid., 519.
9. Ibid., 520.
10. Ibid., 521.
11. Ibid., 523.
12. Ibid., 524.
13. Ibid., 527.
14. Ibid., 534, 536.
15. Ibid., 541.
16. Ibid., 547.
17. Ibid., 549.
18. Ibid., 552.
19. Ibid., 577.
20. Ibid., 578.
21. Ibid., 620.
22. Ibid., 651.
23. Hugh Lefler, *History of North Carolina* (New York: Lewis Historical Publishing Co., 1956), vol. 1, 432, quoting Hassell, 736–37.
24. Lefler, 431.
25. Lefler, 432.
26. Rhys Isaac, *The Transformation of Virginia 1740–1790* (Chapel Hill: University of North Carolina Press, 1982).

Chapter Two

1. Emile Durkheim, *The Elementary Forms of Religious Life*, trans. Joseph Ward Swain (London: G. Allen & Unwin; New York, Macmillan Company, 1915).
2. Max Weber, *The Protestant Ethic and the Spirit of Capitalism*, trans. Talcott Parsons (London: Unwin Paperbacks, 1985).
3. Weber, 99 ff.
4. Weber, 221, n. 19.

5. Weber, 111.
6. Weber, 112.
7. Weber, 114–22.
8. Weber, 118.
9. Weber, 108.
10. Weber, 109.
11. For an elaboration of this aspect of Weber, which is not sufficiently reflected in most commentaries, see James L. Peacock, *Muslim Puritans: The Psychology of Reformism in Southeast Asian Islam* (Berkeley: University of California Press, 1978), 10–14.
12. Weber, 138.
13. Weber, 48. This textual approach to Weber has been ignored by most social scientists, but the following article has come to our attention: Fredric Jameson, "The Vanishing Mediator: Narrative Structure in Max Weber," *New German Critique*, vol. 1 (Winter 1973), pp. 52–89. Also note the astute comments of Harry Liebersohn, "Max Weber: The Allegory of Society," in Liebersohn's recently published *Fate and Utopia in German Sociology, 1870–1923* (Cambridge and London: MIT Press, 1988), and in particular p. 226, footnote 44, where he comments: "Parson's translation is serviceable, but does not attempt to render the dense allusiveness of Weber's prose. Although Weber is often criticized for his stylistic carelessness, *The Protestant Ethic* shows a metaphorical complexity rivaling that of great literature." Liebersohn's entire chapter on Weber is an important contribution to our understanding of this complex figure in social thought.
14. Weber, 56.
15. "The Protestant Sects and the Spirit of Capitalism" in Hans H. Gerth and C. Wright Mills, eds. *From Max Weber* (New York: Oxford University Press), 304–5. This is a translation of "Die Protestantische Sekten und der geist des Kapitalismus" in *Gesammelte Aufsätze zur Religions soziologie*, I, Band, Sei te 207–36. "Die Protestant ethik und der Geist des Kapitalismus" is on pages 17–206 of this work and was first published in the *Archiv für Sozialwissenschaft und Sozialpolitik* in 1904–5, then reprinted with considerable change as the *Gesammelte Aufsatze . . .* in 1920. So the trip to Mt. Airy was part of Weber's ongoing research and writing on the Protestant Ethic. An account of this visit is also given in Marianne Weber, *Max Weber: A Biography*, trans. and ed. Harry Zohn (New York: Wiley, 1975). In addition to these published sources, our account draws on Evelyn Cook, "The Fallensteins of Mt. Airy," unpublished paper, January 10, 1980, and interviews with Julius Miller in Mt. Airy, North Carolina, and Jay Branscomb near Fancy Gap, Virginia, both on November 28, 1986. We are grateful to Professor Edward Tiriakyian, Department of Sociology, Duke University, for providing a copy of the paper by Ms. Cook and the address of Mr. Miller.

16. This genealogy synthesizes the accounts given by Marianne Weber, Evelyn Cook, Julius Miller, and Jay Branscomb.
17. Bronislaw Malinowski, *Argonauts of the Western Pacific* (London: G.Routledge & Son; New York, E.P. Dutton & Co., 1922).
18. Edward Evans Evans-Pritchard, *The Nuer* (Oxford: Clarendon Press, 1940).
19. Ruth Benedict, *Patterns of Culture* (Boston: Houghton Mifflin, Co., 1934).
20. Edmund R. Leach, *Political Systems of Highland Burma: A Study of Technique in Social Structure* (Cambridge: Harvard University Press, 1954).
21. John Middleton, *Lugbara Religion* (London, New York: Oxford University Press, 1960).
22. Victor W. Turner, *Schism and Continuity in an African Society: A Study of Ndembu Village Life* (Manchester: University of Manchester Press, 1957).
23. Victor W. Turner, *The Forest of Symbols: Aspects of Ndembu Ritual* (Ithaca: Cornell University Press, 1967).
24. Victor W. Turner, *Drama, Fields, and Metaphors: Symbolic Action in Human Society* (Ithaca: Cornell University Press, 1974).
25. Victor W. Turner, *On the Edge of the Bush: Anthropology as Experience*, ed. Edith L.B. Turner (Tucson, Ariz.: University of Arizona Press, 1985).
26. Victor W. Turner, *From Ritual to Theater: The Human Seriousness of Play* (New York: Performing Arts Journal Publications, 1982), and "Dewey, Dilthey, and Drama: An Essay in the Anthropology of Experience," in Victor W. Turner and Edward Bruner, eds., *The Anthropology of Experience* (Urbana: University of Illinois Press, 1986).
27. Clifford Geertz, "Ritual and Social Change: A Javanese Example," *American Anthropologist* 59, no. 1 (1957): 32–54. Reprinted in Clifford Geertz, *Interpretation of Cultures* (New York: Basic Books, 1973).
28. Clifford Geertz, "Thick Description: Toward an Interpretive Theory of Culture," in *Interpretation of Cultures* (New York: Basic Books, 1973), 3–30. Geertz's relationship to Weber is explored in James Peacock, "The Third Stream: Weber, Parsons, Geertz," *Journal of the Anthropological Society of Oxford* 12, no. 2 (Trinity Term, 1981), 122–29. Also see Ruel W. Tyson, Jr., "Culture's 'Hum and Buzz' of Implication: The Practice of Ethnography and the Provocations of Clifford Geertz' 'Thick Description,'" *Soundings* 70, no. 4 (Winter 1988): 801–18.
29. James Fernandez, "The Mission of Metaphor in Expressive Culture," *Anthropology* 15, no. 2 (June 1974): 119–33; J. Christopher Crocker and J. David Sapir, eds., *The Social Use of Metaphor: Essays on the Anthropology of Rhetoric* (Philadelphia: University of Pennsylvania Press, 1977).

30. James A. Boon, *The Anthropological Romance of Bali, 1597–1972: Dynamic Perspectives in Marriage and Caste, Politics and Religion* (Cambridge: Cambridge University Press, 1977).

31. Marshall Sahlins, *Islands of History* (Chicago: University of Chicago Press, 1985).

32. Renato Rosaldo, *Ilongot Headhunting, 1883–1974: A Study in Society and History* (Palo Alto, Calif.: Stanford University Press, 1980); James L. Peacock, "Religion and Life History: An Exploration in Cultural Psychology," in Edward Bruner, ed., *Text, Play and Story: The Construction and Reconstruction of Self and Society* (Washington, D.C.: American Ethnological Society, 1984), 94–116.

33. Bruce Kapferer, *A Celebration of Demons: Exorcism and the Aesthetics of Healing in Sri Lanka* (Bloomington: Indiana University Press, 1983); Thomas O. Beidelman, *Moral Imagination in Kaguru Modes of Thought* (Bloomington: Indiana University Press, 1986).

34. Rodney Needham, *Against the Tranquility of Axioms* (Berkeley: University of California Press, 1983).

35. Richard Baumann, *Let Your Words Be Few: Symbolism of Speaking and Silence Among Seventeenth-Century Quakers* (Cambridge and New York: Cambridge University Press, 1983); Joel Brett Sutton, "Spirit and Polity in a Black Primitive Baptist Church," PhD diss., Department of Anthropology, University of North Carolina at Chapel Hill, 1983; Jeff Titon, *Power House for God* (Austin: University of Texas Press, 1988); Rhys Isaac, *The Transformation of Virginia 1740– 1790*. We are citing here not a representative list of works pertaining to the empirical phenomenon under study (Baptists, American religious groups), but only studies that have both this empirical focus and reflect trends in ethnographic study noted. Among other recent pertinent ethnographic analyses of religious patterns in the Southern United States, see Gwen Kennedy Neville, *Kinship and Pilgrimage* (New York: Oxford University Press, 1987), and Carol J. Greenhouse, *Praying for Justice* (Ithaca: Cornell University Press, 1986). Sources on the Primitive Baptists include W.J. Berry, "Primitive Baptists," *Encyclopedia of Southern Baptists*, vol. 2 (Nashville: Broadman Press, 1958), 114–15; Howard Dorgan, *Giving Glory to God in Appalachia: Worship Practices of Six Baptist Subdenominations* (Knoxville: University of Tennessee Press, 1987), chapter 1, 1–54; Byron C. Lambert, *The Rise of Anti–Mission Baptists* (New York: Arno Press, 1980); Arthur C. Pipekorn, "The Primitive Baptists of North America," *Concordia Theological Monthly* 42, no. 5 (1971), 297–314; James O. Renault, *The Development of Separate Baptist Ecclesiology in the South, 1755–1976* (Ann Arbor: University Microfilm, 1982); Melanie L. Sovine, "Studying Religious Belief Systems in Their Social Historical Context," *Appalachia and America*, ed. Allen Batteau (Lexington: University Press of Kentucky, 1983), 48–67; Chester R. Young, "Primitive Baptists," *Encyclo-*

pedia of Religion in the South, ed. Samuel S. Hill (Macon: Mercer University Press, 1984), 612–13.
36. For an overview of this approach, see James Clifford and George E. Marcus, eds., *Writing Culture: The Poetics and Politics of Ethnography* (Berkeley: University of California Press, 1986.)
37. Vincent Crapanzano, *Tuhami, Portrait of a Moroccan* (Chicago: University of Chicago Press, 1980.)
38. Jeanne Favret-Saada, *Deadly Words: Witchcraft in the Bocage*, trans. Catherine Cullen (New York: Cambridge University Press, 1980).
39. Jane Bachnik, *The Japanese IE: An Organization of Self and Society* (Palo Alto, Calif.: Stanford University Press, forthcoming).
40. Hans-Georg Gadamer, *Truth and Method*, trans. Garrett Barden and William Glen (Ocepel, N.Y.: Seabury Press, 1975). For an elaboration and critique of the hermeneutical approach of Gadamer as applied to ethnography, see James L. Peacock, "Form and Meaning in Recent Indonesian History: Some Reflections in Light of the Philosophy of History of H-G. Gadamer," in *Symbols through Time*, ed. Emiko Ohnuki-Tierney (Palo Alto, Calif.: Stanford University Press, forthcoming). See also Tyson as cited in note 28.

Chapter Three

1. A short account of this case appears in James L. Peacock, "Barchester Towers in Appalachia: Negotiated Meaning," in Phyllis Chock and J.R. Wyman, eds., *Discourse and the Social Life of Meaning* (Washington and London: Smithsonian Institution Press, 1986). A superb analysis of a broadly similar case among neighboring black Primitive Baptists is in Sutton.
2. The Minutes for the 1982 Annual Association of the Senter Association read for Saturday, September 11, 1982: On MOTION:
1. The roll call was omitted.
2. The reading of the Constitution and Rules of Decorum were omitted, but they are to be printed in the minutes.
3. The committee on arrangements recommended that we continue seating all orderly, peace-loving Primitive Baptists as visitors; that a committee go to visit, consisting of all the elders of the Senter Association and three deacons . . . Elder R.D. Roten is to be the spokesman for the committee and Elder Samuel Whittington is to be the alternate spokesman. Deacon Bertie Bare, recording secretary for the committee, is to find out the reason why the majority of the members have been excluded. [We have omitted the name of the church we are calling Low Valley in the preceding quotation from the Senter Association Minutes for 1982.]

Chapter Four

1. Cecil Lambert Byron, *The Rise of the Anti-Mission Baptists: Sources and Leaders, 1800–1840* (New York: Arno Press, 1980), 365–68.
2. Walter Evans, *The General Judgement* (Sparta, N.C., 1968).
3. *Minutes of the One-Hundred and Eighty-Fifth Session of Mountain District Primitive Baptist Association* (Atwood, Tenn.: Christian Baptist Publishing Co., 1983).
4. Weber, *The Protestant Ethic*, 104.
5. Weber, 104.
6. This sketch of Primitive Baptist singing is taken from remarks by Daniel and Beverly Patterson. We acknowledge their aid in this and other matters and free them of responsibility for error in our account of their comments.
7. D.H. Goble states: "Care has been maintained in the selection of hymns and spiritual songs, to not only include all the old, familiar ones, and favorites of our brethren in the different sections of the country, but especially that no unsound sentiment be found in any selection; and this is the only apology we would offer for numerous small changes made in a number of selections found in this book. We are fully persuaded that we had as well preach unsound doctrine as to sing it with an attempt at devotion." *Primitive Baptist Hymn Book for All Lovers of Sacred Song*, compiled by D.H. Goble (Greenfield, Ind.: D.H. Goble Co., 1887).

Chapter Six

1. The Minutes for the 1983 Meeting of the Mountain District Association records the following regarding the election for the moderator and the other officers: "3. Organized by move, second, and approval to elect Elder Walter Evans, moderator; Elder [Joseph Reed], assistant moderator; Roy L. Truitt, clerk; and Leslie T. Nichols, assistant clerk." We do not attempt to explain the discrepancy between the voting for officers by private ballot that occurred at the first session and this record in the official minutes. A sample check of the minutes for a number of other annual meetings shows the same formula as quoted here. Perhaps the formula used in recording the minutes was too strong a custom to accommodate the deviation from custom that in fact did occur by the use of private ballot.
2. In 1983, Elder Reed was elected moderator, and Elder Evans retired. The 1984 minutes state: "The Association gives thanks first to God and second to Elder Walter Evans for his twenty-one years of faithful and dedicated service as moderator of the Mountain District Association."

Minutes of the One-Hundred-Eighty Sixth Annual Session of the Mountain District Primitive Baptist Association (Atwood, Tenn.: Christian Baptist Publishing Co., 1984), 3.

Chapter Seven

1. Sacran Bercovitch, *The American Jeremiad* (Madison: University of Wisconsin Press, 1978).
2. An interesting comparison could be made between the Primitive Baptists and another mountain group, the Sons of God. Whereas the Primitive Baptists speak of the female church symbolism of the church positive (e.g., the bride of Christ), the Sons speak of it negatively (the whore of Babylon). Yet where the Primitive Baptists forbid women to preach, the Sons have female preachers who, however, are said to represent the fleshly aspect of the established church from which all should escape in order to become entirely spiritual. On the Sons of God see James Wise, "The Sons of God Message in the North Carolina Meetings," Master's thesis, Curriculum in Folklore, University of North Carolina, Chapel Hill, 1977.
3. Rodney Needham, *Reconnaissances* (Toronto: University of Toronto Press, 1980), 63–105.
4. Weber defines charisma as follows: ". . . a certain quality of an individual personality by virtue of which he is considered extraordinary and treated as endowed with supernatural, superhuman, or at least specifically exceptional powers or qualities," while "An organized group subject to charismatic authority will be called a charismatic community (*Gemeinde*)." Max Weber, *Economy and Society*, ed. Guenther Roth and Claus Wittich (Berkeley: University of California Press, 1978), 241, 243. The original German provides parenthetical examples of charismatic leaders as part of the definitional statement (such examples are prophets, persons with a reputation for therapeutic or legal wisdom, leaders in the hunt, or heroes in war). Max Weber, *Wirtschaft und Gesellschaft: Grundriss der Verstehenden Soziologie*, ed. Johannes Winckelmann (Tuebingen: J.C.B. Mohr (Paul Siebeck), 1980), 140.
5. John Calvin, *The Institutes of the Christian Religion*, ed. John T. McNeill and trans. Ford Lewis Battles, The Library of Christian Classics, vol. 21 (Philadelphia: The Westminster Press, 1960), Book III, xxi, 2, 923–24.
6. Edward A. Shils, "Charisma, Order, and Status," in *Center and Periphery: Essays in Macrosociology* (Chicago: University of Chicago Press, 1975), 256–75.

Chapter Eight

1. Edward Evans Evans-Pritchard, *Social Anthropology and Other Essays* (New York: Free Press, 1964), 61.
2. Aside from the general argument in Weber's discussions of Calvinism and of charisma, respectively, the lack of cross-referencing between the two is confirmed by a check of indexes. In the English translation of *Wirtschaft und Gesellschaft, Economy and Society*, ed. Guenther Roth and Claus Wittich, 2 vols. (Berkeley: University of California, 1978), a detailed index is provided with numerous entries under "Charisma" and "Protestantism" (no entries under "Calvinism"). No reference to "Charisma" appears under "Protestantism" or to "Protestantism" under "Charisma." For *Wirtschaft und Gesellschaft*, 5th ed. (Tuebingen: J.C.B. Mohr (Paul Siebeck), 1980), "Calvinismus" contains only page numbers, not subentries, as does "Charisma," and we have not checked all the pages to see if either is mentioned in relation to the other. In the English translation of *The Protestant Ethic and the Spirit of Capitalism*, trans. Talcott Parsons (London: Unwin Paperbacks, 1985), there are two entries for "Charisma." One is a passing reference to the charisma of disciples as seen by the Zinzendorf branch of Pietism, and the other is a footnote to this passage, which defines the term "Charisma." The German edition that we have consulted— *Die Protestantisch Ethik 1: Eine Aufsatzsammlung*, which includes "Die protestantische Ethik und der Geist des Kapitalismus," as well as other essays (Tubingen: J.C.B. Mohr, 1973)—has no index.
3. Victor W. Turner, *Drama, Fields, and Metaphors*.
4. Victor W. Turner, *On the Edge of the Bush*, 298; *From Ritual to Theater*, 11; Clifford Geertz, "Blurred Genres: the Refiguration of Social Thought," *American Scholar* (Spring 1980): 165–79.
5. Clifford Geertz, "Ritual and Social Change: A Javanese Example," in *Interpretation of Cultures*, 32–54.
6. Clifford Geertz, *Negara: The Theatre State in Nineteenth Century Bali* (Princeton: Princeton University Press, 1980).
7. Marshall Sahlins, *Islands of History* (Chicago: University of Chicago Press, 1985); Anthony Giddens, *Central Problems in Social Theory: Action, Structure and Contradictions in Social Analysis* (Berkeley: University of California Press, 1979).
8. Rodney Needham, *Circumstantial Deliveries* (Berkeley: University of California Press, 1981), 89; cf. Rodney Needham, *Primordial Characters* (Charlottesville: University of Virginia Press, 1978), 75–76, where Needham calls for "empathetic penetration" in ethnography rather like that in literature espoused by Henry James.
9. Kenneth Burke, *The Philosophy of Literary Form: Studies in Symbolic Action*, 3d ed. (Berkeley: University of California Press, 1974).

Appendix I

1. "Epilogue: Independent Protestants in North Carolina and the Study of Living Religion," in *Diversities of Gifts: Field Studies in Southern Religion*, ed. Ruel W. Tyson, Jr., James L. Peacock, and Daniel W. Patterson (Urbana and Chicago: University of Illinois Press, 1988), 204–5.
2. Ibid., 204.
3. Frank Baker, "Methodist Churches," in *The Encyclopedia of Religion*, vol. 9, ed. Mircea Eliade (New York: Macmillan, 1987), 493.
4. Ibid.
5. Quoted in George D. Bond, "Perfectibility," in *The Encyclopedia of Religion*, vol. 11, ed. Mircea Eliade (New York: Macmillan, 1987), 241.
6. Robert E. Cushman, "Arminianism," in *Encyclopedia of Religion in the South*, ed. Samuel S. Hill. (Macon: Mercer University Press, 1984), 70.
7. Ibid.
8. Edwin S. Gaustad, *Historical Atlas of Religion in America*, rev. ed. (New York: Harper and Row, 1976), 76–77.
9. Winthrop S. Hudson, *Religion in America*, 2d ed. (New York: Charles Scribner's Sons, 1973), 123–24.
10. Gaustad, *Historical Atlas*, 80.
11. Quoted in Hudson, *Religion in America*, 124.
12. Ibid., 342.
13. Ibid., 343.
14. Ibid., 343–45.
15. Robert M. Anderson, "Pentecostal and Charismatic Christianity," in *The Encyclopedia of Religion*, vol. 9, ed. Mircea Eliade (New York: Macmillan, 1987), 231–32.
16. Ibid., 232.
17. Edith L. Blumhofer, "Pentecostalism," in *Encyclopedia of Religion in the South*, ed. Samuel S. Hill (Macon: Mercer University Press, 1984), 585.
18. Ibid.
19. Frank S. Mead and Samuel S. Hill, *Handbook of Denominations*, 8th ed. (Nashville: Abingdon Press, 1985), 198.
20. Grant Wacker, "The Functions of Faith in Primitive Pentecostalism," in *Harvard Theological Review* 77, no. 3–4 (1984): 353–54.
21. Grant Wacker, "Pentecostalism," in *Encyclopedia of the American Religious Experience*, vol. 2, ed. Charles H. Lippy and Peter W. Williams (New York: Charles Scribner's Sons, 1988), 935; for an alternative view, cf. Robert M. Anderson, *Vision of the Disinherited* (New York: Oxford University Press, 1979), 43.
22. Hudson, *Religion in America*, 342.
23. Edith L. Blumhofer, "Holiness," in *Encyclopedia of Religion in the South*, ed. Samuel S. Hill (Macon: Mercer University Press, 1984), 326.
24. Anderson, "Pentecostal and Charismatic Christianity," 230.
25. Gaustad, *Historical Atlas*, 11.

26. Edwin S. Gaustad, "Baptist Churches," in *The Encyclopedia of Religion*, vol. 2, ed. Mircea Eliade (New York: Macmillan, 1987), 63.
27. Gaustad, *Historical Atlas*, 12.
28. Ibid.
29. Ibid., 13.
30. Mead and Hill, *Handbook*, 51.
31. Ibid.
32. Ibid.
33. Ibid., 53.
34. Cf. ibid.; also Chester R. Young, "Primitive Baptists," in *Encyclopedia of Religion in the South*, ed. Samuel S. Hill (Macon: Mercer University Press, 1984), 613.
35. Young, "Primitive Baptists," 613.
36. Ibid. We count only 1,347 in 1984 (see Appendix C), served by 864 elders. See *The Primitive Baptist Church Directory* (Cincinnati: Baptist Bible Hour, Inc., 1984).
37. Ibid.
38. Ibid.
39. Ibid.

Index

Appendices F–I and Notes (but not Appendices A–E) have been included in Index.

Absher, Lloyd, 172
Absher, Mr. and Mrs. Bobby, viii, 12, 14
"Absoluters," Absolutism, 42–43, 120, 151, 266
aesthetics (*see also* doctrine, and aesthetics); of ethnographic representation, xiii–xiv, 221, 226; of Primitive Baptists, xiii–xiv, 6–7, 18, 27, 94, 99, 104, 106–9, 112, 114–17, 126–27, 133, 150, 158, 194, 204–5, 216
Alexander, Elder Charles, 14, 187
Alleghany County, N.C., xvii, 131
Amish, 15
Anabaptists, 35
Anders, John, 80
Anglicans. *See* Church of England
Arminianism, 35–39, 67, 120, 179, 226–27, 263–65 (*see also* Calvinism, and Arminianism); and Wesleys, 37, 43, 67, 263–64
Arminius, J., 36, 148, 178, 263–64
Articles of Faith, 209; of Kehukee Association, 96; of Mountain District Association, xviii, 27–29, 95–97, 101, 178 (*see also* Appendix A); of Strict Baptist churches, 30–32, 40, 96; of Union Baptists, 142
Ashe County, N.C., xvii, 12, 40–41
Augustine, 35, 92

Bachnik, Jane, *The Japanese IE*, 65
baptism, 21, 32, 45–46, 141; Primitive Baptist, 2–4, 15, 23–27, 35, 44, 90, 93, 101, 134, 172, 191, 207 (*see also* Evans, baptisms of); Weber at, xix, 59–60
Baptists, xviii, 24–26, 36–39, 44–47, 56, 60, 64–67, 101, 103–5, 115–17, 171, 263–64. *See also* Black Rock Convention; Free Willed Baptists; Missionary Baptists; Primitive Baptists; Southern Baptists; Strict and Particular Baptists; Union Baptists
Bare, Bertie, 272
Baumann, Richard, *Let Your Words Be Few*, 64
Baxter, Richard, 56
Baywood, Va. *See* churches, Cross Roads Church
Becket, Thomas, 62, 224
Bellah, Robert, 66
Benedict, Ruth, *Patterns of Culture*, 61
Bible, 7, 28–29, 34, 39, 45, 89, 95, 124, 140, 142, 154, 179–80 (*see also* King James Bible; scripture; translation, of scripture); as ritual focal point for Primitive Baptists, 107–8, 118, 125; schools and societies, Primitive Baptist attitude toward, 41
biblical characters: Barnabas, 172; Elijah, 6, 137, 182, 185–88, 200; Elisha, 182, 187; Enoch, 184–86, 188; Isaac, 140; Isaiah, 112; Jesus, 21, 32, 39, 45, 89, 91–94, 107, 112–13, 115, 120–21, 134, 141–42, 145, 181, 183, 186, 188, 194, 200, 227;